Remembering D-D

To: Mr. Wouts

From : Alex
Forman

Remembering D-Day

Personal Histories of Everyday Heroes

Martin W. Bowman

Collins

Collins
HarperCollins*Publishers*
77-85 Fulham Palace Road
Hammersmith
London W6 8JB

www.**collins**.co.uk

First published by HarperCollins*Publishers* in 2005
This text-only edition first published by HarperCollins*Publishers*
in 2005

© HarperCollins*Publishers* 2005

1 3 5 7 9 8 6 4 2

ISBN 0 00 719450 1

A catalogue record for this book is available from
the British Library

Printed in Great Britain by Clays Ltd, St Ives plc

Contents

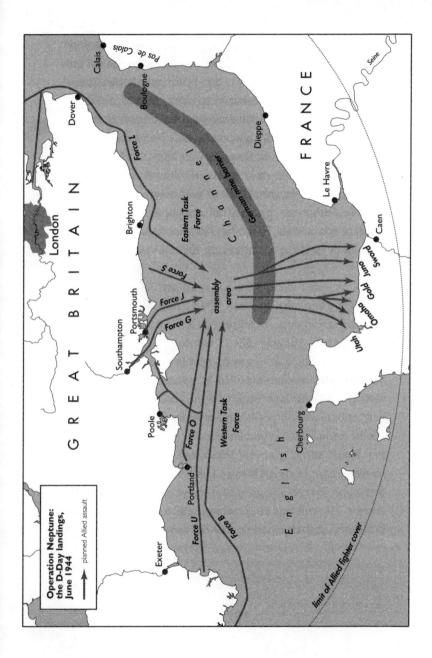

Operation Neptune:
the D-Day landings,
June 1944

→ planned Allied assault

GREAT BRITAIN

London
Dover
Calais
Pas de Calais
Boulogne
Brighton
Southampton
Portsmouth
Poole
Portland
Exeter

Force L
Eastern Task Force
Force S
Force J
Force G
Force O
Western Task Force
Force U
Force B

assembly area
German mine barrier
Channel

FRANCE
Seine
Dieppe
Le Havre
Caen
Sword
Juno
Gold
Omaha
Utah
Cherbourg

English

limit of Allied fighter cover

Normandy by Cyril Crain

Come and stand in memory
Of men who fought and died
They gave their lives in Normandy
Remember them with pride.

Soldiers, airmen, sailors
Airborne and marines
Who in civvy life were tailors
and men who worked machines.

British and Canadians
and men from USA
Forces from the Commonwealth
They were all there that day.

To Juno, Sword and Utah
Beaches of renown
Also Gold and Omaha
That's where the ramps went down.

The battle raged in Normandy
Many lives were lost
The war must end in victory
And this must be the cost.

When my life is over
and I reach the other side
I'll meet my friends from Normandy
And shake their hands with pride.

Countdown

26 January 1942

PFC Milburn Henke, of Hutchison, Minnesota is the first of two million American soldiers to arrive in Britain during the build-up to D-Day.

March 1942

BBC broadcasts a Royal Navy plea for holiday snaps of French coast to help map coastal areas. 30,000 letters arrive the following day.

19 August 1942

In a disastrous rehearsal for D-Day of 6,100 men involved in the landings at Dieppe, France, only 2,500 return. One

German company repels three battalions of mainly Canadian troops, taking 2,000 prisoners and killing 1,000. Enemy losses are less than 600. The raid proves the need for overwhelming force and heavy bombardment and that a floating harbour would need to be taken.

June 1943

Americans are now living in 100,000 buildings in 1,100 locations in Britain. In December, 30,000 further acres of South Devon are taken over and 3,000 residents evicted from 750 properties. Landings are rehearsed in Devon's Bideford Bay, chosen for its similarity to the Normandy coast.

August 1943

During Churchill's voyage aboard the Queen Mary en route to Quebec for the summit with Roosevelt, professor John Desmond Bernal, a scientific adviser, uses a loofah as a wave machine and 20 paper boats as the D-Day fleet. With the PM and aides looking on he proves success would depend on vast floating harbours, Mulberrys – represented by a Mae West life preserver.

November 1943

Thirty directives for *Overlord* issued.

6 December 1943

General Dwight D. Eisenhower appointed to command landings in France.

1 January 1944

General Montgomery relinquishes command of 8th Army in Italy and flies to England to set up his invasion HQ at his old school, St Paul's, Hammersmith. Montgomery will remain in command of ground forces until September 1944 when General Eisenhower will assume direct control. For the purposes of *Overlord*, RAF Bomber Command and the 8th US Air Force are placed under the operational direction of the Supreme Commander to add to the aircraft of the Allied Tactical Air Forces.

I7 January I944

Supreme Headquarters, Allied Expeditionary Force established in London.

2I January I944

Generals Eisenhower and Montgomery agree changes to General Morgan's COSSAC plans which set the invasion date as 31 May, extending the landing area west across the Cotentin Peninsula towards Cherbourg and increase the initial seaborne force from 3 Divisions to 5 Divisions.

I February I944

Revised *Overlord* plan, Neptune, the sea transportation and landing phase of *Overlord* issued.

5 March I944

Supreme Headquarters Allied Expeditionary Force (SHAEF) moves from Grosvenor Gardens to former US 8th Air Force HQ at Bushey Park, near Hampton Court, code name Widewing. Eisenhower lives nearby in Telegraph Cottage, Warren Road, Kingston upon Thames.

April I944

All leave cancelled for troops destined for *Overlord*. Eighteen Allied air forces begin pre-invasion bombing of France. 9th Air Force begins bombing targets in the Pas-de-Calais, railway marshalling yards and important bridges. ACM Sir Trafford Leigh-Mallory remarks that the 9th Air Force is by far the most effective force in knocking out these types of target. (From the beginning of May, the 9th dispatches more than a thousand aircraft each day, weather permitting, against targets in Normandy and the Pas-de-Calais).

10 April 1944

Naval Commander in Chief, Admiral Sir Bertram Ramsay, responsible for Neptune, issues orders for the naval involvement on D-Day. The document stretches to 1,100 pages.

22–29 April 1944

Operation Tiger, realistic US rehearsal for *Overlord* at Slapton Sands between Plymouth and Dartmouth. On the night of 27/28 April two German E-boats in the English Channel find eight LSTs, sink two and damage others, and kill 441 soldiers and 197 sailors.

1 May 1944

Eisenhower and Ramsay, aware Rommel is strengthening the Atlantic Wall (by D-Day 6.5 million mines are laid along the approaches) and covering the beaches with below-the-water obstacles, decide that the landings will be in daylight and at low tide, so that the obstacles will be visible.

A daylight landing also increases the accuracy of air and naval bombardment.

2–6 May 1944

Fabius, final rehearsal for *Overlord* at Slapton Sands.

8 May 1944

SHAEF selects 5 June as D-Day. HM The King, General Eisenhower, Field Marshal Smuts and others attend conference at General Montgomery's St Paul's HQ to review the final plans for *Overlord*.

18 May 1944

German radio broadcast that 'the invasion will come any day now'.

23 May 1944

Camps containing the soldiers who will land on D-Day are sealed with barbed wire. Senior Commanders told that D-Day is 5 June. Detailed briefings begin.

28 May 1944

Time the leading troops are to land ('H-Hour') is set at a few minutes before 06:00 hours and after 07:00 hours. Americans are to land first on Utah and Omaha then minutes later, to allow for the difference in the time of low tide, the British and Canadians agree to land on Gold, Juno and Sword. Eisenhower and Montgomery move elements of their HQs to HMS Dryad at Southwick House, near Portsmouth, to be near the embarkation ports.

31 May 1944

Group Captain Stagg, chief met officer, warns Eisenhower to expect stormy weather for several days to come.

1 June 1944

Admiral Ramsey takes command of the immense armada of ships for Operation Neptune, the naval part of *Overlord*. First regular morning and evening meetings are begun between senior commanders at Southwick House, principally to discuss deteriorating weather conditions in the Channel. Eisenhower begins a daily shuttle between his forward HQ at Southwick, Bushey Park his main HQ, and Stanmore, where SHAEF Air Forces HQ is located. Weather forecast is poor.

4 June 1944

At Southwick House Stagg meets commanders at 04:15 hours.

The forecast is rising wind and thicker cloud. Montgomery is prepared to go despite the weather but ACM Leigh-Mallory is not in favour. With so much depending upon air superiority Eisenhower has no choice but to postpone the landings, scheduled for 4/5 June, for 24 hours. All convoys at sea have to reverse their courses but two British midget submarines continue and just before midnight take up their positions off the beaches to act as markers for the invasion army when it arrives. By 09:30 Stagg predicts 36 hours of relatively clear weather with moderate winds.

Feldmarschall Rommel, convinced an invasion is not imminent, decides to leave the Normandy coast for Germany.

0415, 5 June 1944

With no basic changes to the weather pattern described the previous day, Eisenhower turns to General Montgomery and asks whether he could see any reason for not going on Tuesday, to which Montgomery replies, 'I would say – Go!' The other commanders agree. 'OK' says Eisenhower; 'We'll go.' A coded wireless message sent out by the BBC instructs the French Resistance to cut railway lines throughout France. German intelligence, which had partially broken the code, warns Rommel's HQ but in his absence it seems to have been ignored. Of 1,050 planned breaches of rail lines by the Resistance, 950 are carried out.

Home Front –
Second Front

'Unless we can land overwhelming forces and beat the Nazis in battle in France, Hitler will never be defeated. So this must be your prime task.'

Winston Churchill's orders to Lord Mountbatten in 1942.

In spring 1943 at the Anglo-American TRIDENT conference the British Chiefs of Staff committed themselves to Overlord and the Combined Chiefs issued their Directive to General F. E. Morgan, who had been appointed Chief of Staff to the Supreme Allied Commander (Designate) 'COSSAC' at the Casablanca Conference:

'To mount and carry out an operation, with forces and equipment established in the United Kingdom and with target date 1 May 1944, to secure a lodgement on the Continent from which further offensive operations could be developed. The lodgement area must contain sufficient port facilities to maintain a force of some 26 to 30 divisions and enable that force to be augmented by follow-up shipments from the United States or elsewhere of additional divisions and supporting units at the rate of three to five divisions per month.'

The target date of 1 May 1944 for invasion was later postponed a month to enable extra landing craft to be built and the initial assault was expanded from three to five Army divisions. *Overlord* **proceeded in London under the direction of General Morgan and Brigadier-General R. W. Barker, who set up an Anglo–American HQ for the eventual Supreme Commander and prepared an outline plan for the invasion of North-West Europe from Britain. But where would the attack take place?**

'The Pas-de-Calais has many obvious advantages such as that good air support and quick turn-around for our shipping can be achieved. On the other hand, it is a focal point of the enemy fighters disposed for defence and the maximum air activity can be brought to bear over this area with the minimum movement of his Air Forces. Moreover, the Pas-de-Calais is the most strongly defended area of the whole French coast … Further this area does not offer good opportunities for expansion … the Caen sector is weakly held; the defences are relatively light and the beaches are of high capacity and sheltered from the prevailing winds. Inland the terrain is suitable for airfield development and for the consolidation of the initial bridgehead; and much of it is unfavourable for counter-attacks by panzer divisions. Maximum enemy air opposition can only be brought to bear at the expense of the air defence screen covering the approaches to Germany and the limited number of enemy airfields within range of the Caen area facilitates the local neutralization of the German fighter force ... In the light of these factors it is considered that our initial landing on the Continent should be effected in the Caen area with a view to the eventual seizure of the lodgement area comprising the Cherbourg/Brittany group of ports.

Seine Bay, the area of Normandy chosen for the assault, is some 50 miles across and stretches from Barfleur eastwards to the mouth of the Seine. Because it was ultimately intended that American forces should be supplied directly from the United States, their troops were assigned to the western sector, while the British and Canadian beaches were in the eastern sector. The invasion would necessitate 24 different embarkation points spread over 1,000 miles of British coastline, made necessary by the total loading capacity in 24 hours, since the assault and follow-up had to load simultaneously. The British would load from Yarmouth to Portsmouth and the Americans from Southampton to Milford Haven. Each of the 24 points required its own embarkation camp, marshalling and concentration area and special road layout – many of which had to be either built or greatly improved.

Brigadier Tom Collins
Director of Movements for Continental Operations
October 1943—June 1944.

'Broadly, the requirements for the coastline and hinterland where the huge embarkation operation was to take place, were: no tide, so that loading at the hards or ramps could take place 24 hours out of 24 and hinterland which was hard and flat, with good road access or surface with no need for road building or improvement, with loading points where one wanted them and not dictated by inland access. The hinterland also needed to be suitable for construction of embarkation camps, with marshalling camps behind them where men and vehicles were to get into their craft loads and – further back – concentration areas to which units were to proceed from their home stations. Good road access from one to another was imperative. Added to that, good depth of water at loading points was essential, so that craft could load without danger.

'North Africa for the Sicily landings was perfect: no tide, no road problems on the hard sand, and camps and areas could be established precisely where required. England, on the other hand, could not have been worse. The change of tide around our shores is so great (24 feet each 24 hours), our coastline is intricate and deep water rarely lies close in. Also, the coastal roads and lanes are so winding and the country inland from the coast so enclosed for creating camps or areas, which could feed from one to the other ... The operation, which could have been mounted on 15–20 miles of the African coast, was spread from Yarmouth to Milford Haven ... spreading well over 1,000 miles with its estuaries and inlets. Even with the large number of embarkation points the loading of vehicles for the assault and follow-up had to begin six days before D-Day ... D-Day was not only the greatest combined operation ever undertaken: it was the greatest that ever will be.'

US Supply Officer, May 1944

'We've got a fairly big job on. Something comparable to the city of Birmingham hasn't merely got to be shifted; it's got to be kept moving when it's on the other side ...'

Trucks, jeeps, transports and staff cars caused a vast traffic snarl-up in the days before D-Day. In Andover, Hampshire, office workers were given 15 minutes extra at lunchtime to cross the street.

Pilot Officer R. H. 'Chad' Chadwick
RAF Lancaster navigator.

'The crew was fairly typical of those in Bomber Command. Although we were in a Royal Australian Air Force squadron, the pilot was the only Australian in the crew. I was the only officer. Mick was a flight sergeant and the remainder were all sergeants. This made no difference. We seven were firm friends with tremendous mutual trust and respect and rank or position had no part in our approach to the job. This was highly desirable, of course, in the making of an efficient bomber crew. As an officer, I felt lucky to have one or two privileges that the others did not get and to make up for this I tried to do a few extra chores around the aircraft, before or after a trip.

'We all felt ourselves lucky to be on this particular squadron as we found that Australians were a wonderful race with whom to go to war. They had little time for anyone who pulled rank or position, and basic discipline was good, but it was a discipline coming from natural leaders with a team keen to get on with the job. As RAF chaps found, an Aussie could call a man "a Pommy bastard" and make it sound an absolute term of endearment! On the other hand, any officer who started to put on airs and graces – very few did – merited the derogatory description "He's gone Pommy".'

Mike Henry DFC
Boston air gunner, IO7 Squadron.

'When we lived under canvas at Hartford Bridge Stan Adams [the navigator] and I shared a tent. The tent site, with a large marquee for our messing, was a long walk across many muddy fields from the main camp. It was good fun in a novel kind of way but it had its drawbacks. For one thing I ruined one of my best suitcases which had soaked up the moisture through the coconut matting on the grass floor of our tent. However, it wasn't for long and there was a good reason for preparing us in the event of a dire lack of accommodation when we moved across the Channel. As it happened we never saw a tent when moving to France.

'Apart from the three Boston squadrons at Hartford Bridge, we had two Dutch squadrons using the airfield for a short time – 322 with Spitfires and 320 with Mitchells. Their crews were dressed in the uniform of the Royal Netherlands Navy. When we found out how much they were paid, we gasped. Apart from their set pay scale, which was higher than ours, they received extra money for every flying hour. We didn't see a lot of the Dutch chaps for they messed elsewhere, but we often saw in our mess Queen Wilhelmina and Prince Bernhard.'

2nd TAF's 11 squadrons of Bostons, Venturas and Mitchells in 2 Group moved to Hampshire to be nearer the enemy coast and newer types of aircraft like the de Havilland

Mosquito FBVI fighter-bomber and Mustang fighter arrived. Mosquitoes of 140 Wing (21, 487 RNZAF and 464 RAAF Squadrons) specialized in pinpoint bombing of key targets in France in the run up to D-Day. During March–April to simulate the type of tactical targets against which 2 Group would be employed, Boston, Mitchell and Mosquito crews took part in two-week training exercises in full field conditions.

Major General Francis de Guingand
Chief of staff, 21st Army Group, shortly before D-Day, in a conversation with General Montgomery.

'I'd feel a lot happier if the Australian 9th Division was going ashore with us.'

The Australian government had withdrawn the last of its divisions, the 9th, from the Mediterranean early in 1943 in order to reinforce their armies in the Pacific.

Jan Caesar, 15
an English schoolgirl.

'We lived in a rented house in Derby Road, Southampton, a very neighbourly area. I was one of five sisters who had moved back to Southampton from Bournemouth with our mother after being evacuated in 1939. US convoys were parked all along the streets, waiting for the "off". One was composed of black men – they didn't mix races. My 14-year-old sister and I were besotted with one of them. He was charming. But after a couple of days they moved on. They were replaced by a convoy of white soldiers who included Julius Kupke, a German who had become a naturalized American and hated what the Germans were doing. He was short and squat – no oil painting, but my, could he sing. Whenever I hear "Rose Marie" my mind goes back to D-Day.

'My mother took pity on the men who were desperately tired and had been forced to sleep in their lorries. She invited several into our home where they crashed out on beds and chairs. My mother didn't have much to offer because of rationing but she made gallons of tea and cut up piles of bread for cucumber sandwiches, which they thought so English. In return, they gave us their rations. They made our eyes pop out – tins of meat, fruit, sweets and chocolate.

'When the convoy moved off we said fare-well with promises to write. My mother was upset, knowing where they were heading. Julius returned early the following morning to say thank you again with another parcel of goodies. They had been held up at the docks, waiting for a boat. My mother kept her promise and wrote to him and his fiancée in America for quite a while but we lost touch when we moved around after my father was de-mobbed.'

Bill Goodwin

Bricklayer on the maintenance staff sealed into the US Camps D2 and D4 in Dorset two weeks before D-Day.

'I queued with the Americans for breakfasts, which included a pint of tomato or fruit juice, a large plate of sweet pancakes with eggs and bacon and a pint of coffee with sugar and carnation milk. We also had the US Women's Voluntary Service calling at the camp. They'd walk around with trays loaded with free cigarettes, glucose tablets, chewing gum, and ring doughnuts, chewing and pipe tobacco. In the Big Tent there were also live shows with US artistes.'

Private Ken McFarlane

Anti-Tank Platoon, Ist Battalion Dorset Regiment, 50th Northumbrian Division.

'After a few weeks on Bren Gun Carrier driving at Bowness on Windermere, mechanics at Fords of Dagenham and range firing at Harlech in Wales, I finally arrived at a wooded camp just outside Fawley, Southampton, posted to 1st Battalion Dorsetshire Regiment. Time was spent studying maps and a sand tray model of our next exercise, *Overlord*. We were issued with waterproofing kit (side extensions, gunge for dill and brakes, breathers, etc.). During the week American MPs were posted outside the camp to prevent us from leaving but vehicles and drivers were sent on to the road outside to line up on painted white squares. We outsiders had heard that the lads inside had been paid 200 francs apiece, so thought the next manoeuvre must be the real thing.'

Lance Bombardier Frank Scott, 24

I65 HAA Regimental HQ Royal Artillery.

'Inevitably all good things come to an end and we received our "Marching Orders" to proceed in convoy to the London Docks. The weather was worsening, putting all the best-laid plans "on hold". Although restrictions as regards personnel movements were pretty tight some local leave was allowed. It would have been possible for me to see my folks just once more before heading into the unknown but having said my farewells earlier felt I just couldn't go through that again.

'With the enormous numbers of vehicles and military equipment arriving in the marshalling area and a continuous downpour of rain it wasn't long before we were living in a sea of mud and getting a foretaste of things to come. To idle away the hours whilst awaiting to hear the shout "WE GO", time was spent playing cards (for the last remaining bits of English currency), much idle gossip and I would suspect thinking about those we were leaving behind. God knows when, or if, we would be seeing them again. By now this island we were about to leave, with its incessant Luftwaffe bombing raids and the arrival of the "Flying Bomb", had by now become a front line and it was good to be thinking that we were now going to do something about it!

'All preparations were made for the off. Pay Parade and an issue of 200 French francs (invasion style), and then to "Fall In" again for an issue of the 24-hour ration pack (army style), bags for vomit and a Mae West (American style). Time to write a quick farewell letter home before boarding a troopship. Very soon it was anchors away. I must have dozed off for I awoke to find we were hugging the English coast and were about to change course off the Isle of Wight where we joined the great armada of ships of all shapes and sizes. It wasn't too long before the coastline of the French coast became visible, although I did keep looking over my shoulder for the last glimpse of my homeland. The whole seascape by now was filled with an endless procession of vessels carrying their cargoes of fighting men, the artillery, tanks, plus all the other essentials to feed the hungry war machine.

'That first night at sea was spent laying just off the coast at Arromanches (Gold Beach) where some enemy air activity was experienced and a ship moored alongside unfortunately got an HE bomb in its hold. Orders came through to disembark and unloading continued until darkness fell. An exercise that had no doubt been overlooked and therefore not covered during previous years of intensive training was actually climbing down the side of a high-sided troopship in order to get aboard, in my case, an American LCT. This accomplished safely, with every possible chance of falling between both vessels tossing in a heaving sea, there followed a warm "Welcome Aboard" from a young cheerful fresh-faced, gum-chewing, cigar-smoking Yank. I believe I sensed the smell of coffee and do'nuts!'

Three Batteries, each of two Troops of four 3.7-inch guns; some 24 guns in all, were tasked for 'Ack-Ack' protection of airfields once a foothold had been successfully gained and a position firmly held in Normandy. As it turned out, the Regiment not only fought in an AA role but 275 Battery came under command of Guards Armoured Division for ground shooting; 198 Battery deployed in the AA role defensive Conc. Area, and 317 Battery deployed in the Anti-tank role.

WREN Doris Hayball, 23

'We knew D-Day was coming because we were inundated with young midshipmen. Shoreham harbour became so full of ships you could walk across it on the landing craft. For at least a month before 6 June I couldn't get home from Hove to Worthing without a pass. On the night of D-Day I was on fire duty but when I came off at midnight I was told not to bother to go to quarters. They wanted me to help cook breakfasts at 2 a.m. So we knew this was it. We had a hotplate ten feet long. It was a very sustaining breakfast but I learned later many of the sailors who left from Shoreham were awfully seasick.'

Lieutenant Abe Dolim
a navigator in the 94th Bomb Group, recorded in his
diary at Rougham:

'There have been all sorts of rumours about an imminent invasion of the enemy coast.'

Vera Lynn
Forces Sweetheart, who in June 1944 was homeward bound
and exhausted after a gruelling tour of Burma and the
Middle East when her plane touched down in Jerba,
Tunisia for a night stop over.

'We had been told just before we landed that there was a whisper something was afoot. I was therefore hoping that there wasn't anything going on that would stop me from getting back. We freshened ourselves up and then we went into this little tent where there was just a handful of officers. We said, "Right, let's turn the radio on." There was this little wireless in the corner. And that's when the news came over that the boys had started and the operation had begun. We all gave a little toast in that tent. And we said we hoped that this was the beginning of the end.'

Civilian George Jackson II
'Along with hundreds of other children I was at the Odeon Cinema at Bury Park, Luton. We were practising for a concert when a man walked on the stage and told us that the Allied Forces had landed in Normandy and it was the beginning of the end of Nazi Germany. We all cheered and clapped even when most of us did not know where Normandy was. I ran home to tell my mother. She said, "Well it looks like your brother did not die in vain."'

Civilian Mrs J. Charlesworth

'I was living with my parents in an old pub in Gosport. A lot of noise and commotion woke me early and I went down and opened the door. There were soldiers and army trucks, all making for the harbour. I put my six-month-old daughter in her pram and walked the short distance to the seafront. Little boats were bobbing waiting for the troops to climb aboard. One American boy said he was so afraid. I said to him, "You will be all right, I know it."'

Nurse Helen Pavlovsky USN
The Royal Victoria Hospital, Netley.

'It seemed to me that it took at least a week for all the ships to gather just outside our hospital in Southampton Water. The Royal Victoria Hospital at Netley was a very cold and damp monstrosity and certainly not conducive to treating patients. The Seabees [US Navy construction battalion personnel] remodelled the whole thing to make it usable. We could go outside and sit on the waterfront and watch. One day it seemed like the whole area was full of ships and the next morning there was not a single one. We were on duty 24 hours a day but we didn't know what we were waiting for.'

Civilian P. McElhlnney

'I was 12 and old enough to understand what was going on. At breakfast the radio announcer gave out a carefully worded message to the nation saying our troops had made a landing on the beaches of Normandy, and were fighting for them inch by inch. I sensed that I was witnessing history being made. I lived in Portsmouth and the streets were filled with equipment. I will always remember a young soldier stopping me and putting his hand in his pockets. He pulled out all his money and cigarettes, pushed it all into my hands and said, "Here kid, take this. I won't be coming back from where I'm going." I still wonder if he ever did.'

WREN Jean Irvine
Serving on the planning staff of Admiral Ramsay.

'Once I arrived at Southwick House in May, I was sealed inside the gates until after D-Day. I was working in a Nissen hut adjoining the house and my job was to file, type and organize secret documents. We were under terrible pressure. We worked 80 hours a week for more than four months. It was so exciting to know everything that was about to happen. On 5 June we played cricket, but on the night of the invasion itself I stayed up all night. On the morning of D-Day I fell asleep at my desk – there was such a relief of tension.'

Major Tom Normanton, 27
intelligence staff, Southwick House.

'There was a complete hush in the room – a cool, calm atmosphere and one of quiet confidence. Everything had been thought out but we all remembered the old adage that the finest of plans comes to an end when the shooting starts. The weather was blowing a gale. The wind was howling and the rain was lashing down but inside there was almost complete silence. There was only a handful of people in the map room itself. There were no raised voices and no raised tempers. And there was none of the normal backslapping or laughing. In our hearts we all knew this was it.'

Ena Howes

Duty Petty Officer

'I was Duty Petty Officer on the night of 5 June. It was remarkably quiet and after the previous night's cancellation because of adverse weather conditions, the operation was under way. For once the operators had time to chat amongst themselves, wondering if their boyfriends had sailed off to France too? Would we get any leave beforehand? Would the invasion succeed? How bad would the casualties be? All of these thoughts were bandied about, helping to pass the time – it was a very long night. Because of the use of scramblers we could only anticipate what was happening, but a call from General Omar Bradley at about 02:00 gave us cause to hope that everything was going to plan. The RAF had bombed the coastal batteries between Le Havre and Cherbourg and gliders had landed Airborne Divisions behind the coastline of Normandy. By the end of the Middle Watch we received news that everything was going well and at 06:30 the first seaborne troops were landing on the beaches. I finally went off duty at 08:00 and then came the BBC announcement of the landings. The Mess echoed to an almighty cheer. After all the planning the beginning of the end was in sight. Our lads were in France and we had been part of it! I walked down the tree-lined drive at Southwick House very tired but very happy.'

BBC 8 a.m. bulletin

on the morning of 6 June read by Frederick Allen.

'Supreme Allied Headquarters have issued an urgent warning to inhabitants of the enemy-occupied countries living near the coast. The warning said that a new phase in the Allied air offensive had begun. Shortly before this warning the Germans reported that Havre, Calais and Dunkirk were being heavily bombarded and that German naval units were engaged with Allied landing craft.'

New York bulletin

3:32 a.m., Tuesday, 6 June.

'Under the command of General Eisenhower, Allied naval forces, supported by strong air forces, began landing Allied armies this morning on the coast of France.'

Mary Hoskins, 2I

student nurse.

'As our nurses' home next to the Royal South Hampshire Hospital had been bombed, we had been billeted out in a large house in Highfield, Southampton. For weeks before, we had become used to the movement of troops and the droning of aircraft which had disturbed our sleep. On 6 June someone dashed into our room and gave us the shock news. A reliable source on the wireless had broadcast that we had made a landing on the Normandy coast. We dressed hurriedly and in small groups made our way to catch our tram. The streets were filled with people as we tried to get to work and the tram services were in chaos. Breakfast roll call at the hospital was at 7:30 a.m. We could not be late so we decided to walk, or, as it happened, run! But to no avail. We were 20 minutes late. Home Sister was already doling out the porridge. She said, "What time do you call this?" We tried to explain we had walked because the landings had disrupted public transport. She just said, "You should have made allowances for that", as if we young nurses should have known one of the biggest secrets of the war! Then she sent us on duty without any breakfast! That evening, we walked up The Avenue instead of getting our hospital bus and saw the convoys going down to the docks. Southampton had almost become an American town!'

Lieutenant General George S. Patton
commander, Third United States Army.
'We won't just shoot the sons-a-bitches, we are going to cut out their living guts and use them to grease the treads of our tanks.'

Winston Churchill
to his wife Clementine on the eve of D-Day.
'Do you realize that by the time you wake up in the morning, 20,000 men may have been killed?'

Feldmarschall Erwin Rommel
'We'll have only one chance to stop the enemy and that's while he's in the water. Everything we have must be on the coast … the first 24 hours of the invasion will be decisive. For the Allies as well as Germany, it will be the longest day.'

Feldmarschall von Rundstedt
'The Atlantic Wall was a myth … any resolute assault was bound to make a breakthrough anywhere along it in a day at most.'

Adolf Hitler
German Chancellor.

'If we do not stop the invasion and drive the enemy back into the sea, the war will be lost.'

General Dwight D.Eisenhower's
prepared speech in the event D-Day did not succeed.

'Our landings in the Cherbourg-Havre area have failed to gain a satisfactory foothold and I have withdrawn the troops. (The troops have been withdrawn).

'My decision to attack at this time and place was based on the best information available. If any blame or fault attaches to this attempt, it is mine alone.'

Ron Mailey
4th AGRA Signals, in a holding battalion in Kent.

'On the morning of 6 June we heard on the radio that a large force of both our troops and the Americans had succssfully landed on the beaches near Caen and Bayeux and also further down the coast towards Cherbourg. This was very good news and we felt that it would make up for the defeat in 1940 in which I had taken part. Immediately our own Battalion was mobilized, and we departed for Southampton. In hindsight, Hitler was our greatest ally. He made the mistake of thinking our attack was a diversionary one and that the main attack was to come in the Pas-de-Calais area. It was a mistake he repeated many times in the war and, perhaps, had he left it to his generals, we may have lost, instead of won.'

Gunner Alfred Sewell

I24 Light AA Regiment RA, Lewes, Sussex.

'We were on guns at dawn on 6 June watching huge fleets of planes and gliders bound for France. We were warned to expect dive-bombers, rockets and God knows what. We prayed for the boys going over. *Overlord* had begun.'

Panzer Leutnant Günter Halm

'I was asleep when the invasion began. The first bombardment started at about 01:00, and it was so loud and shocking that all of us knew instantly it was something out of the ordinary. I shot out of bed and went straight to the battalion staff quarters to organize my men. Then we hung around until 07:00, waiting for orders. Feldmarschall Rommel was away and so was our divisional commander so there was no one to give orders. We were told to push on to the coast in our armoured personnel carriers and we had almost got there when we fell upon English troops. I've no idea to this day who they were but they were on foot. During that night, my battalion lost three-quarters of the men. I've no doubt that if we had not wasted those valuable first hours waiting for orders, we could have pushed the Allies back right away. Those hours from 01:00 to 07:00 were critical and our tanks were left idle for too long.'

Andre Heintz, 23

French Resistance fighter.

'I shall never forget that night or the thrill of knowing the Allies were coming to expel the Nazis at last. My mother woke up in the early hours when she first heard the noise and said, "It must be the landings." But I dared not confirm it, even to her, because I knew that the Germans thought it might be a diversionary tactic. So I told my own mother nothing. In the morning a friend called and told me the sea was black with ships. Then the bombing began. I was helping to take the injured to our local hospital, which was run by nuns, but there was nothing to distinguish it from other buildings the Germans had been using. We couldn't paint a red cross because the Germans had requisitioned all the paint so the nuns brought out the sheets, red with blood, that had been in use in the operating theatre and we spread them out in a cross.

'I'll never forget the next RAF plane to fly over us. It waggled its wings, and we all knew it had worked. The bombing stopped in our area.'

Civilian June Telford

'I was catching a bus to work when I noticed things where different. Usually the town was full of commandos and as I stood there, wondering what was different, it came to me ... silence. There were no boots, no troops, not even the usual singing. We were planting tomato plants on the farm, so we didn't miss anything in the air over the Isle of Wight. We saw the planes returning, some on fire, and some with smoke pouring from them and many spaces in their formations.'

Jean Lancaster-Rennie
an English schoolgirl.

'Every day we'd heard the bombers go out and every evening we heard them return. But there was something different enough to send us, at dawn, from our beds to windows that looked out on chimney pots and slates and beyond to the clear blue sky with tiny white clouds. The bombers seemed to come from nowhere in perfect, geometric formation. They kept coming and coming as if the whole sky belonged to them as they roared away to deal death and destruction. It was D-Day.'

Stan Bruce
5th/7th Battalion, The Gordon Highlanders.

'When I joined the 5th/7th Gordons they were training for the invasion of Normandy. I was quite proud to be joining, as my father served in the 7th Battalion Gordons in WWI. Plus we had heard so much about the famous 51st Highland Division and their exploits against Rommel in the desert campaign. All we did was train and you could feel the tension in the air. We knew that the invasion was coming and the old hands knew what was in front of them. I was going to win the war single-handed. Dream on Bruce. What an idiot! Us young lads did not know what it was like to really be under enemy fire and still thought that war was a great adventure. That thought would soon be shattered and quite a few of us did not survive. One day all leave was cancelled, and we were moved nearer the coast and put in a huge compound under canvas. The Battalion was on the move and heading for the embarkation port and the invasion.'

Lieutenant Ed Wanner
B-24 Liberator pilot, 'Asbestos Alice', 700th Bomb Squadron, 445th Bomb Group, 2nd Bomb Division, Tibenham, Norfolk, whose crew were recent replacements.

'Here we were in a foreign land where they drove on the wrong side of the road, where "knocked up" meant they were busy that night, and where the great Normandy Invasion Landing was happening.'

Ben Smith Jr
radio operator-gunner, Chicks Crew, 303rd Bomb Group, Ist Bomb Division, 8th Air Force, Molesworth.

'Stars and Stripes gave American losses over Europe in the five months preceding D-Day as 1,407 heavy bombers, 673 fighters and 100 medium bombers. These figures do not include those killed or wounded when the planes returned to their home base or crashed in the United Kingdom. Over 14,000 men were lost in the heavies alone. The British had parallel losses.

In June, after six months of intense training, we were assigned, as a crew, to a B-17G at Kearney, Nebraska. We flew it overseas to England where we started flying combat missions immediately, just in time to join the D-Day invasion support flights. The first few short-haul sorties were milk runs, giving us the false impression that this combat flying was a piece of cake. But that was to change quickly … It was apparent to all of us that the long-awaited invasion of Festung Europa was imminent. We knew that we would be involved, but expected all-out opposition from the Germans. The night of 5 June we saw the RAF aircraft and gliders coming over, wave after wave. We knew we would be going in the morning and thought there would be hell to pay. We didn't sleep much that night. At briefing we heard Eisenhower's inspirational message to the departing troops. At least it was supposed to inspire. Churchill could have done it with a lot more class.'

Wilbur Richardson

B-17 gunner, 94th Bomb Group.

'Invasion fever was abound. In May all flight crewmen were ordered to carry their .45s at all times. Ground crews were issued carbines to have at the ready, in case enemy paratroops would attempt to foul up any suspected plans. With double summer time in effect, darkness came very late and the nights were much shorter than I was used to, growing up in Long Beach, California. So in order to get some sleep, before the usual crack-of-dawn (or earlier) briefing for a bombing mission, it was necessary to close the blackout curtains to darken the room by shutting out the later evening light. But on the evening of 4 June we were called out to get ready just before darkness was fully upon us. Unusual. The rumours circulated once more. After some night formation flying and speculating, we headed for our target along the French coast sometime after dawn. It was a long day, and again it didn't happen. Just a rumour. Little did we know. Must wait again. It was an even longer day for those in the intelligence unit. About six or seven of them were placed under guard, food sent in, etc., until the dawn of the big day. Next evening, 5 June, we started early again, same as the night before. So, we felt this must be it for sure.

'At briefing, this was it. What a contrast when it was usually groans when we learned of the target. What animated talk and yippie! The weather was better for the Channel crossing. It was a go! The pilots gave a few more details as we repeated last night's run and then to the shoreline targets at dawn before the landings were to begin in about an hour.'

Harry Barker

RAF bomb aimer, 2I8 Squadron.

'In April 1944 we attacked three targets in France and then began training to use a new type of G called GH. This would enable the navigator to direct the pilot to fly to within a few yards of a position on the ground to allow bombs to be dropped blind. We practised during May using Lincoln cathedral as our target and taking photographs to record the results. This work continued in the first week of June and then on 5 June we took part in Operation *Glimmer* to simulate a naval attack on the Pas-de-Calais area in order to deceive the Germans into believing that the D-Day landings were there and not Normandy. This was achieved by flying a progressive square search pattern between Newhaven and Boulogne, dropping Window continuously. The plan was successful and we shared the task with 617 Dam Busters Squadron with additional crew members to ensure that a continual dropping of the packets of Window was maintained. I understood that no aircraft were lost during this risky operation. We returned to Woolfox Lodge after five hours 15 minutes of demanding flying. After the usual breakfast we slept for a few hours and awoke to find out on the 1 p.m. news that today, 6 June, was D-Day and the landings in Normandy had begun. In my diary I noted that it was cold and miserable at home.'

Flight Lieutenant Eric 'Phil' Phillips DFC MiD

2I4 Squadron Gunnery Leader, I00 Group, 22:50 5 June.

'We were cruising on course at 30,000 feet, a brilliant moonlit night with 10/10ths cloud 5,000ft below, the vapour trails from each wing tip standing out for all to see. Inside the Fortress aircraft "N" with its crew of ten fully trained airmen all is silent; just the steady hum of the four engines can be heard. There was a click as the wireless operator Flight Lieutenant Bill Doy switched on his intercom and spoke. "Rear gunner, there is a U/I aircraft approaching very fast from the rear, I confirm that I have it in sight some 2,000 feet astern and approximately 800 feet below." I brought it in by commentary – 1,200 feet, 1,000 feet – at 800 feet it started to disappear under the Fortress. I handed the commentary back to the W/O, who gave the skipper the order, "Corkscrew, starboard go!" On the word go, I fired one short burst blindly with both .5s fully depressed. The next second with the Fortress in a deep dive to starboard the attacking aircraft I now recognized as an Me 410. It was on my port quarter for a second. It appeared to just hang there with the glow of two cannons being fired. I fired two short bursts and also observed an accurate burst from the mid-upper turret. There was no doubt that the Me 410 was hit as I did see smoke. He then disappeared from my view and I did not see the aircraft again. The Me 410 was claimed destroyed.'

Five Fortresses of 214 Squadron operated in support of the D-Day operation in an ABC (*Airborne Cigar*) jamming role. A protective patrol lasting over five hours was flown at 27,000 feet starting just north and east of Dieppe and running almost perpendicular to the coastline carrying out jamming and *Window* dropping in conjunction with 24 Lancasters of 101 Squadron of 1 Group. One Lancaster was shot down. The patrol was outstandingly successful and earned a personal congratulation to all concerned by Arthur Harris to whom he pointed out that 'the work carried out was of paramount importance in connection with the Invasion Forces'.

Flight Sergeant Roland 'Ginger' A. Hammersley DFM

Lancaster air gunner, 57 Squadron, which bombed heavy gun positions at La Pemelle.

'It was at 01:40 hours in JB318/'O' with a bomb load of 11 1,000-lb AN-M and four 500-1b GP bombs that we took off with the other 15 crews for the attack. As we were crossing the English Channel it was apparent that there was either a huge flock of birds, thousands of aircraft or a vast fleet on the sea immediately below our Lancaster – my "fishpond" was swamped with blips. Banking the aircraft to port and starboard, we could see a huge fleet of vessels heading towards the French coast. The expected "D-Day" had arrived and I was there to the fore.'

Sergeant Johnny Cook, I9

(later Flying Officer DFM), Halifax III rear gunner, 578 Squadron at Burn.

'June 5th – INVASION. Target Montfleury – Cherbourg – gun battery. Early morning take off. Almost a daylight operation. Heavy cloud and severe icing over Channel to target. We opened the "Second Front" – D-Day – at about five in the morning. Saw the massive convoy formations in the Channel.'

Franklin L. Betz

B-I7 navigator, 379th BG, Kimbolton.

'To be awakened about 04:00 for a mission was pretty much routine but to be hauled out of the sack at about

01:30 to report to briefing – well something unusual must be up, I thought as I groped sleepily for my clothes. The atmosphere at briefing was invariably sombre. Sitting quietly on benches dozing or languidly puffing on cigarettes that glowed eerily in the soft light of the starkly furnished rooms, there was very little talk while the fliers, officers and enlisted men waited for the CO, Colonel Preston, to arrive.

'"Tenshun!" someone up front bawled when the CO strode in. Everyone arose standing erect, eyes straight ahead. "At ease," the Colonel said. The men sat down quietly, tensely awaiting roll call and the removal of the cover from the huge map of Europe on which the course to and from the target had been traced. If it showed a deep penetration of Germany that meant dangerous fighter attacks and flak encounters throughout the flight; a groan arose from the dry throats of the airmen that trailed off into excited whispers as briefing continued. But at 02:30, when the briefing officer announced, "This is it – this is D-Day!" it was different; a lusty cheer shattered the quiet of a moment before. Whoops, whispers and yells echoed from the grey walls. It was an unprecedented and ecstatic vocal demonstration by the fliers who had doggedly been carrying the war to Germany for many months with considerable losses of men and planes. It was the day they had awaited to share with the ground forces and together they would assault the *Nazi* war machine, hopefully gaining a foothold on the mainland with the ultimate goal of driving the *Wehrmacht* back to the Fatherland and crushing it.'

Flying Officer Kazik Budzik KW VM

Spitfire IX pilot, 3I7 'City of Wilno' (Polish) Squadron, which flew four separate patrols over the invasion beaches.

'We must have been amongst the first fighter aircraft over the beachhead as dawn was just breaking upon our arrival. The invasion armada was enormous. Most of the landing craft were still heading towards the beaches. It really was quite a spectacle. There was flak everywhere though, mostly from the fleet, and that was quite frightening. Watching the start of Europe's liberation was a fantastic experience, particularly the naval bombardment. You could see the guns fire and the shells landing on the coastline, getting further inland the more our troops advanced. It was amazing.'

Manfred Rommel, I5

about to celebrate his mother's 50th birthday on 6 June.

'Father had arrived from France on 4 June and we were planning a simple family lunch for my mother's birthday. Speidel [Generalmajor Hans Speidel, Chief of Staff of the 7th Army in Normandy] kept saying he was not sure the landings had taken place and father should continue with his intention of speaking to Hitler about the strategy of repelling the invasion. My father disagreed with the other generals over this. He favoured a confrontation on the landing beaches while General Karl von Rundstedt wanted the panzer divisions to be kept back to the north of Paris. Father was very calm and cautious, as always. He agreed Speidel should call back in an hour but he began packing immediately. When the call came, Speidel told him the landing had happened. The Navy had told my father before he left France that no landing would be possible because the seas were too stormy. It had not been an easy decision for my father to return to Germany but he had believed the Navy. Now he was getting reports of Allied landings from all parts of the coast. He was calm but he was not happy that he had been at home when it all happened. He left immediately for the 500-mile journey back to Normandy to lead the men who had long expected the invasion, yet had been caught by surprize just the same. Mother took it completely in her stride. I talked to my father a lot about how the invasion happened. For a long time, everyone thought the Allies would land in the Pas-de-Calais because it was the nearest point to the English coast, only 25 miles away. On the other hand, the German fortifications were strongest there, so Normandy began to be considered the likeliest.

'One thing everyone believed was that the Allies would first have to capture and hold a harbour. But, of course, they brought over their own mobile *Mulberry* harbour – a masterstroke by Churchill, which no one could ever have imagined.

'My father was tremendously impressed with the organization and the imagination involved. It was a glorious battle for the Allies and, as a soldier, he admired them greatly. Father knew from North Africa that the British were good soldiers. But, as he said, Normandy showed him they were even better than he had presumed. He knew by then that Germany could not win the war. He had often discussed it with me. He said anyone with common sense could see that the only solution on the Western Front was to achieve a position in which to make peace. He would say: "Even if you have to give in, as long as you are strong, you can achieve peace.'"

Field Marshal Erwin Rommel had travelled back from the Normandy front to be with them and to give his wife a pair of grey shoes. At 7 am Generalmajor Hans Speidel, Chief of Staff of the 7th Army in Normandy, told them the long-feared invasion had started.

'So it's started then!'

Adolf Hitler's unconcerned response after lunch on D-Day when the Führer finally appeared and was told of the 'invasion'.

Hitler held his first meeting about the landings at 14:00. It was not until nearly 17:00 that he finally gave permission to move just two armoured divisions and the counter-attack could not be mounted until the morning of 7 June, by which time the bridgehead was 30 hours old and it was too late. Hitler, and many of his generals, believed that Normandy was simply a diversion for a larger attack on Calais, a view he clung to until August 1944.

Nations Represented On D-Day

Australia

Virtually all 11,000 Australian aircrew participate in *Overlord*. Most of the 1,100 officers and men of the Royal Australian Naval Volunteer Reserve (RANVR) serve aboard British cruisers HMS *Ajax, Enterprise, Glasgow* and *Scylla*, or as commanders of several flotillas of landing craft and MTBs. On *Ajax*, a RANVR officer commands the 6-inch gun bombardment of the German Naval Battery at Longues-sur-Mer on cliffs 200ft above Gold Beach. Australians also serve aboard destroyers HMS *Ashanti*, *Eskimo* and *Mackay*.

Czechoslovakia
310, 312 and 313 Squadrons (Spitfire IXs), 134 Wing, 84 Group, 2nd TAF, and 311 Squadron (Liberator Vs), 19 Group, RAF Coastal Command.

Belgium
Two corvettes, three merchant ships and three Congo boats. 350 Squadron participate in aerial defence of Gold and Sword Beaches. 349 Squadron provide covering fire for US 82nd Airborne Division.

Canada
About 15,000 troops of the 3rd Infantry Division. RCAF commit 39 strategic and tactical squadrons, who fly 230 sorties of the 1,200 mounted by Bomber Command. Nearly 10,000 officers and men aboard 126 Canadian fighting ships, 44 landing craft among them.

Denmark
800 Danes mostly serve aboard ships.

France
329, 340 and 341 Squadrons, 145 Wing (Spitfire IXs) and 88 and 342 Squadrons, 2 Group, (Boston IIIAs) in 2nd TAF, Allied Expeditionary Air Force, and 345 Squadron

(Spitfires) in No.11 Group, ADGB. Light cruisers *Montcalm* and *Georges Leygues*, Western Task Force off Port-en-Bessin, and the destroyer *La Combattante*, Eastern Task Force off the coast of Courseulles-sur-Mer, take part in the naval bombardment. Five frigates, four corvettes, and four submarine chasers perform escort duty. The elderly battleship *Courbet* is towed across the Channel and sunk off Ouistreham to act as a breakwater for the Mulberry harbour at Arromanches.

United Kingdom
Second Army composed of two corps (including three British divisions with auxiliary units and services – some 62,000 men). Provides about 80 per cent of the warships. RAF flies 5,656 sorties.

Greece
Two Royal Hellenic Navy corvettes escort convoys to Juno, Gold and Sword. A number of Greek soldiers, sailors, and airmen serve in Allied Forces.

Norway
Ten warships of the Royal Norwegian Navy in exile and 43 ships of the Norwegian Merchant Navy (two of the cargo ships are scuttled to create a breakwater for landing craft) and three fighter squadrons – 66, 331 and 332, 132 Wing, 2nd TAF, flying Spitfire IXs.

Netherlands
Cruiser, HMNS *Sumatra* and two sloops, *Flores* and *Soemba*, (The latter two fire in support of the landings on Utah and Gold. On D+3 *Sumatra*, its armour dismantled,

is intentionally scuttled near the shore to form part of the breakwater for Mulberry harbour. Nos. 98, 180 and 320 Squadrons, 139 Wing (Mitchell IIs), 2 Group, and 322 Squadron (Spitfire XIVs), 141 Wing, all from 2nd TAF.

New Zealand

By June 1944 more than one-third of New Zealand's overseas manpower, about 35,000 men, are serving in Britain. Of these, about 30,000 are in the RAF or in the six RNZAF Squadrons and they take part in every phase of the operation. 4,000 officers and men of the Royal New Zealand Naval Volunteer Reserve are in the Royal Navy. Junior officers of the RNZNVR command scores of landing craft and flotillas of New Zealand-manned MTBs.

Poland

302, 308 and 317 Squadrons, 131 Wing, 84 Group (Spitfire IXs) and 306 and 315 Squadrons, (Mustang IIIs) 133 Wing, (all from 2nd TAF) and Lancasters of 300 (Polish) Squadron, 1 Group, RAF Bomber Command. Destroyers *Krakowiak* and *Slazak* take part in the Eastern Task Force's naval bombardment of the coast. Four other Polish warships and eight merchant ships play various roles.

United States

First Army composed of two corps (five divisions with auxiliary units and services – about 73,000 troops). Navy provides 16.5 per cent of the Allied warships and hundreds of landing vessels. 8th and 9th Air Forces (6,080 tactical and strategic aircraft) in Allied Expeditionary Air Force.

'Neptune' Factfile

May D-Day is set for 5 June, a time of favourable moon and tides, conditions which would still prevail on 6 and 7 June but not thereafter. Naval units are required to be in their designated assembly positions by 29 May, a directive which involves shipping movements at almost every southern British port from the Mersey to Harwich as well as at Belfast and a number of Scottish locations.

Majority of 300+ large cargo vessels are of the American-built Liberty type, many of them carrying vehicles (mechanized transport) and their attendant troops. Over 1,500 craft and barges are required as ferries between the anchorage position of the larger ships and the shore. After completing their initial task, the LSIs are to head back to the UK to reload.

23 May Because of their slow speed, being old or damaged ships, the section of the *Corncob* (blockship) fleet which had assembled in the estuary of the Forth set out to be scuttled or 'planted' off the French coast.

30 May First of a fleet of coasters, which have been waiting in the 20-mile stretch of the Thames, sail to take their places amongst over 500 ships in an anchorage extending from Hurst Castle in the west to Bembridge in the east. 362 coasters are to help maintain a continuous flow of supplies to the beaches.

2—3 June From their anchorages in the Clyde or Belfast Lough, the battleships of the bombarding fleet sail.

5 June Landing craft with the longest crossings set out. HMS *Scylla*, flagship of the Eastern Task Force, leaves Portsmouth Harbour at 13:40 as the first assault forces pass through Spithead Gate. The US HQ ship *Ancon* leaves Plymouth so as to reach her assigned anchorage at Omaha. Troops joining their Utah-bound LSIs at Torbay anchorage are ferried to their ships in landing craft from Torquay. Troops embarking in Weymouth Bay, where over 80 ships are anchored, and Portland, are similarly transported from Weymouth Quay.

21:30 During the night the biggest invasion force the world has ever seen sails from British ports across the English Channel to France. The two Naval Task Forces total 672 warships for assault convoy escort, minesweeping, shore bombardment, local defence, etc., and 4,126 major and minor landing ships and craft for initial assault and ferry purposes: a total of 4,798. They carry the force of 39 army divisions – 20 American, 14 British, three Canadian, one Free French, and one Polish. To this ship total can be added (A) Home Command for follow-up escort and Channel patrols, plus reserves: 1 RN battleship; 118 destroyers and escorts (108 RN, 4 US, 1 French, 5 Allied); 364 other warships including coastal forces (340 RN, 8 French, 16 Allied). (B) Western Channel Approaches A/S Escort Groups and reserves: 3 RN escort carriers, 55 RN destroyers and escort vessels. (C) 864 Merchant ships (mainly British liners, tankers, tugs, etc) to supply and support the invasion and naval forces. Grand Total, 6,203 vessels. The armada converges on an area south of the Isle of White code-named Area Z but known unofficially as 'Piccadilly Circus.'

6 June 05:00 First of the bombarding ships open fire. The heaviest bombardment takes place during the first 50 minutes after the sun rises at 05:58. Task is to silence, with saturating fire, not only the 13 main coastal artillery batteries but also the beach defence forces and then, after the assault has gone in, to engage other targets assisted by ground and air spotters. Destroyers assist the larger warships in these tasks.

09:00 German 84th Corps informed of seaborne landings.

09:30 Announcement of *Overlord* released to the press. British troops one mile inland on Gold. British capture Hermanville. Tactical surprise is total. Ship casualties are less than anticipated. (Naval action occurs early at the eastern extremity at 05:30 when three German torpedo boats on patrol, finding themselves unexpectedly confronted by an enemy fleet, fire and narrowly miss *Warspite*, *Ramillies* and the Sword HQ ship *Largs* but sink the Norwegian destroyer *Svenner*, 12 miles west of Le Havre, with the loss of one officer and 33 crew. A delayed-action mine sinks US destroyer *Corry* in the western sector while, just inside the northern limit of the eastern assault area, HMS *Wrestler* suffers a mine strike and has to be taken in tow.) Casualties to landing and small craft prove higher than allowed for, although 75 per cent of these are attributed to the weather. All told, 59,900 personnel, 8,900 vehicles and 1,900 tons of stores are landed. By D+50 631,000 personnel, 153,000 vehicles and 689,000 tons of stores, plus 68,000 tons of fuel and oil, are delivered to the bridgehead.

Phantom Fleets

5 June 21:30 First aircraft take off from British airfields. (More than 10,000 aircraft are involved in the invasion.)

By midnight 1,333 heavy RAF bombers drop 5,316 tons of bombs on radar stations and the ten most important German gun batteries in the assault area. In the 24 hours between the night of 5 and 6 June. The RAF drops between 15,000 and 20,000 tons of bombs.

5/6 June Operations *Taxable* and *Glimmer*, both devised by Wing Commander E. I. Dickie, create 'Phantom Fleets' on enemy radar screens. Taxable involves 16 Lancasters of 617 Squadron and is a joint RN/RAF operation aimed at making the Germans believe that an invasion force was attacking the French coast between Dieppe and Cap d'Antifer. Attacks on enemy radar installations had all but destroyed their effectiveness, but care had been taken to leave enough operational to allow the Germans to deceive themselves that their radars were showing an invasion fleet. The RN uses 18 small vessels as tugs to tow balloons, which would show up as large ships on the German radar screens. This 'convoy' occupies an area of sea that measures 14 miles by 15 miles and appears to move at seven knots towards the coast. It is known subsequently that the German High Command has plotted three invasion forces arriving on the French coast.

Six aircraft of 218 Squadron, and a few boats, mount

Operation *Glimmer*, whose 'convoy' is aimed at the beaches of Boulogne. German searchlights are turned on and guns open fire on the convoy. *Luftwaffe* night fighters are directed towards the jammers and spend hours in the area, as do E-boats searching for a fleet that never sailed.

15 aircraft of 138, 149 and 161 Squadrons, giving the impression of a much larger force, drop dummy parachutists called 'Ruperts' between Rouen and Le Havre. At 04:00 the 915th Regiment, General Marcks' LXXXIV Corps reserve, abandons Omaha and sets off to intercept them. It takes hours before the German reserve can be re-grouped and brought back to the beachhead.

16 aircraft of 90, 138 and 149 Squadrons, flying tracks 15 miles south of that taken by the invasion forces, simulate landings at Maligny and Villers Bocage. The Maligny decoy serves to relieve some pressure on US airborne forces around Ste-Mere-Eglise.

24 Lancasters of 101 Squadron and five B-17 Flying Fortresses of 214 Squadron, carrying 82 radio jammers between them, obliterate the German night-fighter frequencies for more than five hours.

16 Stirlings of 199 Squadron and four Fortresses of 803 Squadron USAAF establish a Mandrel screen from Littlehampton to Portland Bill jamming all but 5 per cent of the Freya radars between Cherbourg and Le Havre.

The Allies fly 14,674 sorties on D-Day. Losses, chiefly due to flak, are 113 (0.77 per cent). The *Luftwaffe* flies 319 sorties.

RAAF and RNZAF Participation

The part played by the Allied air forces in the build up to the Invasion was crucial. By day the RAF's 2nd TAF, which had been formed in Norfolk on 1 June 1943 under Air Vice Marshall Basil Embry, and the US 8th and 9th Air Forces, blasted enemy targets in Northern France and Belgium. At night the 'heavies' of RAF Bomber Command added the weight of its bombs to marshalling yards and enemy positions. 2nd TAF and RAF Bomber Command consisted of all manner of foreign and Commonwealth personnel as well as British airmen. The part played by the far-flung dominions is often overlooked but their participation was significant. In May and early June Royal New Zealand Air Force (RNZAF) fighter and bomber squadrons were heavily involved in operations in support of *Overlord*. Tempests of 486 Squadron and Mosquito Intruders of 487 Squadron attacked the railway system of northern France. On D-Day 489 Squadron RNZAF Beaufighters patrolled along the invasion coast and in the week after the landings made 34 separate attacks on E-boats and R-boats.

On D-Day the Mosquitoes of 464 Squadron Royal Australian Air Force (RAAF) attacked transport further east across the Seine. One Mosquito was brought down. Flight Lieutenant D. M. Shanks, navigator, survived and remained hidden until August. Australian piloted Typhoons of 121 and 247 Squadrons made ground attacks south of Caen amid heavy anti-aircraft fire. Three Australian Typhoons were shot down although one pilot, who had severe burns and a broken leg, evaded capture and reached the beachhead. After dusk on D-Day Mosquitoes of 488 Squadron RNZAF took over patrol duty and intercepted several Luftwaffe raids against the beachhead and claims for 20 bombers shot down in the first week were recorded. Lancasters of 75 Squadron RNZAF were among those who bombed Ouistreham on 5/6 June and who participated in other raids in the Normandy area on four of the six succeeding nights. In the attack on coastal batteries on 5/6 June RAAF Lancasters flew 67 sorties, the majority of them against German gun emplacements at Pointe-du-Hoc.

As late as June 1944, 11,000 RAAF officers and men were serving with the RAF or the ten RAAF squadrons. Australia also provided 168 of the 1,136 aircraft committed by Bomber Command, almost 15 per cent of the total. RAAF pilots flew six Lancasters of 617 Dambusters Squadron in a deception operation on 5/6 June and five more flew Stirlings of 199 Squadron in their deception operation. Just after midnight RAAF officers piloted 41 transports of the ten squadrons of 38 Group for the drop of the British 6th Airborne Division, the RAAF providing about one in seven of the pilots. In the week following D-Day 460 Squadron RAAF flew on five of the seven nights and flew 107 sorties. Each of the three other RAAF bomber squadrons operated on four nights.

D-Day Fact File

More than 130,000 men are landed from the sea and over 20,000 men from the air in the first 24 hours. Americans suffer over 6,000 casualties. Casualties in British 2nd Armoured amount to 4,000 from a force of 82,000.

The end of D-Day establishes almost 155,000 Allied troops across nearly 80 square miles of France: 55,000 Americans are ashore, plus 15,500 who have parachuted or glided across the Channel. Anglo–American co-operation had secured a bridgehead in Normandy.

One out of every 11 Americans who has taken part in the cross-Channel invasion is dead, missing or wounded. There are 6,000 American casualties (of whom 700 are airborne troops): more than half the total Allied casualties on the day. By the end of July the Americans are the majority Allied force in France with 980,000 troops compared with 660,000 British. By VE Day three million US troops are fighting on the continent.

As night falls on D-Day all five beachheads are established and 150,000 Allied troops are on French soil along a 50-mile front. 55,000 American and 75,215 British and Canadian troops come ashore during D-Day. In the first six days over 300,000 men, 54,000 vehicles, and 104,000 tons of stores are unloaded.

Screaming Eagles and the All Americans

Bernard M. Job, RAFVR

Flying Officer, Mosquito navigator, 4I8 Squadron, RAF
Holmsley South near Bournemouth.

'Six aircrews were detailed to act as "Flak bait" to cover the paratroop and glider drops in the Cherbourg Peninsula, by drawing searchlights and flak away from these more vulnerable aircraft. So successful was this that two of the six were hit, one so badly that it crash-landed near base and burnt up. The crew ran!'

Extract from 'Currahee!'
by Donald Burgett, 19

506th Parachute Infantry Regiment, 101st Screaming Eagles Division. 'Currahee!' was the only World War II book to be endorsed by General Eisenhower, who called it a 'fascinating tale of personal combat'.

'Inside the other planes I could see the glowing red tips of cigarettes as men puffed away. It was weirdly beautiful, lots of sparks and tracer shells. But I knew that between every tracer shell are four armour-piercing bullets. "Let's go," shouted Lt. Muir and we began moving in what seemed slow motion towards the open doorway as the green "go" light spread a glow across our faces. (In the hours before D-Day we were given our objectives – capture the bridges over the rivers and canals around Carentan and secure the exits from Utah Beach – and told to burn personal possessions like letters from home. There were bonfires across the camp. When the ashes could be raked out we used them to blacken our faces for the drops. We looked like racoons. Several of the guys broke into the Al Jolson 'Mammy' song which helped relieve the tension. Singing might have lightened the emotional burdens, but not the physical ones. If mules were the slave carriers of WWI then the paratrooper of WWII was its two-legged equivalent. Our equipment must have weighed over 100 lb.) It seemed like forever but in fractions of seconds I was at the door and tumbling into space. Tracers were coming up towards me. As I checked the canopy above I hit the ground backwards so hard that I was stunned, unable to move.

His aircraft had strayed off course and dropped them nine miles away near Ravenoville. In the light rain of that early

**morning he crawled on his belly across a field to a thicket …
only to hear rustling.** I thought it was the enemy and I raised
my rifle. Sweat was pouring off me. I knew I was about to
kill a human being and it was a terrible thought. Suddenly
this guy began crawling towards me. As my finger tightened
on the trigger I recognized him as a pal called Hundly. His
throat was so dry with fear he couldn't even speak!'

**After surviving machine-gun strafes across the field from a
gun hidden in a hedgerow, Don linked up with several other
survivors to begin the march on Ravenoville.** 'There were
about 200 Germans down one end of town and only 20 of
us. They began hand-grenading civilian houses. I got a
bead on one of them and squeezed. There was a slight
vapour that came from his body. He buckled and went
down. It was done and it didn't worry me. Another came
around the corner. I aimed and shot him in the chest. He
fell too. But they killed four of our guys from a heavy
machine-gun burst from a window in a house. The guys
lay there in the front garden.

'The next day we began to march on our objectives but
were halted by heavy German machine guns placed
outside of town. Several times we tried to break through
but were driven back. We decided to march the German
prisoners on to the guns, figuring they wouldn't cut down
their own. They did. As the Germans screamed, *"Nicht
schiessen, Nicht schiessen"*, they were cut down. Then they
made a break for it and we shot them down from the
back. None survived.

'On the road to Carentan a Sherman tank used its
tracks to run over three Germans in a fortified trench.
Their screams could be heard above the engine's whine.

Then we came into conflict with an SS battalion and mounted Cossacks [**White Russians on horseback who had deserted Stalin to fight for Hitler**]. On the outskirts of the town of St Côme du Mont there was another vicious firefight in which the Germans were beaten back before launching an even more ferocious counter-attack. The roads, fields, ditches were littered with the dead. I nearly got it from a German except a medic with a long-barrelled cowboy revolver got him first. I shot a blond-haired German crawling to a farmhouse to get more mortar shells to lob on to us. I saw his blond hair and it agitated me. Then the whole thing became clear to me: I wanted his scalp. I started crawling towards him. The prize was nearly within my reach when rifle fire opened up and I was forced to dive behind a hedgerow. Twice more I tried to reach him but each time I was driven back by stubborn squareheads. I decided to forget the whole thing. Finally a tank, one of ours, came by and raked the hedgerows with cannon and machine-gun fire. When he was out of ammo he said he would be back for more. He took off down the road to make better time instead of crossing the fields. It was a mistake. A German 88 opened up and the tank started to burn. The crew were all killed, the commander burning alive in the turret. We called up artillery and those Germans were wasted in a rain of high explosive.

'The next day we were on the outskirts of Carentan and I was told to go back to regimental HQ with vital information on German positions that they didn't trust being radioed. I had to go back through [**where**] the heaviest fighting had been the day before. The road was a river of gore. When I came to the end I felt as if I had left a world of darkness for a world of sunlight.

'Crawling to investigate what lay behind a thick hedgerow I was confronted by a German lobbing a stick grenade into my face. I went after it to return it but it went off inches from my fingertips. It was an orange ball that gave off real furnace heat. I passed out. When consciousness came back I was stone deaf, but otherwise felt OK. I have heard that a person can be just the right place in an explosion and live. I must have found the right spot.

'I was walking to the rear with mortars still exploding around me. Shrapnel from an 88 went into my arm and ripped it open. I didn't lose a teaspoon of blood but my main artery was hanging out like a rubber tube, dangling there as I could put four fingers on the exposed bone.

'D-Day was the most momentous time of my life. I killed so many Germans I lost count. Would I do it again? It's a hard question. Everyone loses in war, everyone. War isn't like the movies, never will be. It was dirty and dehumanizing and disgusting. You never stopped for your buddies in the field, even your best pal. You stopped and they got a bead on you and you were next. You left them behind, dead, dying or just grazed. Hell, war is all politics anyway. We did it to each other because they made us. I just hope that when they make their fine speeches on the beachheads they remember what happened. I do. Every night of the year. The images of the dead always wake me up.'

Don McKeage
of F Company, 505th Parachute Infantry Regiment.
'All went well until arriving near the DZ 'O' the C-47s did not slow up for the drop. Everyone in the 2nd Battalion

agreed that it was the highest, fastest jump ever made.
Eyeballs had to be screwed back into their sockets. The
Second Battalion landed on or near the DZ. Except for one
stick from F Company and they headed for the centre of
Ste-Mere-Eglise.'

In the first few minutes low cloud obscured the target areas
and the 2nd Platoon mortar squad of F Company, 505,
mistimed their exit and landed in the Square of Ste-Mere-
Eglise. Thirty minutes before, two sticks of the 101st
Airborne's 506th Parachute Infantry Regiment had jumped
across the east side of the town. The German guards killed
four and this alerted them to the 505 error.

Lieutenant Charles Santarsiero
506th Parachute Infantry Regiment, IOIst US Airborne
standing in the door of his plane as it passed over Ste-
Mere-Eglise.

'We were about 400 feet up and I could see fires burning
and Krauts running about. There seemed to be total
confusion on the ground. All hell broken loose. Flak and
small arms fire was coming up and those poor guys were
caught right in the middle of it.'

Pierre Huet
a farmer living with his young wife in Pretot near Ste-
Mere-Eglise.

'At 4 a.m. there was a knock at the door. When I opened
it, two Americans walked in. They pulled a printed
message in French from their helmets, which read "My
comrade is wounded. Please help." They led me to a para
with a broken leg and we carried him to my house. By
dawn we had found another six. For two weeks they hid

in my attic, but then the Germans came to arrest me. Someone had informed on me. An Austrian captain interrogated me. He knew who I was but protected me by pretending I was someone else. He told me, "If we find the owner of this farmhouse he will be shot." He saved my life by letting me escape. That night my wife and I crossed the German lines, got through an American minefield and were taken directly to American HQ. I warned them my farm was a German base and asked them to shell it. Half an hour later there was nothing left of my house ... and nothing left of the Germans.'

Frenchman Raymond Paris, 20

who lived in Ste-Mere-Eglise.

'A fire broke out in a house at about 10 p.m. (midnight British time). A German sergeant gave Mayor Alexandre Renaud permission to rouse the populace and for the priest to ring the church bell. The people set up a bucket brigade in the light of the flames. As they were fighting the fire, American planes appeared low overhead, so low that I could see their open doors. Paratroopers began jumping out by the hundreds. I saw one paratrooper drop on the road, but a German killed him before he could get untangled from his parachute. Another was killed near me. I will never forget the sight.'

Private Ken Russell

F Company, 505th Parachute Infantry Regiment.

'I jumped with the 2nd Platoon, it was commanded by 2nd Lieutenant Harold Cadish. I don't remember all the stick in our plane but I know Private H. T. Bryant, Private Ladislaw 'Laddie' Tlapa and Lieutenant Cadish were most unfortunate. They were the fellows who were shot on the power poles. My close friend Private 1st class Charles Blankenship was shot still in his chute, hanging in a tree, a little distance down the street. When we jumped, there was a huge fire in a building in town. I didn't know that the heat would suck a parachute towards the fire. I fought the chute all the way down to avoid the fire. One trooper [Private 1st class A. J. Van Holsbeck of F Company] who had joined our Company shortly before D-Day landed in the fire. Facing the church from the front, I landed on the right side of the roof, luckily in the shadow side from the fire. Some of my suspension lines went over the steeple and I slid down over to the edge of the roof. This other trooper came down and really got entangled on the steeple, I didn't know it was Steele. Almost immediately a Nazi soldier came running from the back side of the church shooting at everything. Sergeant John Ray had landed in the churchyard almost directly below Steele. This Nazi shot him in the stomach while he was still in his chute. While Ray was dying he somehow got his .45 out (sergeants jumped with a .45-calibre pistol) and shot the Nazi in the back of the head, killing him. He saved my life as well as Steele's. It was one of the bravest things I have ever witnessed.

'I finally got to my trench knife and cut my suspension lines and fell to the ground. I looked up at the steeple but there was not a movement or a sound and I thought the trooper was dead. I got my M-1 assembled and ducked around several places in that part of town hoping to find some troopers, but all of them were dead. I got off several rounds at different Germans before they drove me to a different position with intense gunfire.'

Van Holsbeck died falling into the house, which was on fire on the south side of the town square. The Germans allowed the villagers, under guard, to break the curfew to fight it.

Chief-corporal Rudolph May

German soldier who commanded a patrol of ten men, cut the parachute lines with his pocket knife to release Private John 'Buck' Steele, F Company, 505th Parachute Infantry Regiment, 82nd Airborne Division, so he could be taken captive.

'On the evening of 5 June my friends and I were enjoying ourselves trying to break a cycle speed record around the church at Ste-Mere-Eglise, just to kill time. At 10 p.m. I resumed my post in the steeple – a telephone at my side. Around midnight (2 a.m. British time) I heard planes passing overhead and saw "objects" falling from the sky. During this period a house began to burn. It was the light from this fire that made it possible for me to see hundreds of parachutes falling from the sky as the airplane motors droned on. They fell on the roofs, in the streets and even in the trees of the church square. The sky was studded with parachutes.

'Suddenly everything in the steeple became dark. Through an opening I saw that a parachutist had fallen on the steeple, hanging by the ropes. He appeared to be dead, but after a moment I heard his voice. There were two of us on duty at the post, and my companion wanted to shoot him. "Are you crazy?" I said. "If you shoot we'll be discovered."'

2nd Lieutenant Leon E. Mendel

Interrogation Officer, proficient in seven languages, 325th Glider Infantry, Mission 'Galveston' on D+I at Landing Zone 'W'.

'My glider made a beautiful landing at Ecoqueneauville and I made my way south to my assembly point at Les Forges crossroads. Here I got the bad news that I had lost half of my six-man team in glider crashes. The good news was the others had already eight German prisoners for interrogation. I started off with German but with little response, so I switched to Russian with the question, "*Vj Russkij chelovek?*" (Are you a Russian?). Their reply was immediate, "*Da, ya khochu ekhat' na Ameriku*" (Yes, I want to go to America). I slapped both my hands on top of my helmet and shouted at them, "*Durak, durak. Ya tozhe!*" (Crazy, crazy. Me too!)."'

The enemy included 'volunteers' from Eastern Europe and Soviet Russia. The Seventh Army had 13 'Ost' battalions made up of non-Germans.

George Rosie

IOIst Airborne. Captured, he spent II months in PoW camps before being liberated by the Russians south of Berlin.

'We boarded the planes at about 22:30 on 5 June. With two chutes and full combat equipment, we could hardly walk. Some of the men looked like they were scared to death. I was certainly uptight but had no thoughts of being killed. I had the feeling we were part of a big chunk of history. Out of the window, there were planes in every direction and, below, hundreds of ships. As we crossed the French coast, a plane on our right was hit by flak and blew up, wiping out 18 to 20 men. Welcome to the real war.

'The green light came on and we jumped. I hit a road and went head first through a wooden fence, knocking out two teeth. Then I took cover in a hedgerow. A minute later 40 Germans came marching past. I could have reached out and touched them. Being alone behind enemy lines is a unique experience. You feel so helpless, so alone. After a bit I ran into John Gibson, our medic, and Charles Lee, a mortarman. It was as if I had found a long-lost brother.

'I looked up and there was a C-47 transport plane at about 800 feet with the left engine on fire and troopers bailing out. The last one bailed out at not more than 200 feet and the plane went right over the top of our heads, hit the adjoining field and burst into a million flaming pieces. From the direction of the crash, four men came running towards us. We discovered they were from our troop – Phil Abbie, Francis Swanson, Leo Krebs and my high school pal Francis Ronzani. The downed plane had damn near got them.

'We now had an army of seven but we ran into about 100 Germans as daylight was breaking. Abbie and Ronzani were killed and the rest of us were pinned down in a field. Bullets were flying all over the place and Leo Krebs remarked, "God, these guys are lousy shots." A German officer was running back and forth and Krebs said, "What the hell is wrong with that guy? Is he nuts?" We shot at him and he went down. But we were in a hopeless position and were captured in no time.

'Lee had got away into a wood and, a short time later, began shooting at the Germans who were guarding us. I told Leo I still had a hand grenade the Germans had missed. If Leo hit one of the guards I was going to throw the grenade at the other one. But the Germans circled behind Lee and killed him. I left the grenade in the ditch.

'Ronzani had been hit in the chest three, four, five, or six times. I'm sure he never knew what hit him. When I returned to the States after the war and visited his mother and father, one of the things that seemed to be of great relief to them was that Francis had not suffered.'

American Paratroopers' Timetable

D-Day begins with an assault by more than 23,000 airborne troops, 15,500 of them American, behind enemy lines to soften up the German troops and to secure needed targets. The paratroopers know that if the accompanying assault by sea fails there will be no rescue. Departing from Portland Bill on the English Coast, 6,600 paratroopers of the 101st Division in 490 C-47s and 6,396 paratroopers of the 82nd Division are dropped over the neck of the Cotentin peninsula. (Force B of the 82nd Division has a strength of 3,871 glidermen). Two parachute regiments of the 101st Division are to drop just west of the lagoon, silence a heavy battery and seize the western exits of the causeways leading from Utah beach and head off a German eastern advance. One parachute regiment is to drop north of Carentan, destroy the rail and road bridges over the Douve and hold the line of that river and the Carentan canal so as to protect the southern flank of the Corps.

The 82nd Division, landing farther inland, is to drop astride the Merderet River south and west of Ste-Mere-Eglise, block the Carentan–Cherbourg road, and extend the flank protection westward by destroying two more bridges over the Douve and secure the Merderet crossings.

Heavy fog and German guns mean that the pilots are unable to drop the paratroopers precisely as planned. Only one-sixth of the men in the 101st Division reach their destination points. The first regiment of the 82nd Division fare better but the second suffer heavy supply losses and much of the division is left without sufficient arms. Both Divisions form smaller improvized squads and by 04:30 the 82nd have captured Ste-Mere-Eglise.

19:00 Merderet crossing at Chef du Pont controlled by 82nd Airborne Division. Elsewhere paratroops are so heavily engaged fighting for their lives they have no chance of blowing the bridges over the Douve or forming a compact bridgehead over the Merderet.

US Airborne Forces
82nd Airborne Division
Major General Matthew B. Ridgway
505th Parachute Infantry
508th Parachute Infantry
507th Parachute Infantry
325th Glider Infantry

101st Airborne Division
Major General Maxwell D. Taylor
501st Parachute Infantry
506th Parachute Infantry

502nd Parachute infantry
327th Glider Infantry

101st Division casualties total 1,240, of whom 182 are killed. 82nd Division suffers 1,259 casualties of whom 156 are killed. Of the 6,396 paratroopers of the 82nd who jumped, 272 or 4.24 per cent were killed or injured as a result of the drop. Of the 6,600 paratroopers of the 101st Division, only about 2,500 had assembled by the end of the first day.

Paras' Equipment

Paratroopers carried an average of 70 lb of equipment, officers 90 lb. With the parachute, men weighed between 90–120 lb over their body weight. The items carried were:

Standard Parachutist Pack:
M-1 Garand Rifle with 8-round clip
Cartridge belt with canteen
Hand grenades
Parachute and pack
Anti-flash headgear and gloves
Pocket compass
Machete
.45-calibre Colt automatic rifle
Flares
Message book

Officer Pack (British, but similar to American officer pack):

Sten gun

Spare magazines with 9mm ammunition

2 lb plastic high explosives (HE)

2–36 primed hand grenades

Two full belts of Vickers .303 ammunition

Wire cutters

Radio batteries

Small-pack

Basic equipment webbing

48 hours' worth of rations

Water

Cooking and washing kit

Spread throughout pockets:

Loaded .45 automatic pistol

Medical kit

2 additional lb HE

Knife

Escape/survival kit

Toggle rope

Additional personal items

Emergency Rations:

4 pieces of chewing gum

2 bouillon cubes

2 Nescafe instant coffees, 2 sugar cubes and creamers

4 Hershey bars

1 pack of Charms candy

1 package pipe tobacco

1 bottle of water purification (Halazone) tablets

Winged Pegasus

Brigadier S. J. L. Hill
Commanding 3rd Parachute Brigade.
'Do not be daunted if chaos reigns. It undoubtedly will.'

Major General Richard Gale
6th Airborne Division Commander; his orders to
Brigadier Nigel Poett, 5th Parachute Brigade, for the
capture of the parallel bridges over the Canal de Caen
at Bénouville and the River Orne at Ranville.
'The seizing of the crossing intact is of the utmost
importance to the conduct of future operations. As the

bridges will certainly have been prepared for demolition, the speedy overpowering of the bridge defences should be your first object. They must therefore be seized by a *coup-de-main* party, landed in gliders as near to the bridges as is humanly possible. You must accept risks to achieve this.'

Major John Howard commanded the *coup-de-main* party of six platoons (150 men) of D Company, 2nd Battalion, Oxfordshire and Buckingham-shire Light Infantry, and 30 men of 249 Field Company (Airborne) Royal Engineers. After capture their task was to hold the bridges until relieved.

Brigadier Nigel Poett
Commander 5th Parachute Brigade.

'As my small aircraft skimmed over the defences of the Atlantic Wall, not a shot was fired. The red light came on and then the green. I was out, seconds later bump. It was the soil of France. The time some 20 minutes after midnight. The darkness was complete; the silence unbroken except for sound of my disappearing aircraft. A few minutes later the sky to the west lit up – firing, explosions, all the sights and sounds of battle. It was John Howard's assault. He also had been timed to land at 20 minutes after midnight.

'Now I must get to the bridges as quickly as possible and be able, if need be to adjust the Brigade plan. Would the bridges be in the hands of friend or foe? Intact or damaged? Indeed Howard's Company had achieved a splendid success. The bridges were in our hands, intact. All was well!'

Sergeant Edgar Gurney BEM
7th (LI) Battalion, 5th Parachute Brigade.

'Just before midnight Sunday 4 June I was lying on a gas cape spread over wet ground inside a bivouac made of groundsheets on the perimeter of Keevil airfield, going over coming events. The 6th Airborne Division was to spearhead the invasion of Europe and secure the left flank of the Landing Beaches. The next day was spent resting during the morning, a short service after lunch and then a final check of personal equipment. Together with spare clothes I had 100 rounds .303 (50 tracer and 50 incendiary), four No. 36 grenades fitted with four second fuses, anti-tank Gammon Bombs and four spare Bren Gun mags, a Lee Enfield rifle and a telescopic sight (I was a sniper). In addition I had to carry an inflatable rubber dinghy attached to my right leg (to cross any water obstacles if the "Ox & Bucks" failed to capture the bridges). Loading into an adapted Stirling Bomber I learned that the aircraft was to go on a dummy bombing raid prior to dropping us. I found my place in the line of 20 paras, which the aircraft carried. We all sat on the floor; even numbers on one side and odd numbers on the other. No smoking until we were airborne so to ease the tension we sang paras songs to the tune of "Knees up Mother Brown", the end of the chorus going, "I'll always keep my trousers on when jumping through the hole". I wondered if that would be true that night.

'We took off and as we neared the French coast anti-aircraft shells started bursting all around the plane causing it to rock, but the pilot flew straight towards our target area near the village of Ranville. Suddenly, a red light appeared near the rear of the aircraft, which denoted 20 seconds to the commencement of the drop. The tension could have been cut with a knife; we were all as taut as bow-strings. Soon the voice of the Despatcher was heard, "Stand up, Hook up". We formed a single line down the centre of the aircraft and each man hooked up the man in front of him. The Despatcher opened the floor doors and remarked, "There are thousands of ships down there so you'll soon have plenty of company". The red light changed to green and the Despatcher shouted, "GO".

'The first man disappeared through the hole in the floor, swiftly followed by others who were shuffling towards it, until it was my turn at No. 17. I stepped into space, but just as I did so the plane rocked and I hit both sides of the hole during my exit, breaking my army watch which I later found had stopped at 00:36 hours.

'I heard the crack of the chute developing, slowing my descent. I grabbed the rope holding the kit bag on my leg and pulled the quick release, then lowered it to its full length. I had a quick look round, noting the pretty patterns made by the searchlights and tracer bullets. Many searchlights were trying to locate our planes whilst the tracer shells and bullets weaved a beautiful pattern in the night sky. Then in the distance I saw a church with a detached tower, silhouetted against the lighted background, which I instantly recognized as Ranville Church. I had seen it many times before on photographs and the scale model of the dropping area. I heard a thump as my kitbag hit the ground. Then for a full minute, I was violently sick from the fear and the release of tension.

'"Stand with your back to the church and run forward and slightly left, there you will find a road leading to the bridges." These words were imprinted in my brain and I blindly followed instructions. Gathering my kitbag I turned my back towards Ranville Church and ran. I knew I would find the road that led to the bridges now known at Horsa and Pegasus bridges. I shuffled on under my heavy load and then the W/Op shouted "Ham and Jam", the signal that the bridges had been captured intact by the "Ox & Bucks" bridge party. I immediately discarded the kit bag, as the dinghy would no longer be needed. Soon we had made a group of 20 to 30 parachutists, one of whom was a wireless operator, who was trying to make contact with the bridge party. Had they captured the bridges intact?

'We were about 200 yards from the first bridge when the wireless operator signalled the glider troops had captured the bridges intact. We raced onwards and as we approached the Canal de Caen bridge I saw a number of dead bodies amongst whom was an officer, lying in the roadway. On the other side of the bridge there appeared to be a mighty battle in progress but this turned out to be ammunition exploding in a German tank that had been destroyed by the glider troops. We made our way through Bénouville but near the Chateau gates we made contact with the enemy. Private McCara climbed over a hedge and was knifed to death by two Germans waiting on the other side. A No. 36 hand grenade with a four seconds fuse was thrown over the hedge into the slit trench that the Germans had then occupied. A machine gun then opened fire from inside the chateau gates wounding Private Whittingham who later died of his wounds. A German stick grenade exploded near the head of our officer who started to bleed from his eyes and ears, which gave us the impression that he had a fractured base of the skull. So we withdrew, taking our wounded with us.

'We set up a defensive position astride the main Caen–Ouistreham road on a bank of earth bordering a sunken cart track that was about 10 feet wide. On the opposite side of the track and immediately in front of us was a seven-foot brick wall with a wooden door at one end. We were now on the seaward side of Bénouville. Our position enabled us to control any enemy movement along the main Caen–Ouistreham road as well as preventing him from making any attack on the bridges from the western side of the village. The night was taken up with small patrol skirmishes.

'By morning we were completely surrounded but we had to hang on until relieved by the Commandos. The Germans launched several counter-attacks, one of which penetrated to the far side of a wall about ten feet in front of me. A stick grenade landed close to me, which I knocked into a sunken lane in front of me and I replied with one of my grenades, which silenced things a lot. At about 10:30 three large Panther tanks came rumbling along the main road from the direction of Caen. They stopped near the chateau gates and the one to my right opened fire. The shell hit a wall about three or four yards to my left. Private McGee, who was near the main road, picked up his Bren gun, then started to walk up the middle of the road towards the tanks, firing the Bren gun from his hip. As one magazine became empty, he replaced it with a new one, discarding the empty magazine on the roadside. We could hear the bullets ricocheting off the armour steel plating of the leading tank that immediately closed down his visor, thus making him blind to things in front! Corporal Tommy Kileen realized what was happening and ran up the side of the road, taking two

Gammon bombs from his pouches. He threw the first bomb which hit the leading tank where the turret and body meets which nearly blew the turret off. He threw the second bomb but being further away from the second tank, it fell short, landing against the tank's track, which was promptly blown off. This tank now tried to escape, but only having one good track it went around in circles, so the crew baled out and tried to escape. They were shot by McGee.

'Just after midday I heard the sound of the bagpipes from the direction of St Aubin and knew that Lord Lovat's commandos had made it and we were no longer alone. About 21:30 the 2nd Warwicks attacked Bénouville and relieved us with the remainder of my company. I made my way back to the bridge where I had my first meal that day. About 01:00 on 7 June I made my way back to the Dropping Zone where I dug a hole seven feet long, two feet wide and two feet deep, lined it with part of a discarded chute, covered myself with the other part and fell asleep. It certainly had been a very long day.'

Charles Pearson
12th Yorkshire Parachute Battalion (AAC) Independent section, 5th Parachute Brigade.

'The flight in a Stirling to my D-Day drop felt like being in a car driving on new grit. We were battered by anti-aircraft fire and I just hoped I'd come through as I did at Dunkirk. Finally we got the green light and jumped. I landed badly and wrenched my arm. I could still use my toes so I went to a pre-arranged point two or three miles away. I caught up with my regiment and was caught up in heavy fighting at Brevile. My companion was hit when we came across three or four Germans. I fired my Colt revolver to stop them following me. We were near a church and suddenly all hell broke loose. Most of our lads died. One had his helmet blown open like a tin can. He was distressed and yelling. I put him on a jeep and carried him out then went back to pick up the others.'

Albert Gregory, RAMC

D Company, Oxfordshire and Buckinghamshire Regiment, who was in the 3rd glider to land at Pegasus Bridge.

'We took off and sat in silence for a while, just listening to the roar of the wind and the tow aircraft's engines. We were soon over the French coast and all hell started up, the anti-aircraft fire exploded in the night sky, we called the shells "Flaming Onions" because of the way they looked and came towards us in a string. I looked around me, and for once, no one was being airsick. I was scared stiff and yet excited in anticipation of what lay ahead of us.

'Suddenly, the towrope was released by the glider pilot and we were away on our own, just the rush of the wind and the downward spiral to France and our fate. In what seemed only a few minutes the words, "Brace, Brace, Brace" were shouted and we all linked arms, awaiting the impact of the landing. Sparks seemed to stream down the fuselage and we touched down, screeching and crashing, till suddenly we came to a stop. We didn't bother to open the door of the Horsa; we just all seemed to pile out through the gashes in the fuselage. I grabbed a trolley full of mortar bombs and pulled for all my worth, only for one to fall out and smash my toe. Someone else came over to give me a hand and we ran towards the bridge. It is very hard to explain to anyone the feelings of war, exhilaration, fear, excitement and comradeship towards your fellow troops who you have been with for the past months.

'I ran to the edge of the road leading to the bridge filled with a feeling of apprehension of what was going to happen. I must have had a guardian angel watching over me because I was still there with so much death around me. Bullets were flying everywhere. I heard the cry "Medic" and I ran towards a guy lying at the side of the road. As I ran, I looked to my left and saw a German soldier running the same way. We were both trying to survive, not knowing why we were doing what we were doing.

'In just a couple of minutes I had injured men who had been hurt in the crash landing. I herded three men into a hedgerow to treat their wounds. I was in that ditch for hours because we could not cross the bridge until the snipers had been found. It was about 8 a.m. before I eventually transferred them to the café and relative safety. I saw a small French girl, ashen-faced and scared to hell. I reached into my tunic and gave her my bar of chocolate, but still she did not smile. Then I joined up with about half a dozen other men who were making their way to Ranville to rejoin their own companies when the rest of the regiment came in on the dropping zones. It had been hours since I saw a familiar face.

'The guys had taken several prisoners at the bridge. One was a young boy of 16. I crossed the Orne Bridge and passed a Para with six prisoners and later rejoined B Company as we all regrouped at Ranville for the attack on Escoville. We set up our mortars in an orchard near a farmhouse with a long driveway. I dug a trench and felt uneasy so I moved to another spot and soon after we were heavily mortar bombed, suffering many casualties. Three men from our mortar squad were severely wounded. A bomb had landed in my original trench. What made me move I do not know.

'Later we moved to the woods at Chateau St Côme. We all stepped over a German soldier lying dead across the path leading into the wood. I will never forget the awful carnage caused when the battleship *Warspite* opened fire on these woods not knowing the Black Watch of the 51st Highland Division had already cleared it of Germans. The smell of death hung over the place. Dead bodies were everywhere. It was terrible and the stench made one feel sick. Everywhere, dead horses and cows were bloating up. There was an awful smell when someone put a bullet in one of them and they burst. It was a smell of death that none can describe but will never forget.

'I dug a trench only to find water seeping in. We were shelled, mortared and machine gunned during the day and sometimes bombed at night but the worst were the air burst mortar bombs, which showered shrapnel down on top of us and caused many casualties. There was turmoil when D Company was cut off and B Company put in an attack to get them out. We had orders to withdraw and as we pulled out up a gully a German threw a stick grenade over the hedge, which severely wounded Sergeant Stan Bridges in his upper arm. I bandaged and splinted his arm and eventually got him to safety when we were sent back about three fields behind the front line for a rest. It was a nightmare. One bomb landed a few yards from my trench and the concussion caused the side of my trench to collapse on me. I was half buried and really scared stiff. We moved back into the woods but it was chaos.

'During these actions I came across some horrible injuries. The worst was the one where a piece of shrapnel had hit this man in the corner of his mouth and tore a gash to his ear. The side of his face fell down to his neck and looked an awful mess. I gave him a shot of morphine, then put a roll of lint along his gums. Then I pinned his face up with four safety pins, applied a dressing held on with Elastoplasts and got him evacuated to the casualty clearing station.

'I was wounded in the head by an air burst shell as I ran to help Sergeant Bobby Hill who had also been wounded. There was a blinding flash and I fell on top of him. He bandaged me up and got me evacuated to Bayeux. A piece of shrapnel had pierced the top of my helmet and blown a big hole in the top of my head. How I survived all this hell, only God knows. I regained consciousness in a C-47 Dakota while crossing the Channel back to England. A young nurse said, "The war's over for you my lad!" I lost consciousness again and the next thing I remember is waking up in a military hospital in Oxford, with my wife looking down on me. It was only then that I realized I would be all right.'

Helmut Romer and Erwin Sauer, both 18
who were on sentry duty at Pegasus Bridge over the Caen Canal.

'Suddenly, we heard a swishing noise and saw a large, silent aircraft flying low towards the canal bridge. It crashed in a small field next to the bridge, only about 50 metres away. At first we thought it was a crippled bomber. We wondered whether to take a look at it or wake our sergeant. We were moving forward cautiously when we heard what seemed to be the sound of running feet. Before we knew it, a bunch of about ten wild-looking men who were charging towards us confronted us. They were armed, but didn't shoot. I found out later this was because they were under strict orders to maintain silence as long as possible so that they had surprise on their side when they stormed the pillbox by the bridge. We were two boys alone and we ran. We could see that these menacing, warlike-looking men outnumbered us. But I still managed to fire off a signal flare to try to warn the rest of our garrison of about 20 men who were sleeping nearby.

'About 100 metres off, we plunged into some thick bushes by the track running alongside the canal. There were two more crashes. We knew that the British were landing in force. Firing had started all around the bridge and we could see tracer bullets whizzing in all directions. At first it was non-stop, then it died down to occasional bursts. It was clear that the British were rooting out the rest of our garrison from the bunkers around the bridge.

'We remained hidden throughout the night, scared to move in case we would be seen and shot. Sometime after noon next day, we heard and saw some more troops with a piper at their head moving from the direction of the beaches to cross the bridge. I found out later that they were Lord Lovat's Commando Brigade. We stayed under cover for the rest of the day and the next night. Then, hungry and thirsty, we decided to surrender. We plucked up our courage, put our hands in the air and walked out of the bushes. The British didn't fire at us. I'll always be grateful to them for that. We knew it was the end of the war for us and we were bloody glad of it.'

Sergeant Charles Thornton, 27
'Ox and Bucks' Light Infantry.

'... Meanwhile, some of the other lads had knocked on the door of Georges Gondree's café. It became the first house in France to be liberated. He led them to the cellar where his wife Therese and their children were sheltering and she hugged and kissed everyone so much her face became black with camouflage paint. Georges dug up 98 bottles of champagne he had buried in 1940, but unfortunately, I missed out on the celebration! I had been with the other troops taking up defensive positions in a nearby field.'

Sapper Cyril Larkin
He and his twin brother Claude were born in Auckland, New Zealand in 1917. Their parents returned to England in 1920–21 and after leaving school both twins were keen to return to New Zealand but the war put paid to this. In 1939 they tried to join the New Zealand Army via NZ House in London but the following February they were called up for the British Army.

'Claude and I were twin brothers and members of No.2 Platoon, 249 Field Company, Royal Engineers, attached to D Company, "Ox and Bucks" Light Infantry. We were under the command of Major John Howard, Ox and Bucks, and Captain Jock Neilson, Royal Engineers. Gliders 1, 2 and 3 would land on the Canal bridge and gliders 4, 5 and 6 on the Orne bridge. Claude and I were both in No. 6 glider – I'll bet there weren't many twins in that position that night! With blackened faces and hands we got aboard. The doors closed and then we heard the increased power of the engines of the Halifax and then the jerk of the tow rope and we were off! The gliders left at one-minute intervals into the night sky. Thirty men in each glider, five of whom were Royal Engineers. For most of us this was our first time in action and there was almost no conversation in the blacked-out interior of the glider. No lights at all were permitted. We flew at 6,000 feet with fighter aircraft escort and crossed the French coast a few minutes after midnight. Suddenly we felt our glider being released and then seemingly in minutes we had landed, with grunts and groans from both our bucking plywood aircraft and ourselves!

'I had been detailed to check that after we landed everyone had left the glider and so I jumped out from the rear-side door, ran a few yards and flattened myself on French soil. And nobody else was there! Just a few staring cows four or five yards from me and otherwise complete silence! Where had all my mates gone and where were the other two gliders? For a second I thought I might be a one-man invasion force, and so I moved ahead of the glider and found to my relief a bunch of men kneeling by a hedge. "Scout Section," I whispered. "Shut up" was the reply. So I moved ahead and there found the others from my glider and we all moved off at a fair pace, down into a ditch, up the other side and on to a road and there straight ahead of us was "our bridge".

'One shot was all we heard from the enemy and one of our men threw a smoke bomb. In the same instant we charged across the bridge. As we did that the sappers were checking for electric wires that would lead to explosive charges as Intelligence Reports had stated that the bridges had been prepared for demolition. Guns were now firing on the Canal bridge 400 yards away but all I heard from the "defenders" of our bridge was the sound of running feet down the tow-path! The sound of 30 pairs of British Army hob-nailed boots rushing around in the darkness was enough to scare the bravest hearts! But how far would they have gone and where to?

'I went under the bridge to the water's edge and in the patchy cloudy moonlight saw a huge dark object right under the centre of the bridge. A barge filled with explosives? A continuation of single-width scaffold boards had been laid through the girders into the darkness. "That's where the explosive will be," I thought. "Phew." So I called for support and lo and behold my twin brother appeared alongside me. Apparently whilst I was under the bridge all other personnel had moved off. So we went to investigate. Crawling through the girders with rifle and back pack was no joke, and the water rushing below me was not inviting either. The "dark object" turned out to be a huge brick pier containing the bridge opening equipment and, thankfully, no explosives. They were discovered next day in a nearby shed.

'Whilst under the bridge we heard running feet above us. Hopefully from the other gliders, but we weren't going to check! I put out my torch and waited and when it was silent Claude and I climbed back on to the road. It was 30 minutes since we had landed and as we got on to the road we saw the first paras dropping and then amazingly, from somewhere in the distance the "All Clear" sounded. They didn't know we were there! Claude and I made our way cautiously to the Canal bridge, which had by now been captured, and waited for the inevitable German counter-attack. But all we saw before dawn was a German foot patrol, staff car and motorcycle which were quickly finished off by the infantry on the river bridge. A sole German tank approached the Canal bridge but that was quickly destroyed with a Piat bomb.

'Early dawn saw a number of Lancaster bombers twisting and turning very low over a coastal gun-battery prior to an attack by the 6th Airborne and a naval bombardment could clearly be heard. Daylight now and we saw and learned of our casualties. One officer killed [Lieutenant Den Brotheridge], one soldier drowned, six wounded and one glider (No.4) missing. Our glider had been the first to land at the river bridge – hence my being on my own initially!

'Then we saw two German naval craft cautiously approaching upstream to the Canal bridge and we opened fire. From my slit-trench I only managed to fire one round at the wheelhouse before my gun jammed. I had managed to get grit into and over my rifle bolt! But it caused no problems. The boat grounded and the crew surrendered and Claude went aboard to check everything out. The second craft managed to turn back but I presume would have been finished off shortly afterwards by the beach landing troops.

'A little later in the morning now and we were getting problems! There were German snipers in the trees and the church tower, and buildings were in use by German troops. The fire was becoming heavy and accurate. We had limited heavy equipment, but the "Ox and Bucks" had got hold of a German anti-tank gun together with ammunition and started to use it with some success against the church tower. Whilst we were now getting some heavy fire on the bridge I saw Allied fighter aircraft flying overhead quite unmolested! Very frustrating!'

First Lieutenant Richard Todd, 23

7th Light Infantry Battalion, 5th Parachute Brigade,
the star of many post-war film epics such as The
Dambusters, Yangtse Incident and The Longest Day (in
which he played the part of Colonel Howard).

'We were a bunch of young men, weighed down with
guns and equipment, our faces blackened. We literally
dropped out of the night sky behind enemy lines. I knew
thousands of men were landing on the Normandy
beaches. We might have been a total disaster but as a
psyched up 23-year-old you don't think of such things.
Because I was one of the first to make the drop I suppose
I'm thought of as a hero. I'm not. To me the real heroes
were the many thousands of soldiers I saw fight so very
gallantly. Some did not come back. Shortly after I landed,
my best friend, Captain Bobby Delatour (also an actor),
was killed only five or six yards away from me. When we
managed to cross the first bridge and were on our way to
the second bridge, one of the gliders went straight into a
German tank, which blew up, sky-high.

'The first few aircraft got in with a certain amount of
surprise factor on their side but after that, many of them
were shot down. I was damned lucky. Seven Para suffered
very heavy casualties. Some were captured. Some were
killed in the air before they got to the ground. Others were
killed fighting their way through. We dropped 610 men.
By the morning of D-Day there were 240 left. A Company
had borne the brunt of the attack. In C Company, who
were more or less next to A Company, all the officers were
killed and there were only 20 men remaining. B Company
did better as far as officers were concerned, but had more
lost on the ground. When we were relieved we dug in for

the night in the area of Ranville to the east of the River Orne and Caen Canal. That night we were quite heavily attacked with guns coming from Breville. On D+1 we had quite a little firefight, then on the second half of the day we were ordered to move to Le Mesnil, to clear quite a large area of orchard and field.

'I think possibly the most unsung person of the day was Colonel Pine-Coffin. He was not only the man who trained 7 Para Battalion, but he also controlled them and remained cool, calm and collected.'

From a total of five officers and 120 men originally in A Company, there were no surviving officers and fewer than 20 men by the middle of 6 June. Then, under the command of Colonel Geoffrey Pine-Coffin, they held a pocket until late in the evening of D-Day, until a battalion of the Warwick-shire regiment who had been seaborne, relieved them in turn.

Chester Wilmot

Australian reporter, a passenger on a 6th Airborne Division glider. Extract from his book 'The Struggle for Europe'.

'Over the coast we run out of the cloud and there below us is the white curving strand of France and, mirrored in the dim moonlight, the twin ribbons of water we are looking for – the Orne and the Canal. The tug has taken us right to the target, but we can't pick out the lights, which are to mark the landing-zone. There is so much flak firing from the ground that it's hard to tell what the flashes are, and before the pilots can identify any landmarks we are into the cloud again.

'Soon one of them turns and calls back to us – "I'm letting go, hold tight." As it leaves the tug the glider seems to stall and to hover like a hawk about to strike. The roar of the wind on the wooden skin drops to a murmur with the loss of speed and there is a strange and sudden silence. We are floating in a sky of fathomless uncertainty – in suspense between peace and war. We are through the flak-belt and gliding so smoothly that the fire and turmoil of battle seem to belong to another world.

We are jerked back to reality by a sharp, banking turn and we are diving steeply, plunging down into the darkness. As the ground rises up to meet us, the pilots catch a glimpse of the pathfinders' lights and the white dusty road and the square Norman church-tower beside the landing-zone. The stick comes back and we pull out of the dive with sinking stomachs and bursting ears. The glider is skimming the ground now with plenty of speed on and is about to land when out of the night another glider comes straight for us. We take-off again, lift sharply and it sweeps under our nose. The soil of France rushes past beneath us and we touch-down with a jolt on a ploughed field. It is rough and soft, but the glider careers on with grinding brakes and creaking timbers, mowing down "Rommel's asparagus" and snapping off five stout posts in its path. There is an ominous sound of splitting wood and rending fabric and we brace ourselves for the shock as the glider goes lurching and bumping until with a violent swerve to starboard it finally comes to rest, scarred but intact, within a hundred yards of its intended landing place.

'It is 03:32. We are two minutes late. Shouts and cheers echo down the glider, and a voice from the dark interior cries out, "This is it, chum. I told yer we wouldn't 'av ter swim."

'We scramble out into a cornfield, which is the graveyard of many gliders. Some have buried their noses in the soft soil, others have lost a wing, a wheel or a complete undercarriage, several have broken their backs, one has crashed into a house and two have crashed into each other. Few have come through with as little damage as ours and all around us the twisted wrecks make grotesque silhouettes against the sky, now lit by a burst of flame as the petrol tanks of a crashing aircraft explode.

'The wreckage seems to signify the failure of the daring plan to land the gliders by night, but in fact, though we don't yet know it, 49 of the 72 destined for this field have landed accurately and, despite the chaos and the damage, the casualties to men and weapons are comparatively few. Indeed as we move off towards the rendezvous near Ranville church, men are climbing out of the broken wrecks, dragging their equipment and slashing away the splintered fuselages to set free jeeps and guns. Ten of the 18 anti-tank guns have survived and soon they are moving to their appointed positions.

'The flak guns are still firing spasmodically into an empty sky, but otherwise there is little sight or sound of fighting. It seems unreal to be talking about behind the Atlantic Wall unhindered by the enemy, and every moment we expect to hear a shot or challenge ring out of the darkness. In the absence of noise of nearby battle every sound is magnified. The rustle of troops moving through high corn, the muttered curse from a stumbling man, the crash of an axe on flimsy wood, the roar of a jeep engine, the rumble of a gun-carriage, carry far in the night, but the expected crack and thunder of guns is missing. The only challenge is from our own paratroops dug in on the edge of the landing-zone. To their call of "V for", we quickly add the other half of the password – "Victory".'

Sergeant Charles Thornton
'Ox and Bucks' Light Infantry.

'In the early evening we sat in the field and saw the men from the 6th Airborne gliders being towed in by Halifax bombers and parachutists making their way down. Soon there were so many of them you could not see a bit of the sky. It was such a lovely sight that I broke down in tears. So did a lot of the others. It was a joy to behold but we had paid the price. Of the 181 men only 76 were without wounds.'

Sapper Cyril Larkin

'Evening now and the sky suddenly filled with a vast number of gliders and aircraft dropping supplies in the bridge area. A most welcome sight. We knew now that we had more tanks and mobile guns and more comrades with us. A plane was hit by German anti-aircraft guns and came down in flames crashing in a nearby field. For us sappers by the Canal bridge it now meant an all-night guard duty. Certainly a very long and eventful day.

'On D+2 an Fw 190 fighter-bomber flew in very low over the River Bridge and then dropped a bomb on the Canal Bridge. I watched, as the bomb was released, about 200 yards from its target. I said to myself, "You've had it!" I was about ten yards from where the bomb fell but it did not explode. A lump of rag placed in the mechanism had sabotaged the bomb! If it had exploded I would not have survived. We hit the deck at great speed. I was hit by a piece of shrapnel. Claude was hit at the same time but suffered less injuries. I was stretchered on to a French Resistance lorry and taken almost instantly to a beach First Aid Station. In due course I was told I was to be taken back to the UK. Inside this huge Tank Landing Craft many stretcher cases arrived. I was one of the first batch delivered. I wasn't sure what had happened to Claude. I asked an attendant if someone like me, as he was my twin brother, had arrived. "Yes," he replied, "he was in the last load aboard."

'Hospitalized together for a couple of weeks with plenty of humour and care from the nurses and then I was moved on alone for a further two months to another hospital and we both rejoined 249 Company in September.'

Merville — The Red Devils' Greatest Triumph

'Whoever occupies this field will hold the key to the gateway of France and eventually into Germany itself.'
Feldmarschall Erwin Rommel, during his inspection of the Merville Battery in June 1944

'The Hun thinks that only a bloody fool will go there. That's why we're going.'
Major General Richard Gale, commanding 6th Airborne Division, 4 June 1944

Intelligence indicated that the battery contained four 155mm-calibre guns, each capable of bombarding the landing beaches and 160 men in 15–20 weapons pits, each with 4–5 machine guns and possibly three 20mm anti-aircraft guns. (In fact 130 men of the 716th Regiment commanded by Leutnant Raimund Steiner who were billeted nearby in Franceville-Plage and Gonneville manned the battery and the 150mm guns had been removed and replaced by Skoda 105mm field guns). Each of the four casements was built of six feet of reinforced concrete, two of which were also covered by 12 feet of earth, and a 400-yard anti-tank ditch defended the battery, 15 feet wide by l0 feet deep around two sides. Two belts of barbed wire surrounded the whole Battery, the inner being six feet high by ten feet deep. There was also a minefield and other mines had been sown in possible approach routes around the Battery. The 9th Battalion prepared with several rehearsals on a full-size mock-up of the Battery built specially at a farm at West Woodhay near Newbury.

A 750-strong assault force was to land on a DZ 1.25 miles east of the battery after C Company, 1st Canadian Parachute Battalion had captured and secured the DZ and Pathfinder Paras of the 22nd Independent Parachute Company had marked it. A Company, 1st Canadian Parachute Battalion was to protect the left flank of the 9th Battalion in its approach march and attack on the Battery. It was planned to land the paratroops and sappers in 11 gliders. They would clear and mark paths through the minefields before the main assault was launched. A glider assault party of three Horsa gliders, ferrying three officers and 47 OR of A Company, plus one officer and seven OR of the 591st Parachute Squadron Royal Engineers, who carried explosives to destroy the guns, were to land within the Battery perimeter itself. The first group were dropped accurately at 00:20 but the C-47 Dakotas carrying the Canadians dropped over a wide area and only about 30 Canadians landed on the DZ. Pilots of the 32 Dakotas carrying the main body (around 540 paras) were hampered by a huge dust cloud caused by the RAF bombing raid and poor visibility caused by patchy cloud and a strong easterly wind. Almost all the Battalion and much of the Brigade were scattered over a wide area, many landing in the flooded fields. In Otway's C-47 only seven of the 20 men managed to jump while over the DZ, and the Dakota had to make three more runs to get them all out. Otway landed beside a German HQ, which fired at him. The firing only ceased when a para threw a brick through the window and the enemy obviously thought it was a grenade! Also, the gliders carrying the mortars, anti-tank guns, mine detectors, and all the heavy equipment, landed well to the south-east and Otway's only heavy equipment was now a solitary Vickers machine gun.

By 02:50 only about 150 paras were grouped together. No support could be expected from the glider-borne troops either. One of the three Horsas broke its tow rope just after take-off and had to make an emergency landing at RAF Odiham. The second landed several miles east of the battery, and the third flew over the battery and crashed in an orchard about 100 yards away to the south-west, having been hit by AA fire.

Meanwhile, the advance party had cut the outer wire fence but the lack of mine detectors and tape meant that a path through had been achieved by searching for them with bare hands and making them safe one by one. To mark the path they had dragged their feet to scratch two lines in the earth. Otway decided to make two gaps in the wire and send two assault groups through each. These he split into two teams, one for each casement. Another section was ordered to wipe out the German machine gun posts that were outside the Battery. Gaps were blown in the wire and the paras stormed the battery. The diversion party attacked through the main gate and hand-to-hand fighting ensued for 20 minutes until the Germans finally capitulated. Twenty-two prisoners were taken and the Paras put the guns out of action. At 04:45 the success signal was fired. (HMS *Arethusa* was standing by to pound the battery with her six-inch guns at 05:50 if the attack failed.) The 75 paras still standing left for high ground around Amfreville, taking their wounded with them. Later in the day the 736th Grenadier Regiment re-occupied the Battery and a message was received by Major General Richard Gale stating that 'the guns had opened fire'. Next day Nos 4 and 5 Troops, No.3 Commando assaulted the Battery and the defenders were overcome, but the enemy counter-attacked using self-propelled guns and drove the commandos out.

Lieutenant Colonel Otway's short and sharp official report.

'By 02:50 hours the battalion had grown to 150 strong with 20 lengths of Bangalore torpedo. Each company was approximately 30 strong. Enough signals to carry on – no three-inch mortars – one machine gun – one half of one's sniping party – no six-pounder guns – no jeeps or trailers or any glider stores – no sappers – no field ambulance, but six unit medical orderlies – no mine detectors – one company commander missing. The commanding officer decided to advance immediately.'

Sergeant Percy Reeve

'I landed about a mile and a quarter from the battery, up to my neck in a ditch. When I climbed out I met a surprised Frenchman and then the 150 of us met up in a wood. A major problem was the lack of any tape used to mark paths through minefields. It meant we had to feel our way in single file, on hands and knees, most of the way there. I sometimes wonder if the Germans were waiting. It wasn't until the Bangalore torpedoes went in that all hell broke loose. Up to then there was almost total silence. It was uncanny. There was this almighty clatter. I'm sure it must have come from their 20mm gun. I was halfway there, running like hell across the open ground within sight of the target with my Sten and just folded up in the air and came down on my back.'

Private Alan Mower

'I saw an Airedale terrier standing in a section of barbed wire. A corporal told me not to touch it because it was stuffed and booby-trapped because the Germans knew the British like dogs ...There was a lot of hand-to-hand fighting and a terrific amount of small arms fire. We were coming under fire from what I think were 88s. I pressed on to No. 4 Casement to the left of the main road where a dead German was lying near the entrance. I went inside and saw a gun, which was a lot smaller than the 150s we had anticipated. I said we could get rid of it with some grenades in the ammunition nearby but before this could go ahead, there was a bang and all I could remember was my back had been ripped open and my legs were twitching. I thought I'd bought it. I remember calling for my mum – it was my 21st birthday. I felt that bad that I actually asked Paddy Jenkins to finish me off. Then Sid Capon came in ... I got up and found I could walk a few steps and he sort of carried me out of the casement. They sat George Hawkins up in there and he kept shouting, "Don't leave us. Don't leave us. [Hawkins was too badly wounded to be moved.] Then a couple of chaps came up with a bit of door. They carried me a little way on that and then once we got outside the wire some boys came along with this handcart. There was already another boy on there and they laid me on there and got me outside the Battery as far as we could go, and then left me with Major Bestley.'

Sniper John Walker
platoon Sergeant, 9th Battalion, Parachute Regiment.
'Unfortunately, though we were dropped in the right place between two rivers, at ten past midnight, we didn't know that the Germans had flooded the area in three feet of water. There were posts in the ground and coils of barbed wire. It was quite a shock and we lost many men drowned when they got caught up in wire. I was lucky; I was right on the edge but I got sodden wet.

'We all made for the RV, picking up individual people on the way. We weren't at all nervous. We were professionals. Every soldier was reliable. We had to head up through fields and hedgerows. It took us three hours to cover three miles because we could not afford to be seen or be heard. Surprise was everything. On the way I saw one of the gliders that had crashed. On a road we saw two Germans on bicycles but we let them go on. It would have been fatal if they knew we were there.

'At the RV I was reasonably happy. I had three-quarters of the platoon, about 15 men. We waited till we got the OK to go in. No one spoke. It was total silence. Although we had fewer men we would still carry out the attacks on each casement. Colonel Otway simply said, "Go to it!" As soon as the Bangalore torpedoes went off I headed for No.2 casement as quickly as possible. The faster the better. We had eight minutes to do the job and get out. Sergeant Sid Knight and his party of about eight headed for the main gate and I followed on behind them. On the way we passed Colonel Otway standing on the edge of the perimeter. He shouted, "Get those bloody machine gunners!" I was a trained sniper and I carried a shortened Lee Enfield rifle with telescopic sights. The German machine gunner was about 150 yards away. I looked through the sight and fired a shot between the 12-inch opening at the front of the machine gunner's concrete bunker. (Even if the bullet missed, the ricochet inside would probably kill him.) He didn't fire any more.

I carried on to No.2 casement and reached the top where I dropped a Mill's grenade down one of the chimney pipes. Several Germans came out with their hands up. They looked old and dirty. They were handed over to the REs.

Surprise, as far as I was concerned, was total. What efficiency! Two years' training and all over in eight to ten minutes! From there we had to make haste to the LZ to meet the gliders coming in.

Though the big guns weren't there we prevented a bloodbath on the beach.'

Red Devils' Timeline

The 6th Airborne Division is to support Sir Miles Dempsey's British Second Army and Henry Crerar's First Canadian Army. 6th Airborne's task is to seize and hold the left flank of the bridgehead. Brigadier Poett's 5th Parachute Brigade is to seize the ground each side of the bridges over the Canal du Caen and the Orne River and to hold positions on the long wooded ridge beyond the waterways, running from Troarn in the south to the sea. This ridge with the bridges behind will eventually form the critical left flank of the army and the bridges have to be intact to permit Allied troops and supplies to pass easily to and fro. Brigadier James Hill's 3rd Parachute Brigade, made up of the 8th and 9th Battalions and the 1st Canadian Parachute Battalion (1,800 men) is to prevent enemy reinforcements moving towards the British beachhead. The 8th Battalion and the 1st Canadian Brigade are to destroy five bridges in the flooded valley of the Dives. The 9th Battalion, commanded by Lt Col. Terence B. H. Otway DSO, is to silence a battery of four concrete gun emplacements on high ground near the village of Merville, 3 miles east of Ouistreham.

5 June

38 and 46 Groups RAF despatch 264 aircraft and 98 glider combinations, the glider tugs being Albemarles, Dakotas, Halifaxes and Stirlings, the gliders mainly Horsas with a few Hamilcars (carrying light tanks and 17-pounder anti-tank guns).

22:30 *Coup de main* party takes off from Tarrant Rushton, Dorset, in six Horsa gliders towed by Halifax bombers of 298 and 644 Squadrons, who will bomb Caen after the gliders are released.

22:49 Seven Horsas leave Down Ampney behind Dakotas of 271 Squadron.

22:50 Dakotas of 233 Squadron tow six Horsas into the air above Blakehill Farm.

23:10 Four Horsas carrying paratroops and medical staff leave Harwell towed by Albemarles of 295 and 570 Squadrons.

6 June

00:15 At 5,000 ft over Cabourg the gliders carrying the *coup de main* party are released from their tugs and they begin their five-mile glide to the bridges over the Canal de Caen and Orne River.

00:20 Three of the gliders land within 30 yards of the Canal de Caen bridge.

00:20 North of Ranville pathfinders with radar beacons and coloured lights to mark the dropping zones, together with the advance parties of the 5th Parachute Brigade, drop from 27 aircraft.

00:35 Canal de Caen bridge (subsequently renamed 'Pegasus Bridge') is in British hands at a cost of two men killed and 14 wounded. Two other gliders land near the

Orne River bridge (subsequently renamed 'Horsa Bridge'), which is undefended. (A sixth glider lands seven miles away near the Dives River.) Howard has to beat off counter-attacks from German tanks and artillery for more than 12 hours. Spitfires fly over at about 10,000 ft and Howard signals that they have captured the bridge. His men watch as they do victory rolls and one drops a package of the morning papers. Howard says, 'Right then, my blokes forgot about the bridge and the war. They were riveted by the *Daily Mirror* and the sight of Jane taking her skirt off.'

00:50 2,000 men of the 5th Parachute Brigade and 400 containers dropped north of Ranville by 110 RAF aircraft. The 600-strong 7th Brigade is to get to the bridges as fast as possible to relieve the *coup de main* party.

02:30 Main Force of 750 men of the 9th Battalion attacking the Merville battery leaves Brize Norton, Harwell and Tarrant Rushton in Horsas towed by Albemarles.

02:50 9th Battalion para drops are scattered and only about 150 paras are grouped together for the march on the Battery.

03:00—04:00 About 100 Lancasters detailed to 'soften up' the Merville battery with 4,000-lb bombs miss the target in the cloudy conditions prevailing.

03:00 7th Battalion, 5th Brigade, cross the Orne bridge, take up positions in Bénouville and Le Port and for the rest of the day fight off a series of attacks by elements of the German 716th Division.

03:30 Sixty tugs cast off their gliders, which land on dropping zones to disgorge General Gale and his Divisional HQ and the anti-tank batteries with their 6-pounder guns.

04:45 Merville Battery surrenders.

13:30 Brigadier Lord Lovat's 1st Special Service Brigade, composed of four Army and one Royal Marines Commando, reach Pegasus Bridge *en route* to help other units of the Airborne Division.

20:5I—2I:23 Operation Mallard. There are insufficient aircraft to carry the 6th Airborne Division in one lift so 256 tugs of 38 and 46 Groups towing gliders, escorted by 15 RAF fighter squadrons, transport most of the 6th Airlanding Brigade and one regiment of artillery of three batteries armed with American 75-mm pack howitzers. In all, 249 gliders land on their landing zones behind Utah and east of the Orne. One glider crashes and six force-land in England or in the Channel.

The Glider Pilot Regiment loses 34 pilots killed in action on D-Day.

Order Of Battle

6th Airborne Division
Major General Richard Gale

3rd Parachute Brigade
8th and 9th Battalions, The Parachute Regiment, AAC
1st Canadian Parachute Battalion

5th Parachute Brigade
7th, 12th and 13th Battalions, The Parachute Regiment, AAC

6th Airlanding Brigade

2nd Bn The Oxfordshire and Buckinghamshire Light Infantry

1st Bn The Royal Ulster Rifles

A Coy 12th Bn The Devonshire Regiment

Divisional Troops

HQ 6th Airborne Division

6th Airborne Armoured Reconnaissance Regt, RAG

211 Bty, 53rd Airlanding Light Regiment, RA

3rd and 4th Airlanding Anti-Tank Batteries, RA

3rd and 591st Parachute Squadrons, RE

249th Field Company (Airborne), RE

286th Field Park Company (Airborne), RE

22nd Independent Parachute Company

1st and 2nd Wings Glider Pilot Regiment, AAC

Plus Airborne elements of:

Royal Corps of Signals

Royal Army Service Corps

Royal Army Medical Corps

Corps of Royal Electrical and Mechanical Engineers

Bloody Omaha

Franz Rachmann

German Soldier.

'It was in the night and I was sleeping, and my sergeant came running and said, "There are a thousand different ships coming in the English Channel." We could see landing boats of American troops. Then came thousands of men at one time coming on land and running over the beach. This is the first time I shoot on living men, and I go to the machine gun and I shoot, I shoot, I shoot! For each American I see fall, there came ten hundred other ones!'

Flight Lieutenant R. H. G. Weighill

2nd Squadron, 35 Wing RAF, flying a Mustang to spot the
fall of shot of HMS 'Glasgow'. Weighill was probably the
first eyewitness of the landings.

'The sea was littered with ships of all descriptions
ploughing doggedly towards the enemy's coast, looking
very grim and very determined. The bombardment was
terrific and one could actually see the shells in the form of
red and white lights as they left the ships and flew towards
the shore... I stayed at 1,000 feet and watched five of the
naval vessels, which were about a mile from the beach
and turned broadside on, proceeding to belch flame and
destruction. It was a most terrifying sight, for as they fired
rockets, a sheet of flame 50 yards long completely
enveloped the ship. By this time, the first boat was almost
ashore, and, as I watched it, the front came down and the
men inside jumped into the water and ran towards the
beach. It was a wonderful moment when I reported that
the first men had actually landed.'

Lieutenant Commander Joseph H. Gibbons

USNR, CO, US Navy Combat Demolitions Units in Force 'O',
which were awarded the Presidential Unit Citation.

'The Naval Combat Demolition Units (NCDU) were
charged with the responsibility of clearing sixteen 50-yard
gaps on the beaches assigned to that force. They worked
in conjunction with the Army engineers whose job it was
to clear the shoreward obstacles ... The plan called for the
NCDU to land at H-hour plus three minutes. Unfortunately, gunfire was not neutralized and as we approached
the beaches we were subjected to heavy enemy gunfire of

88 mm, .75s, .50 machine-gun and rifle fire. In the engagement we suffered 41 per cent casualties, 20 per cent killed, 21 per cent wounded. This excluded those who were wounded but were not evacuated from the beaches. The gunfire was intense, but we were successful in clearing initially six gaps [of] 50 yards each and three semi-partially cleared gaps. By the end of D-Day we had been successful in clearing ten gaps completely. By D+2, 85 per cent of the enemy obstacles on the beaches had been cleared and by D+4 the beaches on Omaha were cleared of all enemy obstacles dangerous to invasion craft.

'Some of the unusual events which occurred were, first, the complete decimation of one crew, which was killed by a direct hit of an 88-mm gun. The boys went into the beaches carrying 40 lb of specially prepared explosives. We carried 300 lb of additional explosives in rubber boats. This particular unit had placed their charges on the obstacles and in placing these charges, they were all hand placed. They were prepared to pull the fuse detonating the charges, when an 88 shell made a direct hit on one of the rubber boats exploding the auxiliary ammunition. The concussion therefrom set off the explosives on the obstacles, which in turn killed all members of that crew with the exception of one man who had gone up the beach to place markers to guide in subsequent craft.

'Another crew received a direct hit by an 88 in the boat and all except two men were killed. In another case an officer was standing by to pull the fuses after the charges had been placed when rifle fire cut his fingers off and the fuse assemblies. In still another instance enemy rifle fire set off the charges which had been placed on the obstacles which cleared the gap but unfortunately also caused casualties. One unit was decimated, with the exception of three men, by enemy sniper fire. Throughout the entire operation the loyalty and bravery and devotion to duty of the men was most outstanding. All of those who were killed died with their faces toward the enemy and as they moved forward to accomplish their objectives.

'Three of my officers were walking down the beaches, which were strewn with mines. They were walking in the wheel ruts of a truck. Twenty paces behind a soldier came by, stepping in the footprints made by the last naval officer. He set off the mine and was blown to pieces. One officer had a sniper shooting at him for five minutes, without success but unfortunately he did hit the man adjacent to this officer, shooting him between the eyes.

'On the enemy-placed obstacles on the beaches they had also placed teller mines. These were placed on approximately 75 per cent on top of stakes, at the apex of ramps and at the top of the elements "C" and in some cases in the center of hedgehogs [beach obstacles constructed of clusters of wooden or metal stakes sticking into the air at different angles]. In order to detonate those mines, it was decided that they should be detonated at the time the obstacle was destroyed in order to avoid having those mines blown into the beach unexploded, to be a hazard later.

'To accomplish that, it was necessary to place a charge alongside the mine to assure it being detonated when the obstacle was demolished. To accomplish this, men shinnied up the stakes and stood on each other's shoulders all in the face of heavy enemy gunfire.'

James Roland Argo

Pharmacist Mate Ist class.

'Our LCI pulled up to Omaha Beach just at daybreak. We hit an obstacle in the water and were not able to get right up on the beach. I was on the bridge/conning tower with Lieutenant Montgomery. Suddenly all hell broke out. Montgomery yelled, "Get off the bridge" and we abandoned the bridge immediately. The German bunkers that were supposed to have been blasted out in an air raid weren't. Fire started coming from everywhere. To make things worse, the water was very rough. We carried men from the 1st Division (the Big Red One) to Omaha Beach. Wood timbers/cross ties and barbed wire were attached to mines. I saw a couple of dead men draped over these obstacles in the shallow water. The fighting on the beach seemed to be the most horrendous for the first five to six hours. It eased up a little around what I thought seemed like lunchtime, but the shelling continued for two days. You should have seen my helmet. I wish I had saved it for my kids to see. I was told that the Germans wouldn't aim fire directly at men in the Red Cross helmets. A few hours into battle, I took my helmet off because I was certain they were aiming right at that Red Cross. I guess the Germans figured for every hospital corpsman they took out, the more overall casualties there would be. Dead corpsmen can't save lives.'

Ben Isgrig

448th Bomb Group, 2nd Bomb Division, 8th Air Force at Seething, Norfolk.

'We were called to the briefing room at 23:00 and Colonel Jerry Mason said, "This is it". Our target was Omaha

Beach. The first mission was primarily concerned with the neutralizing of enemy coastal defences and front line troops. Subsequent missions would be directed against lines of communication leading to the bridgehead ... It was just getting light as our formation left the English coast and the clouds broke enough for us to see the hundreds of ships in the Channel heading for France. We could plainly see the heavy warships shelling the coast, which was shrouded in smoke. Besides seeing more ships than I had ever seen before, there were also more heavy bombers in the air than I thought possible to put up in one area. The coast itself was covered in clouds. We didn't see our target at all; neither did we see flak or fighters.'

Leading Stoker Henry 'Buck' Taylor
LST 63.

'We sailed from Felixstowe with about 300 Americans and 40 Shermans on board. Everyone on our LST was tensed up. I shall never forget the sight, as we joined the main fleet in the Channel of the unbroken line of boats going over and coming back and plenty of aircraft cover overhead. We formed part of the second wave, landing at Omaha six to eight hours after the first wave. As the LST crashed through the spray and the ramp slammed down, the mighty Sherman tanks roared off. Down below you could distinctly hear the roar of gunfire and shells exploding as they rained down on enemy defences. We were supposed to get in and get out as quickly as possible but the ballast tanks were blown too quickly and we got stuck. We were marooned there for eight or nine hours until the next high tide before we could slip away.

'The Yanks had really been hit badly. I went up top and saw on the beach the dead and the wounded being tended by medics, discarded rifles and shells and a smashed LST crippled by a German 88-pounder. The beachmaster was shouting his head off: "Where's the crew for these tanks?" The drivers couldn't find the crews and had dumped them.

'Another stoker and I saw a knocked-out German tank and went searching for souvenirs. There were dead inside and we found rifles and pistols. Also some wooden bullets tipped with poison. We couldn't go much farther because the area was still mined and we returned to our boat. Our souvenirs were later confiscated.'

Ben Smith Jr
Chicks Crew, 303rd Bomb Group.

'We flew two missions on D-Day, bombing behind the German lines. We did not see a single German fighter or even a burst of flak. Amazing! I could see a battleship out in the Channel, I believe it was the *Texas*, firing at shore targets. There was a solid mass of ships offshore, and we could see the beached landing crafts and others streaking in with their precious burdens. At least we knew we had made a beachhead.'

Tom Bradley

'I was in the green sector of Omaha beach. The sea was very rough. When we got there the little hatch opened and bullets showered the people near the front of the boat. Then another craft landed next to us and the attention of the bullets turned to the then we got out ... it was over so quickly, I never knew how lucky I was.'

Wilbur Richardson
B-17 gunner, 94th Bomb Group.

'All of us flew a second mission and the few that didn't go with us made theirs toward evening just after we returned. We stayed on the ramp between flights as our B-17s were refuelled and re-armed. I was interviewed by the press as we waited. By the second sortie, the cloud cover was broken up and we could see even more of the action and the hundreds of vessels in the Channel. I saw the *Texas* firing her big guns and watched the three 1,400-lb shells travel to the target. The view from the ball turret was an awe-inspiring sight. The crews were very tired with the loss of sleep and so much time (15 hours total) in the air. But the events of the day left us keyed-up and talkative.'

Henry Tarcza
B-17 El's Bells, 95th Bomb Group, 8th Air Force.

'... I gazed with awe at the hundreds of ships and boats off Omaha Beach below. All were headed toward the beach landing site and it appeared from our altitude that one could almost step from one vessel to another and walk between England and France. Our group of about 40 B-17s in close formation began to ease its way into the narrow corridor for the bomb run. At this time the bombardier instructed me to activate the bombs. I climbed out on to the catwalk and after cautiously removing the safety pins from each bomb I notified him that they were now "live". For the first time since take-off I now experienced a sense of fear. This was mostly for the unknown because I now began to wonder what the Germans had in store for us in that critical area. As we reached Omaha Beach the lead plane released a smoke bomb, which was a signal for all 40 aircraft to drop their bombs simultaneously. Thus, more than 100 tons of bombs exploded in a matter of a few seconds. This was the only mission over Europe when I actually felt the concussion of our own bombs. The explosions caused our aircraft to bounce and vibrate.

'Obviously, the long-planned invasion had remained a well-guarded secret. We encountered no German aircraft in the target area and enemy gunfire was very light and inaccurate.

'We were a little apprehensive on our return because of a diminishing fuel supply. We landed at an RAF base in southern England, refuelled and flew on to Horham where we gave an Associated Press reporter our views on the historic mission. Emotions varied. Many of our thoughts, feelings and opinions we kept to ourselves. My pilot, Mathew McEntie, said, "Thank you men for your fine co-operation as a combat crew. It is doubtful if any of us will ever in our lifetime, participate in a historic undertaking of this magnitude."

'So far nobody has.'

Private Lee Ratel, 18
16th Infantry Regiment, 2nd wave.

'It was waist deep when we went in and we lost, I'd say, probably one-third between getting off the boats and to the edge of the water and then probably another third between there to the base where you got any protection at all because it was straight down and they were zeroed in there. They're very, very good defensive soldiers, but they're not trained the same ... they're trained to think how they're told to think and Americans are more independent they can think on their own resources and this makes a lot of difference in a battle. Most, except myself, were seasoned men, they knew what to do ... there were landing craft blown up in the water, lying in the water, they never got in ... direct hits ... bodies of men who didn't even get into the sand and there were a lot of them lying on the sand ... there was crossfire from pillboxes ... the beach here cost an awful price in men, good men ... it was a job that had to be done and we were allotted to it. That's it. You do what you have to do.'

Diary entry
Lieutenant Abe Dolim
navigator, 94th Bomb Group.

'Tuesday, June 6. Mission No. 18. We bombed a highway junction back of the invasion beaches flying at only 14,000 feet and using radar for the drop. There was no flak. Above the solid undercast at 10,000 feet. We saw nothing but bombers and escorting fighters.'

Wing Commander 'Johnnie'
Johnson DSO, DFC
Spitfire IXb pilot, Wing Leader, I44 RCAF Wing at Ford.
Johnnie finished the war as the top scoring British
fighter pilot with 34 confirmed victories.

'From the pilot's viewpoint, flying conditions were quite reasonable – better than we expected after the gloomy forecasts of the previous two or three days. The cloud base was at about 2,000 feet and the visibility between five and six miles ... We swept parallel to the coast beneath a leaden grey sky, and I positioned the wing two or three hundred yards offshore so that we should not present easy targets to the enemy gunners. Our patrol line ended over the fishing village of Port-en-Bessin, while farther to the west, beyond our area of responsibility, lay the two American assault beaches Omaha and Utah. When we carried out a wide, easy turn to retrace our flight path, a wing of American Thunderbolts harried our progress and for a few uneasy moments we circled warily round each other. Formations of different types of Allied air had attacked each other during the preceding months, but in this instance recognition was soon effected and we continued our flight to the south of the Orne. For the present there was little doubt that we were the undisputed masters of this little portion of the Normandy sky ... Four times that day we made our way across the Channel and never a sign of the Luftwaffe!'

New Zealand Flight Lieutenant John Houlton

pilot, Spitfire IXb MK950, 485 Squadron RNZAF, 135 Wing, 2nd TAF at Selsey, describing how he destroyed the first enemy plane on D-Day. On 8 June he destroyed a Bf 109 and he shot down another Bf 109 on 12 June to take his overall score to four destroyed, two shared destroyed and four damaged.

'In mid-afternoon I led Blue Section during the third patrol of the day, the other Section pilots being Maurice Mayston, Keith Macdonald and Eddie Atkins. South of Omaha Beach, below a shallow, broken layer of cumulus, I glimpsed a Ju 88 above cloud, diving away fast to the south. Climbing at full throttle I saw the enemy aircraft enter a large isolated cloud above the main layer, and when it reappeared on the other side I was closing in rapidly. Our aircraft were equipped with the gyro gunsight which eliminated the snap calculations or guesswork required to hit a target aircraft – especially one in a reasonably straight flight path; and it also enabled the guns to be used accurately at a far greater range than before. I was well aware, however, that most pilots were sceptical of the new instrument and preferred to use the conventional type of sight, which was still incorporated on the screen of the new sight. Normally one would open fire only at ranges below 250 yards; but I adjusted the gyro sight on to the target at 500 yards with a deflection angle of 45 degrees, positioned the aiming dot on the right-hand engine of the enemy aircraft and fired a three-second burst. The engine disintegrated, fire broke out, two crewmembers baled out and the aircraft dived steeply to crash on a roadway, blowing apart on impact.

'As I turned back towards the beachhead I sighted a second Ju 88 heading south and made an almost identical attack, which stopped the right-hand engine. This aircraft then went into a steep, jinking dive with the rear gunner firing at the other members of my Section who all attacked, until the Ju 88 flattened out and crash-landed at high speed. One of its propellers broke free, to spin and bound far away across the fields and hedges like a giant Catherine wheel. As we reached the beachhead, radio chatter indicated that other pilots (349 (Belgian) Squadron) were dealing with another German bomber, so this belated effort appeared to have been a costly exercise for the Luftwaffe.

'By now, two lines of ships were ranged towards the beaches, with two more lines of unloaded ships heading back. As we flew back over the in-bound lanes, the two lines of ships advancing up and down the Channel to the turning point for Normandy stretched right back to the visible horizon. The Squadron's fourth patrol at dusk was uneventful. And so ended D-Day. Intelligence reports confirmed that the Army was ashore in strength, there was no doubt that the invasion had succeeded, and an overwhelming mood of relief had replaced the tension of the preceding days.

'Supreme Headquarters nominated the first Ju 88 I had destroyed as the first enemy aircraft to be shot down since the invasion began, putting 485 (NZ) Spitfire Squadron at the top of the scoreboard for D-Day. Some days before the invasion I had casually suggested we should run a sweepstake for the first pilot to shoot down an enemy aircraft after the invasion began, and I duly collected a few shillings from the pool. When we later had time to unwind and celebrate, my modest winnings were well short of the cost of that party. By coincidence Flying Officer R. E. Lelong – later Flight Lieutenant, DFC – from Auckland destroyed an Me 410 on the eve of D-Day when flying a night intruder patrol with 605 (Mosquito) Squadron over the German aerodrome at Evreux.'

Houlton finished the war with five confirmed victories. In all, Spitfires of 485 Squadron shot down two Ju 88s over Omaha Beach on 6 June, and in the following week, another seven Luftwaffe fighters, including four rocket-firing Fw 190s. 2nd TAF and ADGB flew around 90,000 sorties in June, by far the greatest monthly effort ever recorded in the history of aerial warfare. About a quarter of this effort was directly above the Allied beachheads.

Account by the US War Department's Historical Division of the Ist Battalion, II6th Regiment

which directly assaulted Dog Green and which experienced the severest fire of all on Omaha, from a bluff commanding the western end of the beach and from the Vierville exit.

'As if this were the signal for which the enemy had waited, all boats came under criss-cross machine-gun fire … As the first men jumped, they crumpled and flopped into the water. Then order was lost. It seemed to the men that the only way to get ashore was to dive head first in and swim clear of the fire that was striking the boats. But, as they hit the water, their heavy equipment dragged them down and soon they were struggling to keep afloat. Some were hit in the water and wounded. Some drowned then and there … But some moved safely through the bullet-fire to the sand and then, finding they could not hold there, went back into the water and used it as cover, only their heads sticking out. Those who survived kept moving forward with the tide, sheltering at times behind under-water obstacles and in this way they finally made landings.

'Within ten minutes of the ramps being lowered, A Company had become inert, leaderless and almost incapable of action. Every officer and sergeant had been killed or wounded … It had become a struggle for survival and rescue. The men in the water pushed wounded men ashore ahead of them, and those who had reached the sands crawled back into the water pulling others to land to save them from drowning, in many cases only to see the rescued wounded again or to be hit themselves. Within 20 minutes of striking the beach A Company had ceased to be an assault company and had become a forlorn little rescue party bent upon survival and the saving of lives.'

Sergeant John R. Slaughter

116th Infantry. 29th Division was a National Guard Division. The leading companies of the Ist Battalion were A, B and D, recruited and based respectively around the Virginian towns of Bedford, Lynchburg and Roanoke.

'The journey across that Channel, 12 miles, we were up in it, we were gonna be on the water at least four and a half hours. And so it was everybody immediately became seasick. There was a foot of water in the bottom of the boat and we had to take the bilge pumps but they couldn't evacuate the water fast enough so we had to use our helmets to bail the water. Everybody was seasick. I'd never been sick before and some of my buddies had filled their puke bags already so I gave my puke bag and my Dramamine tablet away. Then I got sick. What caused me to get sick was the cold. It was probably in the 40s, the wind was blowing and we were soaking wet. I was just shivering. I went into my assault jacket and found a gas cape that we had in case of mustard gas and got under it to shield myself from the wind and the water. Of course lack of oxygen under the cape caused me to get really get sick and I came out from under that thing. I started vomiting and I just pulled my helmet and vomited in my helmet, threw it out and washed the helmet out, vomited some more and that's the way we went in.

'We were about 300 yards from touchdown. The Germans opened up on us and as we got in closer, kind of shuddered to a halt as we bucked over a sand bar and the ramp went down. The first man off was on the middle of the ramp and he just went over on it. Oh Dammit! The ramp was going up and down, up and down. I guess a wave had caused the landing craft to surge forward and it just smashed and killed him. It was a terrible sight and a terrible shock to everybody to see that man a healthy young man one minute and the next minute he's smashed to smithereens. You couldn't tell what he was.

'Everybody went off the sides. From then on it was screams and hollering and people drowning and getting hit and fear. It was bedlam, chaos, and it took a while to get it all sorted out and under control before we realized we've got to get organized, get across and get on top of the hill and get dug in. The first person I saw get wounded was a guy who was trying to run across the beach from the craft just to our right. He was staggering and looked like he had a lot of baggage – he was just kind of lumbering across. He was about 25 yards away from me and he got shot. The bullet hit him and he went down in a runnel of water. I watched the water turn red. He was screaming for a medic and one of our medics went over to help him and the medic got shot. Both of them were screaming and I wanted to go out there and help them but I knew if I did I'd get shot, so I just lay there. Within three or four minutes it just went silent so I guess they died. That was the second shocking thing that I saw that day. Then it was just people all around screaming because the water was over their head and getting hit and artillery getting closer and closer to where we were. We knew we had to go. We didn't have any choice. We couldn't stay where we were. We couldn't retreat because there was nowhere to go back there. So the only option was straight ahead.

'We landed in columns of companies. A Company about 06:30, B Company some ten to 15 minutes later and D Company about 07:10, though we probably all were late. We hit the eye of the storm. The battalion was decimated. Hell, after that we didn't have enough to whip a cat with.'

Lucille Hoback Boggess
who was 15 years old in June 1944, living on her family's farm near Bedford, a small town of 3,000 people, which lost 23 men on D-Day, 22 of these from A Company, 116th Regiment.

'I remember well the devastating impact on my family when we received telegrams two days in a row stating that my two brothers were killed or missing in action on D-Day. Shortly after we got the telegrams my mother received a letter from a Corporal Creighton in West Virginia saying that on D-Day plus one that he was walking on a beach in France and he spotted a Bible in the sand. And, as anyone would do, he picked it up. Having thumbed through it, he found my mother's name. He was also very careful to word the letter to say, "By now you have probably heard from your son and he is fine." I think he was even clever enough not to send it for some time to make sure that she had received word that my brother was all right. She has always treasured the Bible so much. She said that, next to her son, she would have wanted to have his bible.'

There were three sets of brothers in A Company. Raymond and Bedford Hoback were killed. Raymond was wounded and lay on the beach. Then when the tide came in he was washed out to sea and drowned. His body was never found, but he was carrying a Bible and it washed up upon the sand. On the Saturday the family got a telegram that Bedford was killed and then Sunday they got another one saying that Raymond was too. There were two Parkers killed. Roy and Ray Stevens were twins. Roy was wounded and Ray was killed.

Private Roy Stevens
(later Tech Sergeant) II6th Infantry Regiment, 29th Infantry Division.

'The relative I had at D-Day was a twin brother. He was on a boat of an even number, and I think mine was number five. When we were loading off the large boat to go on the smaller one, he was standing alongside, and he stuck his hand out for me to shake. I said, "I'll shake your hand in Vierville-sur-Mer at the crossroads there in the night or this morning sometime." And he just sort of dropped his head. He had a feeling that he wasn't going to make it, and he just kept telling me that. But, anyway, he just dropped his head. And the lieutenant with him couldn't understand that either. That has haunted me quite a bit since that happened, because I should have shaken his hand. I was just so sure that we were going to meet there, but he wasn't.'

Sub-lieutenant
George 'Jimmy' Green RNVR
Divisional Officer, 55I LCA Flotilla from the Empire Javelin.

'551 LCA Flotilla had trained with US Rangers in Scotland and we presumed we would be taking them into Omaha beach on 6 June. We were surprised when we heard we were taking the 116th Infantry Regiment on board the SS *Empire Javelin*, as they were a National Guard Regiment from Virginia – pleasant friendly country lads but not assault troops. My task as leader of the first wave of six LCAs was to land A Company at Vierville-sur-mer at 06:30 so they could secure the pass leading off the beach for the following troops to move inland.

'Captain Taylor Fellers, the Officer Commanding A Company, confided to me his misgivings of the task he had been given. His troops had never seen action and he wondered how they would react. He asked me if I could go flat out for the beach and give his troops covering fire as they advanced up the beach. I assured him that if I saw any Germans I would certainly open fire on them with my machine guns.

'On D-Day I was called early as the lowering time was brought forward to 04:00 hours because of the rough seas. We were supposed to take in two LCAs from HMS *Prince Charles* carrying US Rangers but we had to leave before they arrived and they followed us in.

'On our way to the beach we came across a group of LCTs carrying DD tanks, which were to land ahead of us. This was the first I had heard about these tanks and I told Taylor Fellers that they would never make it on time as they were wallowing in the heavy seas. We left them behind and never saw them again.

'About 06:00 it began to get light and we could make out the French coast. It was a strange experience to be out in front facing goodness knows what. The bombardment stopped and there was only the sound of the sea and wind. Then some LCT(R)s appeared and launched all their rockets into the sea well short of the beach. I was just about to give the signal to go into line abreast from two columns when LCA *911* immediately behind me sank by the bows. We could not stop to pick up crew and troops but shouted out we would be back. We then went into line abreast and made full speed ahead for the beach. Because it was so flat the LCAs grounded about 30 yards from the shoreline. The ramps were lowered and the troops who had been sat down in three rows filed off as arranged, with Taylor Fellers leading the way. I wished him good luck as every sailor has great respect for the troops he carries. It took some time for the troops to disembark as the craft was bouncing up and down in the heavy surf and the soldiers were hampered by the amount of kit they carried. They had certainly come to stay. When they reached the beach the troops lay down and made no attempt to advance towards the obstacles 50 yards away or the menacing cliffs 250 yards further on where the hidden Germans were popping off mortars at us. As there was nothing more I could do at the beach after picking up some survivors from the Rangers LCA I made for the spot where LCA had foundered and picked up those left in the water. I then returned to the *Empire Javelin* with as many soldiers as I started with.

'It was some time before I heard that Taylor Fellers and all the men in LCA *910* had been killed. Practically everyone else in that first wave we landed at 06:30 was wiped out shortly after landing.'

On 9 May 1941 Ordinary Seaman Green participated in what King George VI called 'the most important single event in the war at sea' – the capture of U-110 by HMS *Bulldog* and what remained of its crew and equipment, including an Enigma cipher machine with the 9 May settings still on its rotors, and several codebooks. Jimmy finally left the Royal Navy in 1946 and he subsequently re-mustered in the British Army, retiring as lieutenant colonel.

Sergeant Thomas Valence

'We proceeded toward the beach, and many of the fellows got sick. The water was quite rough. It was a choppy ride in, and we received a lot of spray. Our boat was one of six of A Company in the first wave, and when we got to the beach, or close to it, the obstacles erected by the Germans to prevent the landing were fully in view, as we were told they would be, which meant the tide was low.

'I was the rifle sergeant and followed Lieutenant Anderson off the boat, and we did what we could rather than what we had practiced doing for so many months in England. There was a rather wide expanse of beach, and the Germans were not to be seen at all, but they were firing at us, rapidly, with a great deal of small-arm fire.

As we came down the ramp, we were in water about knee high, and we started to do what we were trained to do – move forward, and then crouch and fire. One of the problems was we didn't quite know what to fire at. I saw some tracers coming from a concrete emplacement, which to me looked mammoth. I never anticipated any gun emplacements being that big. I attempted to fire back at that, but I had no concept of what was going on behind me. There was not much to see in front of me except a few houses, and the water kept coming in so rapidly, and the fellows I was with were being hit and put out of action so quickly that it become a struggle to stay on one's feet. I abandoned my equipment, which was very heavy.

'I floundered in the water and had my hand up in the

air, trying to get my balance, when I was first shot. I was shot through the left hand, which broke a knuckle, and then through the palm of the hand. I felt nothing but a little sting at the time, but I was aware that I was shot. Next to me in the water, Private Henry G. Witt was rolling over towards me. "Sergeant, they're leaving us here to die just like rats." I certainly wasn't thinking the same thing, nor did I share that opinion. I didn't know whether we were being left or not.

I made my way forward as best I could. My rifle jammed, so I picked up a carbine and got off a couple of rounds. We were shooting at something that seemed inconsequential. There was no way I was going to knock out a German concrete emplacement with a .30-caliber rifle. I was hit again, once in the left thigh, which broke my hipbone and a couple of times in my pack, and then a bullet severed my chinstrap on my helmet. I worked my way up onto the beach, and staggered up against a wall, and collapsed there. The bodies of the other guys washed ashore, and I was one live body amongst many of my friends who were dead and, in many cases, blown to pieces.

Brigadier General Norman 'Dutch' Cota, 5I

assistant commander, 29th Infantry Division, who, pinned down by the seawall on 'Dog White Beach', said to Lieutenant Colonel Max Schneider, 5th Ranger Battalion, 'Well it looks like the Rangers are going to have to get us off the beach.'

'The air and naval bombardment and the artillery support are reassuring, but you're going to find confusion. The landing craft aren't going in on schedule and people are going to be landed in the wrong place. Some won't be landed at all. The enemy will try, and will have some success, in preventing our gaining a lodgment. But we must improvize, carry on, not lose our heads. Nor must we add to the confusion."

Schneider's men, reinforcements for the attack on Pointe du Hoc, had not been needed and had therefore moved to Dog White as planned. Cota directed specialists armed with Bangalore torpedoes to blow vital gaps in the thick barbed wire just beyond the seawall and finally the others began to trickle then flood through the steep hillside. After helping take Vierville (where a group of men met Cota on the main street, "twirling a pistol on his index finger like an Old West gunfighter" and greeting them with: "Where the hell have you been, boys?") Cota returned to the landing area to help speed the flow of vehicles, including a bulldozer loaded with TNT needed up forward. On 7 June Cota and his men stormed a house in St. Laurent occupied by Germans. In July he became commander, 28th Infantry Division.

First Lieutenant P. Clough

'Of our six assault landing craft only three made Omaha beach. We were surrounded by casualties in the water. They were clinging to the various obstructions – anything they could find. On our way back out we pulled a wounded American soldier aboard. We were told that a serviceman's Bible with a steel-backed cover had deflected the bullet that hit him. On cleaning our craft we found a bloodstained cardboard case that had contained the Bible. I kept it as a souvenir.

Mate Frank R. Feduik, 19

Pharmacist, USS LST 338.

'... *Arkansas* and the *Texas* were behind us as we were going in and these shells would sing their way right over the ship. It was such a din! Some of the targets were eight and ten miles inland. Every once in a while you would hear or see a big explosion way inland and we knew they had hit an ammunition dump or something. It was such a hectic thing, everybody firing this way, beach fire coming at you. They were firing at us from the pillboxes on the beach. You would hear the shells coming at you. You could hear them whirring by and when you saw them hit the water ... well if you were in the wrong place, forget about it. Those German 88s were awful. Once you heard them bark and you were still alive, you knew they hadn't gotten you because that shell would be on top of you before the noise got there.

'We did get hit by shrapnel every once in awhile. When we got hit I was directly beneath one of the gun mounts trying to set up an aid station under gun No. 4. As I was coming up the ladder, I heard this noise and then heard a fellow who was in the gun mount, say, "Round and round she goes and where she stops nobody knows." Evidently, a piece of shrapnel had gotten into the gun mount and wound its way around until it exited. I couldn't imagine how cool he was.'

Madelaine Hardy, 15

a farmer's daughter living with her father and three sisters in Baynes, 11 miles from Omaha beach.

'All day there was a rumbling noise like thunder but no natural sounds at all. It was as if nature had simply stopped. Finally, my father plucked up courage to investigate and returned, elated. "It's the Americans," he said. That evening an infantry regiment set up camp in our fields and we took them milk and cheese. The GIs were only a few years older than me and they were like big brothers. To me they will always remain heroes.'

Lenny Hickman
one of 'Mountbatten's illegitimate children'

'All hell was breaking loose as we pulled away from Omaha Beach. It was 06:30 and we were already on the way back home. Our job was done. We had been among the first servicemen in France on D-Day, parachuting at 00:03 to establish communications posts for the first units landing at Omaha beach to report back. Formed from submariner volunteers, we were nicknamed "Mountbatten's illegitimate children" and known as the 62nd simply because that comprized our number.

'We thought it was another practice run until a gunner on the Halifax bomber dropped the bombshell: "Right; lads. This is It. It's the second front." We were dumbfounded. Complete with a few choice adjectives, the general response was, "Bloody roll on." The plan had been to drop half a mile behind Omaha Beach but we finished three miles further inland and had to snake our way back, avoiding pockets of German troops in the dark.

'We reached our target area at about 04:15, working feverishly to set up camouflaged communications posts just off the beach, and then crawling on our bellies across the sand to defuse mines with magnets, spanners and screw drivers. The beach was generally deserted. A couple of sentries came by – I saw one smoking – but we had dug ourselves in and went unobserved. The first ships appeared on the horizon at about 06:15 and a battleship blasted the enemy positions. Landing craft streamed in and men and machines poured off. Our job was done and we rushed aboard a boat, which took us back to *Glenearn*, an LCA carrier. We were then transferred to LCA *3904* and home to Portsmouth. As we pulled away, all hell was being let loose in the barrage of bombs and shells that were raining down on German coastal defences. I was glad to be out of there.'

Reg Lilley

Royal Navy stoker.

'We landed American troops and tanks on Omaha Beach. We then ferried supplies from Southampton to Normandy for 19 days until we became beached in a storm. After five days food was getting scarce and we were living on herrings in tomato sauce. Eventually I could take it no longer. I grabbed the cook and said, "Take some of those tins to the Yanks and see if you can swap them. Don't come back with those herrings – Or else!" He returned after 30 minutes with two five-gallon tins of pears, the first we'd seen since the war started. We were most grateful. The Americans must have taken pity on us.'

Waverly Woodson, 2I

320th Barrage Balloon Battalion, detached to serve as a medic with the 49th Infantry and one of the handful of black American soldiers who landed on D-Day.

'Off Omaha Beach all hell broke loose. Our LCT hit a mine when we were still a couple of miles from the beach and lost power. As a result we drifted onto the beaches with the tide and landed at 05:30 with the demolition men, earlier than planned. We took fire from artillery and mortars, and I got some shrapnel in my backside. It hurt, but it wasn't bad enough to stop me functioning. We had a tank on board but when the ramp went down it was hit and blew apart. I waded ashore with my medical equipment in about four feet of water. The scene was pretty bad. Scared? You bet. Some of the troops were pinned down under some cliffs. I reached them and did what I could for the wounded. At that time, they didn't care what colour my skin was. That's what I got my Bronze Star for.'

Official report, 16th Infantry

'As the landing craft reached the beach they were subjected to heavy artillery, mortar, machine-gun and rifle fire, directed at them from the cliffs above the beach. Men were hit as they came down the ramps of the larding craft, and as they struggled landward through tie obstacles, and many more were killed or injured by the mines attached to the beach obstacles. Landing craft kept coming in with their human cargoes despite the heavy fire and continued to disgorge them on to the narrow shelf from which no exits had been opened. Several landing craft were either sunk or severely damaged by direct artillery hits or by contact with enemy mines.'

Chaplain Burkhalter's
letter home.

'Dear Mable,

… Just before landing we could see heavy artillery shells bursting all up and down the beach at the water's edge under well directed fire. As I stood in line waiting to get off the LCI to a smaller craft to go into shore, I was looking toward land and saw a large shell fall right on a landing craft full of men. I had been praying quite a bit through the night as we approached the French coast but now I began praying more earnestly than ever. Danger was everywhere; death was not far off ....We finally landed and our assault craft was miraculously spared, for we landed with no shells hitting our boat.

'The enemy had a long time to fix up the beach ... mines were everywhere. The enemy was well dug in and had set up well-prepared positions for machine guns and had well-chosen places for sniping. Everything was to their advantage and to our disadvantage, except one thing, the righteous cause for which we are fighting – liberation and freedom. For the moment our advantage was in the abstract and theirs was in the concrete. The beach was spotted with dead and wounded men. I passed one man whose foot had been blown completely off. Another soldier lying close by was suffering from several injuries; his foot was ripped and distorted until it didn't look much like a foot. Another I passed was lying very still, flat on his back, covered in blood. Bodies of injured men all around. Sad and horrible sights were plentiful.

'In from the beach were high hills which we had to climb .... We filed over the hill as shells were falling on the beach back of us, meaning death for others who were still coming in. Later, one of the soldiers told me that on this occasion he saw a shell land right on top of a wounded man and blow him to bits. Before going over the top of the hill we crouched for a while close to the ground just below the top. While lying there I did most of my praying. The shells were falling all around and how I knew that God alone was able to keep them away from us. I shall never forget those moments. I am sure that during that time I was drawn very close to God.

'Later, about ten of us were crossing along the edge of a field when we heard sniper bullets whiz by. We all fell to the ground. As we lay there hugging the earth, that we might escape shrapnel from shell fire and bullets from sniper's guns, the birds were singing beautifully in the trees close by. As I lay there listening I thought of the awfulness of it all; the birds were singing and we Human Beings were trying to kill each other. We are the greatest of God's creation, made in the image of God, and here human blood was being spilt everywhere. About three minutes later and only about forty yards away we filed by one of our own boys lying by the side of the hedge, crouched over with a hole in the back of his head. His eyes were open but he was dead, hit by a sniper. We didn't have time to stop; we were pushing on inland making a new front as we went. Someone behind and hours later would move him.

'... Our business was to keep fighting on inland and pushing the enemy back. On the roadside my assistants and I saw a dead German officer. He was a tall fellow; must have been about six feet four. We turned him over and stretched him out the best we could. I looked at his face and was surprized to see how young he looked. No doubt he was in his twenties but he had the face of a boy. I thought: surely, this fellow was too young to die. It almost seemed that he had asked for it. I became conscious of an awful evil force behind it all to cause a young fellow like this to seemingly hunger and delight to kill and be killed. We slid his body into a mattress cover and left him by the side of the road.

'... As I look back through hectic days just gone by to that hellish beach I agree with Ernie Pyle, that "it was a pure miracle we even took the beach at all." Yes, there were a lot of miracles on the beach that day. God was on the beach D-Day; I know He was because I was talking with Him.'

US Rangers Assault Pointe-du-Hoc and Pointe de la Percée

Allied intelligence pinpointed 73 fixed coastal gun batteries that could menace the invasion. At Pointe-du-Hoc, a cliff rising 100 ft high from a very rocky beach, 3.7 miles west of Vierville, a six-gun battery (thought to be 155mm, with a range of 25,000 yards) could engage ships at sea and fire directly onto Utah and Omaha. The gun positions were bombed throughout May, with a heavier than average attack by both day and night three days before D-Day, and then again during the night of 5 June. Then, at 06:30 three companies (225 men) of the 2nd Ranger Battalion (Force A) led by Lieutenant Colonel James F. Rudder, using rocket propelled grapple hooks attached to climbing ropes and portable extension ladders were to scale the cliffs within ten minutes after landing and capture the position. Company C, 2nd Ranger Battalion meanwhile, was to scale the bluffs of Pointe-de-la-Percée, 1.25 miles NW of Vierville. Lieutenant Colonel Maxwell Schneider's 5th Ranger Battalion and the 2nd

Battalion's A and B Companies constituted Force C, reinforcement, which were to wait offshore. If Schneider did not receive a signal by H+30 he was to land his men on Omaha and proceed overland through Pointe-de-la-Percée to attack Pointe-du-Hoc. (Schneider's men were not called upon so they moved four miles east, to Dog White, where they spearheaded the advance off the bloody beach and had captured Vierville by evening).

At Pointe-du-Hoc, in addition to the main concrete emplacements, many of which were connected by tunnels or protected walkways, there were trenches and machine gun posts constructed around the perimeter fences and the cliff edge. The garrison numbered about 200 men of the static 716th Coastal Defence Division, mostly non-Germans. In anticipation of commando landings, 240mm shells attached to trip wires had been placed at 100 yards intervals along the cliff. The fortifications came under heavy fire by *Texas* from H-40 minutes to H-05 minutes and 18 medium bombers hit the German positions just before the Rangers (who were 40 minutes late) arrived. But when the sea bombardment had been lifted according to schedule and when the Rangers landed, the Germans had filtered back into the fortifications and were waiting for them with machine-guns, rifles and hand-grenades, which they rolled down the cliffs.

Ray Alm, B Company

US 2nd Ranger Battalion

'We were about 200 feet from the beach when a shell blew off the front of our landing craft, destroying the ramp. My two best buddies were right in front of me, and they were both killed. When we went over the side of the landing craft (to avoid machine gun fire), the water was about 12 feet deep. After the shell hit, it was pretty much everyone for themselves. I was holding a .45 pistol and carrying a bazooka with eight shells; it was so heavy that I just went right under the water, so I had to let everything go except the shells. Eventually when I got to the beach I picked up a German rifle that I used. When we all got together on the beach, things were getting kind of bad. Fortunately, Colonel Schneider called the battleship *Texas* for support fire and it made a direct hit on the German pillbox. Two destroyers [USS *Satterlee* and HMS *Talybont*] took turns all day long firing at targets. They saved us; they were terrific.

When we were on the beach, there were two other Rangers and myself running, and a German machine gun was firing at us. We hid behind an anti-tank obstacle. The three of us ducked behind it. We then headed towards the front again, towards the street. It was terrible; there were bodies all over the place. They wiped out almost the entire 116th Infantry Regiment; they just murdered them. They were floating all over the place, there was blood in the water – it was just dark.

Ranger Alban Meccia

'We were late in getting to the beaches. Our rope ladders got wet on the way over. We were dumped out and had to wade several hundred feet in to the beach, and all the time the Germans were firing at us from the top of the big bluff we had to storm. Some of us were shot crossing the sand to the foot of the cliff. When we climbed, the Germans shot down at us. Finally, we threw grenades at the cliff, making furrows up the side and giving us some protection.

'Then we all went up and chased those Germans, killing a lot of them. They had left a little dog up there in a shack. He would respond to English, but he would stand up when you talked to him in German ... But that dog turned out to be a fifth columnist. He licked the wounded and annoyed them until we had to slit his throat.

'I saw a German officer shoot one of his men in the back when he started to walk over to us with his hands up. One of our guys saw a flag of surrender, and stood up to wave to the Germans to come over, and was shot between the eyes.'

Sergeant Leonard Lomell

Who received the Distinguished Service Cross.

'We landed and fired off our rockets. The ramp goes down and ... I stepped off into water over my head. The guys pulled me out and we just rushed to the base of that cliff and grabbed any rope we could get, and up the cliff we went just as fast as we could go. The wound wasn't bad; it had gone through the muscle on my right side.

'Captain Baugh of Company E was the first person I ran across on top. He had been shot and had his hand practically blown off and wasn't in such good shape. We kept right on going saying, "Captain, we'll send you back a medic." My platoon couldn't wait for nothing. We had our assignment and we in Company D depended on a lot of speed. My second platoon went ahead in a rush. We had some confrontations coming out of shell craters. As we were charging out of a shell crater, a machine gun opened up and Morris Webb, one of my sergeants, jumped back into the crater right on top of one of his men's bayonets that went right through his side.

'We didn't stop; we played it just like a football game, charging hard and low. We went into the shell craters for protection because there were snipers around and machine guns firing at us. We'd wait for a moment and if the fire lifted we were out of that crater and into the next one. We ran as fast as we could over to the gun positions – to the one that we were assigned to. There were no guns in the positions!

'There was an anti-aircraft position off to our right several hundred yards and a machine gun off to the left. There was another machine gun that we had gotten on our way in. The anti-aircraft gun was firing flat trajectory at us and by the time we got to the road I only had about a dozen men left. We were up on top of the cliffs around 19:30.

'The road was our next objective. We were supposed to get into the coastal road and set up a roadblock, which we did. We were the first ones at the coastal road. We were in the midst of doing this when all of a sudden we heard noise and clanking. We laid low in our ditch on the side of the road. It was an armed combat patrol of Germans loaded with heavy equipment, mortars and machine guns headed in the other direction toward Utah. I'd got ten or twelve guys and I was about to take on fifty or sixty when we've still got our mission to accomplish, so we let them go. Sergeant Koenig destroyed the communications along the coastal road by blowing up the telephone poles. Then Jack Kuhn (my platoon sergeant while I was the acting platoon leader) and I went down this sunken road not knowing where the hell it was going, but it was going inland. We came upon this vale or little draw with camouflage all over it. Lo and behold, we peeked over this hedgerow and there were the guns. [Five of the six guns were well camouflaged but unguarded in an orchard 2.5 miles further inland. One had been damaged by bombing and had been removed for repair]. It was pure luck. They were all sitting in proper firing condition, with ammunition piled up neatly; everything at the ready. But they were pointed at Utah Beach, not Omaha. There was nobody at the emplacement. We looked around cautiously and over about a hundred yards away in a corner of a field was a vehicle with what looked like an officer talking to his men. We decided let's take a chance. I said, "Jack, you cover me and I'm going in there and destroy them." All I had was two thermite grenades – his and mine. I went in and put the thermite grenades in the traversing mechanism and that knocked out two of them because that melted their gears in a moment. Then I broke their sights. We ran back to the road, which was a hundred or so yards back and got all the other thermites from the remainder of my guys manning the roadblock and rushed back and put the grenades in traversing mechanisms, elevation mechanisms, and banged the sights. There was no noise to that. There is no noise to a thermite, so no one saw us. Jack said, "Hurry up and get out of there, Len." I came up over the hedgerow with him and suddenly the whole place blew up. We thought it was a short round from the *Texas* but it was another patrol from Company E, led by Sergeant Rupinski, around to the left of us. They came upon the ammo depot and blew it up. We went flying. Dust and everything was settling on us and we got up and ran like two scared rabbits as fast as we could back to our men at the roadblock.

'We had the guns out of action before 08:30 and Sergeant Harry Tate volunteered to go back to Colonel Rudder and report the mission was accomplished and that we had the roadblock set up; and Sergeant Gordon Luning volunteered to take the message via a different route.

'Those guns had not been recently moved to that position. They'd been there a long time. There wasn't one bomb crater near them. They were so well camouflaged that the air force and whoever did the bombings of them never saw them, and their photos never saw them. The rest of the Pointe was perforated. They'd been blowing the hell out of that for four months. No wonder they'd moved those guns. You couldn't find a straight piece of land to do anything on at the Pointe.'

To this point, the 2nd Ranger's casualties were probably 30–40 but later that day the German 1st Battalion, 914th Regiment began a series of counter-attacks that nearly wiped out the small bridgehead and caused most casualties. That night the 2nd Rangers were driven into a small enclave along the cliff, barely 200 yards wide, but the they held out until noon on 8 June, helped by fire from destroyers, when they were relieved by Lieutenant Colonel Schneider's men. By then 2nd Ranger casualties were 135 killed, wounded and missing – a casualty rate of 60 per cent. Company C, 2nd Ranger Battalion suffered 50 per cent casualties (38 out of 64 men) clearing the German positions at Pointe-de-la-Percée before proceeding overland to Pointe-du-Hoc.

US Assault Divisions Omaha Beach

Ist US Division
Major General Clarence R. Huebner

116th Infantry	2nd Rangers
16th Infantry	5th Rangers
18th Infantry	741st Tank Battalion
26th Infantry	111th Field Artillery Battalion
115th Infantry	7th Field Artillery Battalion
	81st Chemical Battalion

Beach Timetable

02:20 Fire support ships led by *Arkansas* and including two French cruisers, arrive.

02:50 Assault elements of 1st and 29th Divisions in 16 large transports, 205 beaching craft and numerous small craft arrive

03:55 Minesweeping by British and Canadian minecraft, which began before midnight, ends.

04:30 Naval Force 'O' (Rear Adm J. L. Hall Jr.) concerned about fire from coastal batteries, begin lowering assault craft 12 miles off shore (the British are lowered less than eight miles from shore). Leading assault craft have to start their run in while it is still dark. The heaviest landings are to be made directly in front of the enemy strongpoints covering the natural exits off the four-mile long beach instead of between them. Bradley and his staff will rely on a heavy aerial and sea bombardment followed by a direct assault by troops to swamp the fortifications, which are believed to be under-manned.

05:50—06:25 USS *Texas* and other gunfire support ships pound the beach exit leading to Vierville amid low cloud and bad visibility and smoke and dust makes further identification of targets difficult. Rocket ships open fire at extreme range and most fall short, among the landing craft. *Texas* fires 250 rounds at the six-gun battery at Pointe-du-Hoc overlooking both Omaha and Utah beaches. 2nd Ranger Battalion land 45 minutes later to begin scaling the cliffs leading to the battery. Battleship USS *Arkansas* and cruiser HMS *Glasgow* pound the Les Moulins area; French cruiser *Georges Leygues* and other ships hit St Laurent plateau. The weather and smoke and dust also hamper aerial bombardment and bomb release is delayed to avoid hitting US troops. Most tonnage dropped by 484 B-24 Liberators lands three miles inland.

06:30 Less than half the companies in assault battalions are landed within 800 yards of their sectors. In the first wave eight companies (1,450 men in 36 landing craft of Major General Leonard T. Gerow's US V Corps' 1st Infantry Division head for the beaches in heavy seas which swamp at least ten LCVPs during the run in. 26 artillery pieces aboard DUKWs are lost. 32 DD tanks destined for the eastern half of Omaha are launched 6,000 yards from shore and all except five are lost. Infantry storm ashore without sufficient armour and suffer terrible losses as they are pinned down on the beach by the battle-hardened 352nd Field Regiment. It takes some companies' survivors 45 minutes to reach the cover of the sea wall. 40 per cent of the 270 specially trained demolition men are killed or wounded. Only six of the 16 armoured bulldozers reach shore and three are immediately destroyed.

08:30 Movement inland halted in the western sector and

little movement in the east. Congestion on the beach becomes so great that the head beachmaster orders no more boats to land until it is cleared. Omaha is on the point of catastrophe. The absence of special tanks offered by the British to demolish fortifications and obstacles and lack of sufficient DD tanks and heavy bulldozing equipment means lightly armed troops have to make frontal assaults on pillboxes and strongpoints without armour. US casualties are heavy but the Germans cannot halt the attack and on the second tide of the day 25,000 more men and 4,000 vehicles are ashore. 5th Rangers blast a hole in the sea wall and 35 men get behind the defenders.

09:50 Admiral Carleton F. Bryant, Naval Gunfire Support Group "O", orders his 17 US, British and French ships in closer to provide artillery support for the beleaguered troops on Omaha. Employing pairs of Spitfires to air spot because of the absence of any surviving fire control officers, the ships, some as close as 800 yards from the beach, open up on inland strongpoints and batteries. *Texas* (his flagship) and *Arkansas* between them fire 771 rounds of 14-inch shells (1,400 lbs each).

10:00 US troops reach clifftops overlooking Omaha.

11:00 US soldiers enter Vierville-sur-Mer.

13:00 101st and US 4th Infantry Division link up at Pouppeville.

13:30 Gerow signals Lt Gen Omar Bradley, 1st Army, "Troops formerly pinned down on beaches ... advancing up heights behind beaches."

13:35 German 352nd Division reported to have thrown the Allies back into the sea from Omaha.

16:00 US tanks begin moving inland from Omaha.

By nightfall Against all odds a perimeter up to a mile deep beyond Omaha is secured although at the start of the day it had been hoped that by nightfall V US Corps might have a beachhead 16 miles wide and five to six miles deep. US casualties are the highest of all the beaches. The 29th Division had 2,440 casualties, the 1st Division, 1,744, most of these in the first two hours. The divisions took 2,500 Germans prisoner.

Utah

Franz Goekel

German Soldier.

'The heavy naval guns fired salvo after salvo into our positions. In the beginning, the ships lay at 20 kilometres, but the range slowly decreased. With unbelieving eyes we could recognize individual landing craft. The hail of shells falling upon us grew heavier, sending fountains of sand and debris into the air. The mined obstacles in the water were partly destroyed.

'The morning dawn over the approaching landing fleet exhibited for us approaching doom. Bombs and heavy-calibre shells continued to slam into the earth, tossing tangles of barbed wire, obstacles, and dirt into the air. The fight for survival began. The explosions of naval gunfire became mixed with rapid-fire weapons. I attempted to seek shelter under my machine-gun position.

'Our weapons were pre-set on defensive fire zones; thus we could only wait. It appeared that the enemy would land in the approximate centre of the beach. We had planned that he should land at high tide to drive the boats over the open beach, but this was low tide. The waterline was 300 metres distant.

'Surprisingly, we had not suffered heavy casualties. We used every available minute to contact one another throughout the rain of shells, and although we saw no possibility to escape from this chaos, we clung desperately to every minute won.

'Suddenly the rain of shells ceased, but only for a very short time. Again it came. Slowly the wall of explosions approached, metre by metre, worse than before – a deafening torrent – cracking, screaming, whistling and sizzling, destroying everything in its path. There was no escape, and I crouched helplessly behind my weapon. I prayed for survival and my fear passed.

'Suddenly it was silent again. There were six of us in the position, and still no one was wounded. A comrade stumbled out of the smoke and dust into my position and screamed, "Franz, watch out! They're coming!"'

Log book entries
Flight Lieutenant Tony Cooper
Spitfire VB pilot, 64 Squadron, Fighter Cover for UTAH beach. 0I:40 hours.

'Patrolling at 05:20 hours – Navy shelling west coast Defences – first landing made at 06:20 hours – Nearly shot down by Thunderbolt – Spitfire in front actually was – another Spit hit by naval shell & blew up – General Brock's "benefit".

'... Fighter Cover for Omaha Beach. Hun bomber attacked invasion fleet. Tremendous return fire from ships – one bomber destroyed.'

Claude V. Meconis
785th Bomb Squadron B-24 Liberator co-pilot, 466th Bomb Group, US 8th Air Force.

'As we passed over the southern coast of England and headed south over the Channel, I began straining my eyes to see some of the invasion fleet our briefing had disclosed. A low undercast in patches obscured most of the water, but whenever open spaces permitted, I could see landing craft and large ships moving south and southeast on a fairly rough sea. Also below us, just above the clouds, I saw B-26 formations assembling. Didn't see a single friendly fighter, though we were expecting 35 squadrons as cover. They were probably at a low altitude, below the clouds, actively aiding the first assault on the coast. We didn't need them.

'I know each man on the crew prayed for the success of whatever those in the landing barges below us had to do. Their job was infinitely more dangerous than ours. We were scared a bit, yes, because we didn't know exactly what kind of air opposition 'Jerry' would throw at us. Frankly, I expected to see a sky full of fighters and flak, all confusion. But those boys in the barges knew they'd meet steel and concrete and a tough fight!

'It was daylight, with the sun shining above the clouds in the east, as we turned right to head 270 degrees for 90 miles until we were west of the Cherbourg peninsula. Several bursts of flak came up. A group to our right passed too close to either Cherbourg or the islands just west of it. A ball of flak, like that I'd seen over Brunswick once, came up at them.

'Our let down over England was gradual. Clouds broke up and when we arrived back at our base area, only small fair weather cumulus and haze existed. The sky was a trifle overloaded, but we managed to cut our way through the snag and land safely.

'I was so sleepy on the trip back that I contemplated taking a pill to keep awake. Glad I didn't because we were allowed to go to bed immediately after landing. We'd be called if we were needed, they told us.

'An S-2 man, Hodges, met us at the plane for interrogation. We asked for news, but all he could say was, "The invasion is on."

'Back at the barracks, Smith had appropriated our radio and was listening to newscasts. Our troops were 10 miles inland already.

'I wrote another letter to Mary, adjusted my gun and went to bed. Someone said Nazi paratroops had landed near us.

Allen W. Stephens

'We awakened at two o'clock in the morning on 6 June. This was my 21st mission and take-off was at 04:20. It was still dark. A steady rain was falling and we could hardly see to taxi, much less fly. But there was no holding back and we poured on the coals, taking off at 20-second intervals between shifts. By the time we cleared the end of the runway, we could barely see the lights of the airplane ahead of us. We climbed on instruments and when we broke out on top of the cloudbank, we could see B-26s and all kinds of other airplanes circling around. It was really a beautiful sight.

'By following prearranged signals, we tacked on to our squadron leader and subsequently were on our way across the Channel. We were part of the spearhead of the invasion, entering the coast of France near Cherbourg over Utah Beach. Our targets were coastal guns and blockhouses along the beach, which we were to hit in collaboration with shelling by naval vessels. We were among the very first aircraft to hit the invasion target.

'As we moved in toward the beaches, we could see an armada of invasion vessels in the Channel below us, their courses converging toward the several invasion beaches. I had the surging feeling that I was sitting in on the greatest show ever staged – one that would make world history. As we flew nearer to the target, that feeling increased to exhilaration and excitement, for it was truly a magnificent operation. We saw hundreds upon hundreds of ships below, moving toward the coast of France, and when we approached the target area, we could see the big naval guns shelling the coast. The Germans were not idle, however, as they threw heavy barrages at the landing craft.

I saw one large ship going down but still throwing shells at the coast. We saw hundreds of discarded parachutes that had been thrown off by paratroopers who had landed simultaneously with the other attacks. These were quite a way inland from the beachhead. I saw one B-26 Marauder explode in mid-air near the target area.

'We went through the heaviest concentration of anti-aircraft fire I had yet seen. Tracers and flak explosions were so thick that it looked impossible to get through without being hit, especially knowing that for every tracer there were six other rounds. The barrage literally filled the air all around us and the flak explosions made the air alive with fire.

'On the beachhead, there was a tremendous wall of smoke all along the shore where the bombs and the shells were exploding. The landing craft were moving up as we turned off the target area after dropping our bombs. Every move was timed to the split second. We went in at 4,500 feet on this first mission. Our bombs went away at 06:30, the precise time planned.'

Lieutenant Robert A. Jacobs
564th Bomb Squadron, 389th Bomb Group DR (Dead Reckoning) navigator, in the first Liberator, Liberty Run, over the beaches.

'... This was what we had been waiting for. Our mission was to lead the 446th Bomb Group to bomb the invasion beaches of Normandy immediately prior to the ground assault. We had been selected to be the first heavy bomb group to cross the French coast on the day. We took off at 02:20, climbed to 10,000 feet and circled in our prescribed forming area firing specific flares as the 446th aircraft assembled in formation behind us. The mission went precisely as planned except for an undercast, which necessitated bombing by radar. As we approached the French coast, the radar navigator called me over to look at his PPI Scope. It clearly showed the vast armada of the invasion fleet standing just off the coast of Normandy – a thrilling sight even on radar. Bombs were away at precisely 06:00! We led our aircraft back to Bungay via Portland Bill and returned to Hethel. Much to our surprise, no flak or German fighters were observed. Our fighter cover was everywhere.

'As we started to undress to get some rest, we were again told to get over to Bungay for another mission. During the course of the briefing the flight surgeon gave each aircrew member a pill with instruction to take it only 'when you feel you can no longer keep awake'. We had been up since 02:30, 5 June and it was now the afternoon of 6 June, some 36 hours later; we were running on reserve energy.'

Bob Shaffer
Bombardier, 'Naughty Nan', 93rd Bomb Group, 8th Air Force.

'We took off at 14:00 hours. The flak was light and the mission successful. I flew as lead bombardier in *Naughty Nan* piloted by Lieutenant Sneddon. There was a full moon and I have never seen as many ships of all descriptions as there were crossing the Channel. I saw battleships firing at gun emplacements. It was quite a sight – quite a show. The flak was light and the mission successful.'

Allan Healy

467th Bombardment Group, 2nd Bomb Division, 8th Air
Force at Rackheath near Norwich, Norfolk.

'The D-Day missions were disappointing. No results of our
action could be seen and we had not been able to do
what we had in our potentiality to do; to further the great
undertaking. Nevertheless, the presence of nearly every
flyable plane in England, the gigantic and continual roar of
their engines, and the bombs hurtling down through the
overcast, must have given the Germans pause, aware of
the destruction capable of being sent him from on high,
and given our own men a sense of security in the air
power overhead.'

Brigadier General
Theodore Roosevelt Jr., 57

son of US 26th President, 'Teddy' Roosevelt, in
conversation in a beach foxhole with Commodore James
Arnold, NOIC.

'... If you have any authority here, I wish you would stop
bringing in my troops down on Red beach. They're being
slaughtered. Navy ought to know better than send them
into that sector where the darn' Krauts have them
bracketed.'

Roosevelt, a veteran of WWI and three assault landings in
WWII already, had finally convinced Major General
Raymond O. Barton, 4th Division Commander, that he
should take part in the landings. Roosevelt, whose
enthusiasm and powerful voice – 'a bellow only a few
decibels higher than a moose call' – were well known to the
troops, went ashore in the first wave, carrying only a cane
and a .45-calibre pistol, set an example of coolness under

fire and, realizing that the lead regiment had landed in the wrong place, improvized and attacked inland. His leadership contributed directly to the 4th Division's success and earned him the award of the Medal of Honor. Roosevelt remained the 4th Division's assistant division commander until he died of a heart attack on 12 July 1944.

Carter Barber, American

with Force U.

'We slowed to a snail's pace and at around 04:45 the anchors rattled down into the water and I could hear some of the curses of men swinging their assault barges over the transport's side. At five the barges were circling around in the water off their looming mother ship and the terrific barrages started from the battlewagons that had preceded us into the bay of the Seine. One of the most beautiful sights ever was the quadruple balls of fire that streaked across the sky with their salvos. Blue-azured little Roman Candle stuff, hard to realize tons of HE behind them.

'It was like a review, the way we took those barges into the beach. You couldn't see the heads of the troops over their sides ... just the coxswain's helmet sticking up from the stern. For some reason I thought of Mitchell Jamieson's oil [painting] of the men going into Sicily in their landing boat. I saw that picture at Corcoran in Washington, which locale reminded me of flags. I looked aloft, saw our cutter's flag twisted around the mast, and in a spurt of patriotism, climbed aloft, to free the banner.

'Just as I came down from the mast we saw our first bunch of men. It was light then and the scene was quickly changing from one of an even line of boats knifing in orderly rows behind their leaders towards the beach to a scene of carnage. One Higgins boat was completely disintegrated by a direct hit from shore. There were no survivors, and I couldn't even see the dismembered parts of the troops aboard come down after they'd been blasted sky high.

'The noise was terrific as we neared the beach. For the first time I felt no need to kind of talk myself into "This is IT! D-Day! What we've been waiting, working, and worrying for for months and years. This is going to be terrific." I knew it WAS terrific when the noise started, and the fact that the invasion had rushed upon me so swiftly in the past 24 hours didn't seem strange then.

'When we saw the LCF get hit, and rushed to her aid, I noticed plenty of men already floating face down in the water. They might have just been stunned, sure. But I had to agree with the skipper that we couldn't stop for them just then but must keep on to get the other men floundering about. We passed one boy floating high and dry on a raft and nosed alongside the first big bunch of men, and started to haul them aboard.

'The first bunch I took pictures of with my borrowed camera. Three minutes was enough, and I put the camera down and went forward to throw heaving lines to other men in the water. Twos and threes of them were screaming, "Oh save me ... I'm hurt bad ... please please please," and I yelled back, "Hang on, Mac, we're coming," and looked astern at the guys on our boat hauling other wounded men aboard, and wondered at the inadequacy of everything. We needed ten pairs of hands more.

'One big fellow, who afterwards admitted he weighed 250 lb stripped, had two legs broken and was in intense pain. We had a hell of a time getting him aboard because his clothing was waterlogged and he was weighted down with helmet, rifle, pack, ammunition, *et al.* The man screamed as we helped him aboard but we had to be a little callous so that we could get the man on deck and move to another group of survivors.

'I watched one man from the bow. He shouted "I can't stay up, I can't stay up." And he didn't. I couldn't reach him with a heaving line and when we came towards him his head was in the water. We didn't stop and went on to seven or eight more men who were just about ready to sink too. When we got them aboard, the first lad had completely disappeared, apparently slipping out of his lifejacket.

'Although it seemed like hours, we quickly got all the men aboard, including one old man who was so soaked in water that he was almost drowned. His face was almost awash and his head was laid open almost to the brain. His eyes fluttered and his jaw moved, however, so we knew he was alive. It took five of us on our boat's fantail to hoist this man aboard, by placing boat hooks under his armpits. We got him on deck, got the water out of his chest and covered him with a tarpaulin. After we picked up the rest of them, including the boy who had drifted for an hour or so on his raft, we took the men to the *Bayfield*, which directed us to the [USS *Joseph T.*] *Dickman*, which was leaving immediately for England. We got all the men aboard, including the guy under the tarpaulin … still alive.

'This was when the transport surgeon looked at the boy in the lazarette and pronounced him dead. This kid had crawled into the lazarette by himself, although vomiting blood the whole while. He lay there for an hour while we picked up his mates, and at the *Dickman* had apparently gone into a coma. Four hours later, the kid reappeared from the lazarette and went aboard the LST. "You were supposed to be dead," said one of our boys. "Yeah," said the kid onerously, although spewing blood from his mouth.

'We were low on gas when we put the men on the *Dickman* and almost went back to Poole, but decided later not to. Good thing too, for we had another rescue coming up. First, however, we disposed of the one man we hadn't put aboard the *Dickman* excepting the kid in the lazarette. This man was our only casualty.

'Apparently from shock, this man had died with his eyes open. Rigor mortis had already set in and we couldn't close his eyes. When we searched his pockets for identification, I thought it was the first time and last time anyone ever rolled this guy right under his eyes. He had a watertight wallet secured in a condom, with hundreds of pound notes, and an American silver dollar around his neck. Been in the Navy five months, 39 years old. We stripped his clothes from him to his underwear, tied him to a rusty piece of steel the *Dickman* had given us, and prepared to bury him. I tried to cross his arms over his chest, but they were too stiff. His flesh was green.

'McPhail, the skipper, reappeared on deck with his Bible, intoned the words, and we stopped the cutter's engines. I took off my helmet and the rest of the boys followed suit. We slid the body into the sea.

'I've covered the story of the burning ammunition ship pretty well in my yarns. Only matter uncovered was the gruesome sight of one man with broken ankles, swollen to the size of grapefruit and coloured like an avocado. This man shrieked, even after morphine. Then we saw his

Z-shaped spine. He was the first man lifted yelling over the side of the LST.

'After we had these men on the LST, and had no one else aboard and no other swimmers or survivors in sight, we called a wee time out.

'"What time do you think it is, Barber?" asked McPhail.

'"Way past noon, at least. Maybe four o'clock."

'"It's nine-thirty this morning."

'We looked around at the heaps of clothing strewn on the deck, gear of the rescue, some abandoned and some cut off. I went below to look around, and it was even worse. There were clothes in the smaller sink, on the stove, in the fo'c'sle, in the head, on the bunks. I stepped on a soggy bunch and blood oozed out. The whole boat below decks stank of blood, vomit and urine.

'We turned to, tossing all the clothes from below topside, and swabbed out the decks as best we could. We brought some K-rations up from the lazarette and ate lunch. Then, with only the helmsman, and motor machinist, we all sprawled on the deck, on the sodden heaps of clothing, and went to sleep. The next I knew it was afternoon.

'The sun had come out and there were no more boats in distress for the rest of that day. At night-time I sat in the pilothouse and listened to the radio avidly for news of the landing. I think I was listening to Danny Kaye when we passed into D+1.'

The USS *Joseph T. Dickman*, a US attack transport (APA), formerly the United States Lines' *President Roosevelt*, embarked 2,050 troops at Torbay anchorage from landing craft from Torquay, arrived Utah at 02:40 on 6 June. The *Bayfield*, a US APA and HQ ship for Force U, embarked 1,545 troops at Plymouth, arriving at Utah on 02:29 hours on D-

Day. LCF (Landing Craft, Flak), were British LCT's with two-pounder (40 mm) guns for anti-aircraft and E-boat defence.

Jack Culshaw
water barge LBW I, 34th Flotilla which landed at about I0:00.

'It was exactly 06:30 and without warning the USS *Nevada* let off a broadside of its 14-inch guns in the direction of the coast. Following the belch of flame, huge clouds of brown cordite smoke veiled the ship. HMS *Black Prince* took up the challenge and it too fired a thunderous broadside. From the rear a barrage of fire from the USS *Tuscaloosa* flew over the shore-bound armada. Shaken to the core, our adjectives seared the paintwork as our tiny barge and its crew trembled with the impact. Three fearful sailors, startled by the roar of gunfire, shot up from the engine room and watched the display with astonishment. Mesmerized by the flames belching from the huge guns we stiffened ourselves for the next ear-splitting blast. The shells whistling overhead with terrifying potential and devastating results were at first nerve-shattering. The creeping realization that these weapons were after all on our side helped to allay these fears. At each broadside and scream of shells rushing overhead, three pairs of anxious eyes peered nervously towards the open hatch above. By the time we had reached the upper deck the shore batteries had begun to retaliate and shell bursts peppered the water nearby. Remembering our orders we continued sailing towards the beach, careful to keep between the two lines of bobbing Dan buoys, the line of markers placed in position the previous night to prevent ships straying into unswept mine fields. I marvelled at the courage of the men who had so bravely ventured to plant the buoys under the noses of the German coastal defence forces the night before.

'The gunfire increased as landing craft mounted with rocket launchers let off their devilish cargo. The sound of their release rendered the onlookers immobile, as a thousand rockets trailing fire and smoke screamed towards the shore. It was now fully light and the battle was at its height. Shells from the battleships behind the diminutive barges continued to scream overhead. The American 4th Infantry Division was dashing towards the beach in their assault craft, returning fire from those shore batteries not yet immobilized. While everyone around us appeared to be engaged in a task to ruthlessly destroy each other, we could only sit tight and forage slowly towards the beach.

'A sleek, grey patrol boat drew alongside. A British naval officer waved an arm in the direction he advised us to proceed. "Take station off shore, between the two petrol barges you see anchored yonder." The tankers were easy to distinguish, as the hoarding above decks plainly spelt out "HIGH OCTANE FUEL" for the benefit of those craft needing refuelling. It also spelt out to any German gunner with an eagle eye, "Why not aim at us?" The water barge had a similar sign "WATER", in large letters painted over the tank. Turning the wheel, Irons made for the spot 200 yards from the beach. No sooner had Smithy and Manchester dropped the anchor, than a procession of assorted craft that had been on station for a few days began to arrive to replenish their meagre water reserves. Small patrol boats and American-designed tugboats sidled alongside to fill their tanks. A stream of assault boats filled with GIs passed by and landed on the beach to spluttering bursts of small arms fire.

'While the frenzied activity below at sea level continued, a buzz of low flying Dakotas droned in from the sea, towing camouflaged gliders. Heavy with troops they swayed and disengaged their tow ropes to weave and turn and drop immediately behind the sand hills. Sounds of splintering wood and canvas filled the air as each vehicle landed clumsily in the small fields, some hitting and killing terrified cattle, others landing badly and ripping themselves in two pieces. Bodies were thrown like rag dolls across the grassy turf. Glider wings crumpled as the limited landing spaces became overcrowded. We could only stare, no grief or shock, no emotion registered itself as the carnage ended as quickly as it started. It was just another episode in the battle.

'By early evening the sound of gunfire had receded into the distance. Activity to and from the shore was increasing as every conceivable type of transport was being thrown on to the beach. Tanks and trucks emerged from beached landing ships, wave after wave of troops ferried from transport ships anchored a mile or so off shore dodged huge motorized pontoons laboriously ploughing towards the beach loaded high with hundreds of tons of battle equipment, medical supplies and rations.

'A startling explosion nearby blew the stern from one of our companion barges as it was about to beach. We could only stare at the tragedy as the remnants of crew scrambled to safety. A pack of LCIs, already beached, stood silently awaiting the next tide after disgorging their cargo of American troops. Once the smoke had subsided, it revealed the burnt-out shells of military equipment on a disordered beach. The blackened skeleton of a troop carrier, and a battle-scarred tank, lay on its side, a sad reminder of the battle. The task began of retrieving the mercifully few bodies of those that gave their lives. The personal mementoes of the same brave men littering the high water mark were being reverently collected. A posse of field grey uniformed prisoners rounded up by the efficient US guards were herded into a hastily erected barbed-wire cage before being shipped to the UK for the duration.

'For those who had reached the coast in the early morning, after surviving a horrendous sea journey and experiencing the barrage of sound, an exhausting quietness emerged. The sea had ceased its furious battle with the invaders; the ground swell rocked the small craft in a kind of remorseful lullaby, perhaps regretting the savage beating it had enforced on us earlier. Content, for us the battle was over, though very aware that their war had just begun.

'... In a strange way it seemed as if the war was now passing us by. I scratched the growing stubble on my cheeks and mused. "Was it only yesterday this sandy piece of land was the centre of confusion and noise?" I sat gazing at my companions resting on this grounded, unattractive, rusting piece of metal which had become our home. Twenty-four short hours ago, black smoke choked the poor devils that dared venture on to this shore. Red-hot chunks of steel seared and whizzed into its sandy core. I cast my eyes over the pockmarked sand hills, where a short time ago I had watched as American soldiers scorched a path through the German bunkers with terrifying flame-throwers. The smoke-blackened concrete bore witness that it had not been a horrible dream after all.

'... A lull in the barge activity prompted some of us to take a walk along the beach. Manchester and Sammy Yates, anxious to see for themselves the scene of the previous day's battle, joined Bentley and me. Veering around beached landing craft and pieces of discarded military equipment, dodging fast-moving jeeps and trucks pouring from beached landing ships, we plodded past the caged German prisoners, guarded by white helmeted GIs attentively nursing their loaded carbines. On past a deserted first-aid post and up into the sand hills. On the other side the land was flat and scrubby. A farmhouse stood in isolation. The bloated bodies of black and white cattle lay in the fields, legs pointing skyward, either having been shot or died of fright. Wrecked gliders, displaying their white identifying wing chevrons, lay abandoned by the airborne troops that had landed the previous day, eerily straddling the fields between the early summer flowering hedgerows. We walked in silence along the ridge of dunes towards the eastern end of the concrete fortifications. Pulling up sharply, we almost fell across the body of a young American soldier lying hidden in a dune. Silently staring at the efforts to revive him, the plasma tubes held in place by his rifle, stuck bayonet end in the sand then inserted in his ridged body proved useless. The boy's wounds were too severe. A fleeting, silent chill accompanying the terrible realization of death passed through my mind. A lump came into my throat as I walked slowly away from the scene, chastened by the futility of war.

'Further along the sandy ridge a concrete German gun emplacement came to view, the huge muzzle pointed ominously out to sea ... inside, we found remnants of meals and discarded wine bottles. After a brief inspection we escaped through a narrow exit tunnel. Straightening and blinking in the bright sunlight, the body of a soldier wearing the uniform of a German trooper confronted us. A pair of jackboots lay tidily beside the body, his steel helmet a few feet away. I murmured, "He was someone's son I suppose." Without malice, I picked up the helmet intending to keep it as a souvenir. Manchester's face contorted in rage as he lifted an iron bar, which lay discarded in the sand and took a vicious swipe at the dead man's head. Cursing and swearing vengeance for reasons he alone understood, we stood horrified by his actions.

"I'm 'avin' that ring on his finger," he snarled, "I'm going to cut his finger off to get it." Not believing what we were hearing we stared inert as Manchester dropped his arm and retrieved the sheathed knife he carried on his belt. The man had flipped. The resentments of the last few months had surfaced. Some would call it traumatic shell-shock. Maybe the poor sod had been through hell once too often. One thing for sure, we were not going to let him carry out his threat. We stepped forward to restrain him. I saw the gaunt, tormented face beneath the untidy black beard relax. His dark ringed eyes turned moodily away from the scene, staring as if transfixed. For what seemed an eternity we stood silent and rigid. Ramming the knife back in its sheath, Manchester kicked into the sand and walked slowly down the dunes.'

The idea of using River Thames Lighters as Landing Barges came from Lord Louis Mountbatten, Chief of Combined Operations. Over 400 of these craft were converted as Supply and Maintenance Flotilla and for the transportation of vehicles, stores and ammunition in beach landings. Two Chrysler six-cylinder engines where hastily bodged, with a

primitive steering assembly; a tank to hold either water, petrol or diesel fuel was then installed, all without prior deliberations as to whether the thing would float or sink when the contents where put aboard. Some were made into Kitchen Barges to feed isolated troops or other seamen, others fitted out for Engineering Maintenance. The flotillas were split between the invasion beaches. Most arrived safely at their destination, others did not. A basic seagoing crew of five men were on most of the barges, supplemented by extras prior to D-Day: two engine men, two seamen and one Coxswain seaman, supplemented, where appropriate, by engineers, cooks, etc.

US Assault Divisions Utah Beach

VII Corps 4th US Division
Major General Raymond O. Barton
8th Infantry 12th Infantry 70th Tank Battalion
22nd Infantry 359th Infantry (attached from 90th Division)

Beach Timetable
02:00 Thirty-four British and US minesweepers under Commander M. H. Brown, Royal Navy, begin sweeping the transport area ten miles offshore, the fire support areas, and the approach channels for boats and bombardment ships.
05:30 Attack by 276 B-26 Marauder aircraft destroy Blockhouse W5 and all five artillery pieces.

05:36 Rear Admiral Morton L. Deyo, Commander Task Force A aboard the heavy cruiser USS *Tuscaloosa*, orders the pre-landing shore bombardment to begin earlier than scheduled because German gun batteries have already begun firing at the Allied ships. *Tuscaloosa*, in a fire-support line with *Quincy* and *Nevada* about 11,000 yards offshore, unleashes its nine eight-inch guns of its main battery and then opens up shortly afterward with its eight five-inch Anti-aircraft guns. For 50 minutes following H-Hour Battleship USS *Nevada*, cruiser HMS *Black Prince*, monitor HMS *Erebus*, and *Tuscaloosa*, provide abundant and accurate naval gunfire support, especially on the remote and large-calibre batteries inaccessible to the ground troops.

06:30 US 4th Cavalry squadron land on Iles St. Marcouf.

06:31 One minute behind schedule the first wave of up to 20 LCVPs each with a 30-man assault team from the 8th Infantry Regiment, 4th Infantry Divison, come within 100 yards of the shore. Twenty-eight of the 32 33-ton amphibious DD Sherman tanks are landed. Because of a strong current 4th Infantry Division have actually landed 2,000 yards south of their intended target but the beach is less heavily defended than the original.

By 07:30 All resistance by the German 709th Division ends. Twenty-six assault waves are landed before noon.

16:00 German 7th Army HQ informed of Utah landings.

By 18:00 21,328 men and 1,700 vehicles are ashore and by midnight they have advanced six miles. Casualties, 4th Infantry Division, 197 killed, 60 missing, presumed drowned.

Sword

John Gough,

radio-operator aboard a destroyer at Harwich.

'Early in the evening of 5 June the entire ship's company who could be spared from duty mustered on deck and our captain briefly put us in the picture as to the part we were assigned to play in the events planned for the next day. To close the proceedings he removed his cap, lowered his head and spoke the opening words of the prayer Lord Nelson had confessed in his cabin before Trafalgar. "May the Great God whom I worship grant to my country and for the benefit of Europe in general a great and glorious victory, and may no misconduct in anyone tarnish it, and may humanity after victory be the predominant feature in the British Fleet." Those words were as relevant as they had been way back in October 1805.

'Within half an hour or so we slipped anchor and headed into the Channel to catch up and overtake the grey columns of troop transports and landing craft which for several hours had been leaving the Solent and now stretched to the horizon and beyond. We had our own rendezvous with the pages of history when the next day we would, in company with many other naval vessels, lead them to the beaches of Normandy. D-Day dawned and Sword beach came into view. Ahead of us were a group of minesweepers and astern a mighty fleet of transports and landing craft filling the scene as far as the eye could see. Overhead the sky was filled with an aerial armada of bombers. The din was tremendous and added to it was the roar of the big guns of the heavier ships bombarding the shore. Before long the bombardment ceased and the first of the assault craft began ferrying the army ashore from the big transports.

'From our viewpoint a mile or so off the beach it was evident that the operation was going well. There was sporadic opposition from hidden German guns, which had escaped the initial bombardment, and here and there landing craft were hit but the majority were reaching the beach unscathed. At 08:00 I had to return to the wireless office to take my turn on watch and so for the rest of the morning had to rely on a running commentary provided by off-watch staff. That night we returned to Portsmouth carrying 20 wounded Canadians who had been transferred to us by an assault craft.

Les 'Tubby' Edwards

signalman, HMS 'Locust', a gunboat in LSH Force S1,
which was escorting landing craft.

'The whole sky was filled with friendly aircraft of all types
– Stirlings, Halifaxes and Dakotas. Inevitably some were
hit. A Stirling, which was well ablaze, seemed to be
heading for our ship. But suddenly the plane banked to
her right and dived into the sea. It was our belief that the
pilot deliberately ditched in order to avoid our ship, thus
saving many lives.'

Mission diary
Ed 'Cotton' Appleman

engineer-gunner, B-24 Liberator 'Duration Baby', 93rd
Bomb Group, 2nd Bomb Division, 8th Air Force.

'Mission No. 14 and the day that everyone has been
waiting for. They ran four missions today but we didn't
have to go on but one of them. We carried 12 x 500 lb
bombs and hit bridges near Caen, France where the boys
were making their landing. The Channel was full of Allied
boats of all kinds and we could see them just off the
French coast making their landings. They had good fighter
cover and we had none, but I imagine they needed it. We
saw no flak and no fighters. Made two runs on the target
and still didn't get our bombs away, but everyone else did.
For some reason we didn't get our bomb bay open in
time. I hope those boys on the ground had it as easy as
we did. Sixteen to go. Six hours, 35 minutes.

Gunner Len Woods,

53rd Medium Regiment Royal Artillery.

'On 1 June we embarked on to an LST at Gosport. On board were men from various regiments but from the 53rd there were just seven with a 15-cwt [hundred-weight] truck. We were the Survey and Recce party. We laid in the Solent in the most appalling weather until 19:30 on 5 June when we set sail, arriving off Sword beach at 10:00 on 6 June. A Reuters newsman who was on board sent the first bulletin back to the UK by pigeon, as there was strict radio silence. The LST had a top and bottom deck. The lower deck was first to unload and then a lift brought the vehicles from the upper deck to the lower deck for their turn. We unloaded by driving on to pontoon rafts, which then ferried us to the beach. After the lower deck had been cleared a German plane (remember there were only supposed to be two German planes over the whole beachhead) machine-gunned our ship and dropped a bomb, which exploded under the bow doors. This distorted the bow doors and wrecked the lift. In order to finish unloading we had to pull away from the beach and tie up alongside another LST that had already unloaded and run our vehicles across from one ship to the other by means of wooden planks. It was a quirk of fate that with the thousands of ships in the area, one of the two German planes in the air managed to hit us.

'I arrived in France on D-Day, travelled through Belgium, Holland and Germany and yet remained unscathed. My brother-in-law landed in Normandy two weeks later and was killed within days of his arrival.'

The only *Luftwaffe* presence over the invasion beaches that morning were two Fw 190s flown by Oberstleutnant

Josef 'Pips' Priller, Kommodore, *Jagdgeschwader* 26 '*Schlageter*', and his regular *Kacmarek* (wingman), Uffz. Heinz Wodarczyk of the *Stab* flight at Priller's Lille-Nord command post. These were the only two fighters available to *JG26*. Near Le Havre the pair climbed into the solid cloudbank and emerged to see the invasion fleet spread out before them. Priller, in his usual Fw 190A-8 '*Black 13' Jutta*, and Wodarczyk each made a full-throttle (400 mph) 50-foot, low-level strafing run over Sword beach with cannons and machine guns before landing at Creil. Priller scored his 100th victory on 15 June when he shot down a B-24 Liberator of the 492nd Bomb Group. Wodarczyk was killed in action on 1 January 1945. Oberst. Priller survived the war with 101 victories.

Hobart's Funnies

After the disaster at Dieppe a whole gamut of brutal new weaponry was devised (some by Churchill himself) specifically to break through concrete, wire and minefields along the French coast. Churchill personally rescued from the Home Guard a talented expert, Major General Percy Hobart, who formed, trained and then led a huge secret armoured division, which stormed the Normandy beaches and helped take all the Channel ports and every major river crossing. All these tank-based secret weapons, usually with animal names (Crab, Crocodile, etc.), supported every British and Canadian army formation and many American units in the 11 months of fighting in north-western Europe in 1944–45. 79th Armoured Division was by far the largest formation in the British Army, although it never fought as a division or a brigade, and rarely as a regiment. In vital 'penny pockets' of AVREs, flails, flame-throwers, or armoured troop carriers, they were indispensable. They were unique and every fighting formation in Europe was grateful for Hobart's Zoo. This irascible, bullying Major General formed 7th Armoured Division in North Africa, 11th Armoured Division in Yorkshire, and created the monsters of 79th Armoured.

J. A. C. Hugill

aboard LCT 7073, one of 70-odd petrol-driven boats ordered hurriedly in November 1943.

'We reached the North Foreland Buoy, just north of Deal, at 22:00. Just now the paratroops would be dropping. I wished them luck. Parachuting is rather a nerve-racking business. There must be many people in the Whitehall area walking about with their fingers crossed tonight, I thought. I was feeling detached about the whole thing now, but never let myself stray far from a piece of wood to touch. The wind freshened still more, and it looked as if the landing was going to be really foul. There was an angry sky as the light faded, and I was reminded of a somewhat fanciful picture of the Battle of Jutland that used to hang in my grandfather's house when I was a little boy. (At least they said it was Jutland.) The sky was just like that.

'I warned everyone to sleep with a clasp knife handy, in case anything happened, so that they could cut themselves clear of the camouflage net, which was stretched over the tank deck. Then I went up on the bridge and waited for the shells to come over from Gris-Nez. None came. We were passing through the Straits at the not exactly breakneck speed of five knots. At 03:30 I went below to turn in. The sub-lieutenant in charge of the mobile naval radar set which was with us had elected to sleep outside, in the interests of fresh air and space. Sleep came to us with difficulty. But it came. In addition to the two pongos and me, there was also the flotilla engineer officer, a pleasant Canadian with a snore like the open diapason of an organ.

'At 05:00 the sub came into the wardroom dripping wet from the rain. We cursed him sleepily as he fitted himself into the group on the wardroom floor like the last piece of a jigsaw puzzle. For some reason we all awoke exactly at 07:25 and looked at one another.

'"Did someone talk about an invasion taking place this morning?" asked one.

'"Don't natter," we answered.

'It was hard to realize that this was *Der Tag*.

'The wind was freshening and the old cow was waddling and ducking more and more disagreeably. So much water was coming over the bows that we couldn't get the hydro-cooker alight. The sub and I dived down into the starboard locker for some tins of self-heating cocoa to warm the shivering men. They were all pretty wet. So were we by the time we had finished.

'After breakfast we took turns standing by the gun pits as extra lookouts or sat in the wardroom reading. There was an air of complete unreality about the whole business, and the bright sun, and the cold wind and spray, made me feel brittle for some reason. I finished reading *Humphrey Clinker*, which was perfect escapist literature and opened *Triple Fugue*, which was not. As we passed Beachy Head I began to wonder if my stomach wasn't full of butterflies. Up forward, a lot of the troops were being or had been seasick, some, I found, with a whole-hearted abandon not entirely admirable. I must try not to be sick in front of the pongos, I thought, and climbed up to the bridge to talk to the 1st lieutenant. There were miles of LCT ahead and astern of us and the large LST at the head of our convoy looked like Roman triremes in the distance.

'At 13:00 we disobeyed all rules and regulations and switched on the BBC, rather in the manner of one pinching oneself to make sure he is awake. Yes, there it was, sure enough. The airborne had landed and the first flight was doing well on the beaches. Our turn soon. Just before 14:00 we turned south and were on the last leg of our journey. We were due to land in about five hours. "I shall be sorry to leave the LCT," I thought, 'though she's so uncomfortable and dirty.' If anyone had told me three days before I was going to be sorry to leave the old bitch I'd have laughed.

'We passed numbers of homeward-bound landing craft, all blackened from firing their rockets, and scores of other craft. Large troop transports went proudly past, but we saw that only about half their LCA were still aboard. The remainder had been left on the beaches. A flotilla of fleet minesweepers passed three miles to starboard. Five miles to starboard something went up with a flash and left a pall of smoke. A sweeper detached herself from the flotilla and went to the rescue. We passed through several patches of oil where some poor wretches had bought it earlier on. A monitor [HMS *Roberts*] nosed past. There was a smug look about her, such as you'd expect to see on the face of a cat after a successful raid on the larder.

'Darkness came and we reduced speed. The wind freshened still more. We were three hours late already and still ten miles from the coast. The camouflage net was rolled back and the ramps were ready to lower. We began to see gun flashes ahead. I asked the skipper what he had been warned to expect in the way of opposition when we landed. He told me that several batteries would probably still be firing, mostly at random, as they were not among the First objectives.

'We crept slowly up to about a mile and a half from the beach. A big fire was burning just ahead. There was an air raid in progress over the beaches, and strings of orange-red tracer climbed and wriggled slowly through the sky like chains of bright caterpillars. A deep rumble forced itself through the purr of our engines. Then German aircraft began to throb over us. There was a flash and a thud as a ship received a direct hit about a mile away. We all put our tin hats on, and I sent the troops below for cover. A German aircraft flew down our column and all the Oerlikons in the Force stammered noisily into action. It was a relief almost, after so much inaction. Every now and then there would be bursts of tracer and flashes from the bigger guns of the now, invisible myriad ships lying offshore.

'A signal came from our escort, delaying our beaching until first light. Weather unsuitable, said the skipper. We dropped our hook. It was cold, so I gave the chaps a tot of rum each and talked to them about nothing in particular. We were all pretty excited but very annoyed at not landing exactly on D-Day. Still, the intention had been good.

'At four the first light came timidly from the east. It was bitterly cold. There was a spasmodic air attack and I saw a Focke-Wulf dive out of the clouds over the column a couple of cables' length to starboard. Four bombs fell, each between a pair of the vessels for which they were intended. It was like a draughts-player going one–two–three–four across the board.

'The first Spitfires arrived at 04:30 and an hour later we got the signal from the shore: Prepare to land. Two cruisers sat like broody hens surrounded by drifters and landing craft. As we passed, their guns spoke from time to time. I hate the noise of a cruiser's guns. Widgeon and teal flew low over the water, looking like black tracer. Every now and then there was a big flash and clouds of smoke and a noise as some part of the beach was cleared of mines by sappers. We elbowed our way past many other craft. As one looked round there were so many thousands of ships that it was impossible to see the horizon and the eye became, so to speak, blasé. It was almost unimaginable, but it was true.

'It was an absolute skipper's nightmare: craft going ashore, craft leaving, barges, DUKWs, rhino ferries, LCT, all moving like slow and independent-minded insects over the surface of a huge pool.

'There was the coast; its shape and contours began to become recognizable. It was exactly as it had appeared in the low-level oblique photographs. Over to port was La Rivière, on the port bow was Montfleury, at the top of a rise. To starboard was Le Hamel. There only seemed to be about a couple of square inches of space to manoeuvre in, and minor collisions happened from time to time. An LCT let down her ramps too soon and a three-ton lorry slid gently and irrevocably into ten feet of water.

'It was possible to see the houses on the front in more detail. They looked a little knocked about. The emptiness in their windows was the emptiness in the eyes of a blind beggar.

'I took breakfast; dry biscuits and self-heated cocoa. There was no opportunity for further cooking.

'We could see tanks climbing up a little hill to their transit area, just short of the top. There were a number of LCA and LCT lying near the beach, some with their sides torn out, some on the bottom. One petrol barge was being unloaded with ill-concealed haste.

'It was 08:30. My mother would be having breakfast. But somehow to think of normal things was just not on. It was hard to believe that one had ever come down to bacon and eggs and coffee and opened *The Times* and leaned it against the coffee pot.

'The 1st lieutenant handed us some packets of cigarettes each in an almost apologetic way. He wouldn't let us pay. I asked him to say goodbye to the skipper for us. We jumped into our vehicles. The ramps started to lower themselves. We ground on to the coast of France. We drove quietly ashore. That was all. There was no shelling, no excitement. It seemed very much of an anti-climax.'

Most LCT were diesel-driven. HMS *Roberts* (15-inch gun), whose lack of speed precluded her from sailing from the Clyde with other units of Force D, left at 17:30 on 5 June, arriving Eastern Task Force Area at 05:25 on 6 June and expended 69 rounds of main ammunition by 16:00.

Lieutenant John Avis, 27

'It wasn't until we got closer to Sword beach and saw dozens of khaki-clad bodies that I realized the real danger. There was debris everywhere. Broken-down jeeps. Tanks. Absolute chaos. My job was to fill up the food dump on the beach. There were also dumps for petrol and ammunition. A bomb landed on one of the petrol dumps, sending a ball of fire thousands of feet into the air, setting alight all the ammunition. I was blown over, but escaped unhurt except for some bruising and some singed hair. What a spectacular firework display! For a while it looked as if we would have to evacuate the beach but one of the officers recruited a gang who made a corridor through the fire … I wouldn't have missed it for the world.'

K. D. Budgen
5th Assault Regiment, 1st Assault Brigade Royal Engineers, 79th Armoured Division.

'After an almost interminable sea journey in a rolling, lurching LCT, dawn revealed the immensity of the operation we had embarked upon. There were ships everywhere. Closer to the coast of France, a smoke screen was laid. An escorting destroyer cut in two by torpedo attack, floated semi-submerged, forming a V with its bows and stem.

'This was H-Hour. The noise increased as the beach got closer, quite deafening now. To starboard a LCT fired a rocket salvo, which upon landing in unison shook every bone. My diaphragm oscillated in sympathy with shock waves, visible as they pulsed upwards through smoke and clouds. We started the 350-b.h.p. engines of our Churchills, which contributed to the general noise. Lion-sur-Mer was in sight, the tide was out, revealing a beach covered with large tripod obstacles with mines attached. Seconds went by like hours, waiting to go down that ramp, or to eternity, we were carrying a large amount of HE. The tank preceding us was on the sea bed in six feet of water, when the rear louvre extension fell off, blocking our exit. Something, probably a mortar bomb, hit the 20-foot bridge we had attached to the front. We went down

An Army Field Kitchen Unit on LST 506 of Force B that loaded at Falmouth and Plymouth and arrived in the Western Task Force Area on 6/7 June.

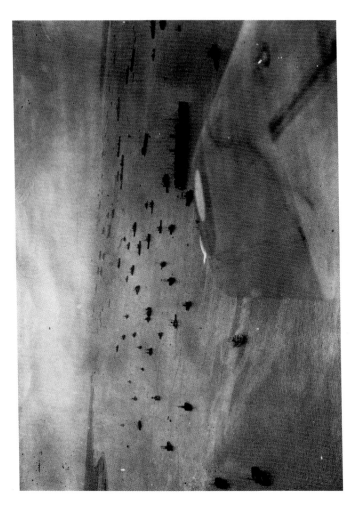

Shipping off Lee-on-Solent looking towards the Isle of Wight on 5 June. In the background are some of the roadway sections waiting to be towed to the Mulberry harbours.

Waco CG-4A glider lands at a D-Day airstrip.

Capt Robert Kirkwood smoking a cigar and Lt Pat Ward, battalion intelligence officer, with twenty men in the stick from 505th Infantry waiting to board their C-47 on the evening of 5 June at Cottesmore.

General Eisenhower talking with paratroops of the 502nd Parachute Regiment, 101st Airborne Division at RAF Greenham Common on 5 June. An aide noticed that there was a tear in Eisenhower's eye.

The Heavy Cruiser Augusta, Flagship Naval Commander (Adm Alan G. Kirk) Western Task Force, with landing craft heading for the shore at Omaha.

Assault wave going ashore
off landing craft.

Wounded soldier on Omaha is helped by his buddies.

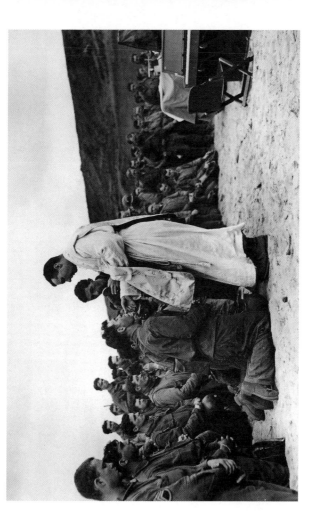

American soldiers receive Holy Communion as mass is offered by Rev John McGovern, US Army Chaplain.

US soldiers coming ashore at Utah.

B-26 Marauder over Lion-sur-Mer in the Sword beach area.

Burnt-out German transport on and off the road between Bayeux and Caen photographed by an FPU Mosquito of 2nd TAF.

A Rhino ferry carrying trucks, guns and stores going ashore.

British troops going ashore from LCA 431. In the background are LCT's 670, 710 and 858.

Troops of the North Nova Scotia Highlanders going ashore from HQ ship Hilary at Bernières-sur-Mer. Though suffering slight damage in a bomb near-miss, Hilary became Flagship, Eastern Task Force on 24 June.

Canadian troops wading ashore from LCT 2079 of the 102nd Flotilla.

into the sea, missing the other tank as we pulled away, by now half full of water. My visor revealed green sea; at last we were on solid ground. Driver left, halt, reverse right. We went every way but sideways. When at last we emerged, a flail tank was leading us up the beach. The Atlantic Wall was not completed here rendering our bridge redundant.

'Once upon the promenade we drove through the chaos of what was once a town and dropped the bridge. A young woman wearing a Red Cross armband rode along the road on a bicycle towards the town, undeterred by sporadic machine-gun fire. When night came, the Luftwaffe dropped anti-personnel bombs to let us know that the war was not over yet. There was a lot more and worse to come.'

Private Edward 'Teddy' W. D. Beeton, 2I
79th Assault Squadron, Ist Assault Brigade, Royal Engineers, Churchill Tank AVRE driver.

'We were the first wave in on D-Day and the first to land on the Beach. Our Churchill Tanks were fitted with special mortars called Petards whose purpose was the destruction of the pillboxes and concrete defences. We had a very rough crossing and most of us were seasick. As we neared the French coast we encountered incoming fire and two of the escort ships were sunk. The LCRs (Landing Craft Rockets) opened fire and as we were the next to run in to the beach all the crew mounted the tanks through the turret, the front hatches being sealed so that the tanks could operate if needs be in up to six feet of water. The drivers mounted in first to start the engines. We beached safely. The ramp was lowered and the first two Sherman "Crabs" fitted with flails went down the ramp. Both were knocked out immediately and burst into flames — it was not a very good sight seeing your mates trying to bail out of their tanks on fire. I was Troop Officer's driver and drove the third tank down the ramp. There were mines everywhere on cross pieces about two feet off the ground. I picked my way through the mines the best I could. Just before I reached the edge of the beach we hit a mine, which blew a bogey off, but the track held. One of the crew put the windsock up. Our Troop Officer and Troop Sergeant had both been killed and we had lost over half the squadron.

'I drove behind a sand dune where we unsealed some of the hatches. By now the commandos were with us. The squadron leader who had lost his tank came up and took over command of our tank and directed us along a road where we came under small arms fire, which we returned until we came to a bridge over a canal. This was defended by a pillbox on the other side. As our Petard Mortar had only a short range the Squadron Leader decided to cross the bridge to the other side to deal with it. On commencing to cross, the enemy blew the bridge, the section we were on held and I was able to reverse off; the commandos then took over.

'I was then directed into an open space where we were clear of the houses and where the Squadron Leader left us. The engine was running hot so I got out and commenced to unseal the hatches. I had just started when I heard an aircraft. I thought it was one of ours until I saw it release a bomb, which came straight at the tank. I promptly lay down on the engine hatches and prayed. All my strength seemed to ebb away and I felt terrible; however, the bomb just cleared the tank and burst in front of it. I lay there for some time until I had regained my strength and then got smartly into the driver's seat and closed the hatches.

'We stayed there all night, amids bombs, shells, small arms fire and burning houses. We pulled back next day to regroup and maintain our vehicles.'

Corporal Walter William Oliver
Reconnaissance Troop, Staffordshire Yeomanry.

'We had to do training for stand up tank battles and we were fairly good after all this. We trained harder than anyone else, as most of the boys were green troops (green being not battle-experienced). So came the glorious 6 June 1944. Recce Troop was told by Major General P. C. S. Hobart, who commanded the 79th Special Armoured Division, "A good recce gives a successful victory." The 79th Armoured Division was special in as much as they had flamethrowers, which threw a flame approximately 200–300 yards and God help you if you were on the receiving end. Bobbins with chains were fixed in front of a Sherman tank. The chains whirled round and blew up mines in front. There were also bridge layers and buffaloes (amphibians).

'About May 1944 we were sent down to Weymouth where some US Rangers and us were. On 2 June we were taken to Southampton, where we loaded our tanks on to landing craft. Other Divisions were loaded on to landing ships, the difference being landing craft are smaller and faster and lower in the water. The enemy could pick out a landing ship but not a tank landing craft until it had dropped its tanks up his nose so to speak.

'All along the French coast the Germans had used forced labour to build what they called Fortress Europe. Full massive pillboxes with dirty great guns pointing at us. The three divisions on the British sector all had special assault teams provided by 79th Armoured. We hit the beach at La Breche with my old friends from No. 4 Commando. We were to race as fast as we could to relieve 6th Airborne who had been dropped by parachute and glider to take the Orne Bridges. They had held out all day and we arrived with about two tanks left, so we joined the rest without tanks. In the village, not far from us some paratroops were holed up with some wounded. My Troop Officer Mr. Duff said, "Just take six blokes down there and get those chaps out." I only had to find four blokes as I knew Jock would come with me. So we set off amongst shot and shell with a few little shots coming our way. But we all made it into the village. The first cottage had some paratroops, gear and a dead paratroop outside so we figured that's where our blokes must be. Jock kicked open the door and a British voice said, "We are in here, wounded." It was slightly dark inside so then when I asked how many wounded, a good old Norfolk voice said, "Six and who the hell are you." I told him who I was and out of the darkened room he said, "Bloody Ginger Oliver, for f**** sake get us out of here." Well we did get them out. The voice from the darkness was Ronnie Gant, my old mate from childhood. Were we pleased to see each other? We shared rations and found some French wine and drank our old toast, "sod 'em all". We were eventually relieved. Ronnie came home with an arm wound and we went on to more glory.'

Platoon Sergeant Albert Pattison
Ist Suffolks.

'It was the worst 48 hours in my life on that landing craft. Worse than swimming two miles off the Dunkirk beaches in 1940, aged 17. Isn't it marvellous what fear can make you do!'

Captain Douglas Munroe
Royal Artillery, aboard the Royal Navy's latest cruiser, HMS 'Diadem', fresh from her Newcastle shipyard and equipped with eight 5.25 electronically controlled guns.

'We arrived off Normandy at first light. The Channel was full of ships and we could see lots of puffs of smoke on the coast. We were in touch with 29 planes on D-Day – British, Canadian, Polish, whatever. They found German gun emplacements and we directed fire on to the targets. We were firing beyond the range of the guns. By moving water and fuel from one side to the other, we were able to tilt the ship to give us a higher angle of sight and a longer range. We engaged targets from Courseulles to Ouistreham and were able to reach Carpiquet aerodrome, the airport for Caen. That was quite an effective shoot, I believe.'

Diadem kept her station off the British beaches for three weeks, firing 3,800 rounds from each gun and literally wearing out the barrels.

Trooper 'Slim' Wileman, 24
I3th/I8th Royal Hussars.

'As we progressed up the beach we saw that one of our tanks had gone over a mine and been blown onto its side.

I recognized it at once as Sergeant Johnny Hardie's tank. We feared the worst. We approached it, expecting to find the five-man crew dead inside. To our amazement we discovered Johnny and his crew completely unharmed, sitting on empty ammunition cases in the lee of the tank, calmly drinking tea. They offered us some of the brew, and we were about to join them when the beach marshal appeared and told us in real soldier's language what to do with our mugs of tea. When I asked Johnny why he and his men had stopped for tea in the middle of battle he shrugged, "We're not infantry. We're not equipped to fight. What else could we do?"

'Rather sensible when you think of it.'

Private Geoffrey Duncan
10th Platoon, 'B' Company, 1st Battalion
The Royal Norfolk Regiment.

'There's an old saying: "you never hear the one that gets you", but I must admit it gave me little comfort at the time. Most of the houses on the beach road were in a sorry state, roofs missing, gaping holes in the walls, some on fire; this was the price of liberation, the havoc of war. Moving between the houses I saw my first dead men – two German soldiers lying on the floor in a room where the wall had been blasted away by a shell. I could see no wounds as such but they were covered by a fine layer of plaster dust, a most uncanny sight, probably killed by the blast of the shell. Once clear of the beach area we got ourselves sorted out and headed for the assembly area, having checked around the Platoon there did not appear to be anyone missing which was most reassuring for all concerned.

'Everything seemed to have gone to plan and we prepared to push on inland in the wake of the 8th Brigade. I could hear huge shells fired from the offshore battleships screaming overhead on their way to inland targets. Was I glad I wasn't on the receiving end of those! Each shell weighed a ton so I could imagine the destruction they caused among enemy positions.

'Some villagers were out waving the Tricolour and giving out glasses of Calvados. What wouldn't I have given for a mug of tea just then! A short halt was called and was I glad to get the weight of my feet for a few moments and enjoy a cigarette. Never mind the future I lived each minute as it came. Orders came through and it was "On your feet lads, we're moving forward".

'I struggled to my feet and off we marched en route for Colleville-sur-Mer. As we cleared the outskirts of Hermanville we lost the cover of the buildings and trees on either side of the road and emerged into open country. We were soon spotted and it wasn't long before the .88s (German field guns) and mortars were giving us a pasting. We didn't hang about too long but we lost several lads on that stretch of road. As we approached the western outskirts of Colleville-sur-Mer we could hear that there was stiff opposition on the far side of the village. In the village itself there were knocked out vehicles, German dead sprawled on the road and several lads from The Suffolk Regiment laying dead in various places. One lad had been shot down in the middle of the road and a tank had run over him. It was a gruesome sight but war is a gruesome business. It was unbelievable how quickly one got hardened to the sight of death and accepted it with very little emotion except when it was one of you own particular friends. Perhaps it's the way it had to be if you wanted to survive in a world gone mad? Self-preservation is a very strong instinct.

'Everyone "Stood to" as dusk approached. I strained my eyes to peer into the gloom. I was having my own private battle now trying to keep my eyes open. My thoughts wandered back over that historic day, thankful that me and many of my pals had made it safely. We had gained a foothold in Normandy. What would tomorrow bring?'

Duncan was wounded in the second major attack on Lebisey Wood and he was evacuated to England.

Troop Sergeant Chris Clancy

67 Anti-Tank Battery, 20th Anti-Tank Regiment RA.

'I had to land immediately behind the assault infantry and carry out a reconnaissance of the brigade area for anti-tank purposes. One troop of self-propelled M10s had landed immediately behind the infantry and the remaining eight guns would be going ashore as soon as possible after midday. I stepped into three feet of water on Queen Red beach. The area was under intense shell and small arms fire, with casualties drowning and floundering around.

'Dead ahead was a low beach wall at La Brêche. Fortunately, my inelegant scramble exposed a Tellermine (a booby-trapped anti-tank mine) linked to several others. I gingerly pushed the sand back to further expose the trap and got out on to the lateral road in front of strong-point Cod, which was under assault by the East Yorks. I hared off to catch up with the South Lancs entering Hermanville. There was a deal of sniping by a scattered enemy. My reconnaissance took me south to the open country near Mathieu and then back seawards to Colleville.

'In a wooded clearing not far away I came across a railway wagon surrounded by dozens of Tellermines and other booby traps in various stages of assembly in what was obviously a workshop. As Wellington said; "A close run thing."

'From an anti-tank point of view the fields with barbed wire aprons and festooned with *"Achtung Minen"* signs raised doubts. Which were *ruses de guerre?*'

Prudent Boiux, 16

who lived on the seafront at Asnelles with his fisherman father, mother and older brother. He saw the Second British Army land at Sword beach.

'We went to our air-raid shelter that evening and settled down. But at 1 a.m. I awoke to a low, rumbling noise. At 5 a.m. my brother left the shelter. Suddenly, he shrieked with excitement and we all ran upstairs. There, about a kilometre out to sea, was a sight I shall never forget. The bay was black with ships – there was absolutely no sea left. Within minutes the earth began shaking with the constant hail of shells, machine-gun fire and bombs. And all the time thousands of soldiers poured out of landing craft. At 10 a.m. three tanks rolled up outside our house and my father ran into the garden, ripped up the rose bush and gave it to the soldiers.

'I shall be grateful to the British for as long as I live.'

Lance Corporal Peter H. Gould

1st Battalion, The Royal Norfolk Regiment.

'We boarded our landing craft at Newhaven and set sail at about 18:00 on 5 June. The sea was a bit choppy and a lot of the lads were very seasick, including me. I was a very bad sailor. I had my hair cut on board, as did so many more of the lads, as we did not know when we would be able to get another one. We were not a pretty sight I can tell you!

'After all night at sea we approached the Normandy beaches at about 07:00 on 6 June. One could not hear one another speak for the noise that was going on around us. Almost every warship in the Navy must have been firing their guns at the same time. Shells were screaming over our heads in every direction. Also, the Germans were firing at us in our assault craft. We were ordered to get prepared to land. One could hear the German machine gunners hitting the side of our landing craft (LCI). We were pretty scared. Except for one or two old soldiers we were all young men. I was a lance corporal at the time I/c of the Bren gun in my section. We hit the beaches at about 07:15. We were expecting a very wet landing but the skipper of the craft got us in close, which we were very glad, as there was nothing worse than getting wet up to one's waist or above.

'Once we were on the beach we had quite a long run to get to cover, of which there was not much. We lost a couple of the lads but most of us made it to the dunes, which we were glad to see. Once the Germans realized what was really going on they started to shell us continually with mortar fire. We got up to the roadway where some of our tanks were. I got to the side of one and advanced with it, as did others. We thought that if we were going to get hit the tank would get it first.

'When we got ourselves together we started to move towards the built-up area, which gave us a bit more protection. Our objective on D-Day was the city of Caen.

We knew we had a long way to go before we got there and a lot of fighting and bloodshed would come but we kept going the best we could, losing a man here and there. Shrapnel from the mortar bombs wounded lots of our boys. Sometimes, one or two of our own shells would drop short causing a bit of panic. We got into the open country and we had fields of corn to go through, which we did on our hands and knees as the German bullets were whistling through the corn. We kept our heads down! There was a lot of sniping going on at the same time. The German soldiers were very good at sniping. Many times our officer had to call in the artillery to try to stonk him out.

'As we got nearer to our objective we were stopped by a German counter-attack. We were getting a bit close to the German dugouts and I don't think he liked it much. All this occurred on a hill called Lebisey Wood, where a lot of our men form the Norfolks and from other regiments lost their lives. We met stiff opposition but as our objective was Caen we had to gain this dominating ground to give us a clear view of our objective. So this was a very sad day. We retreated a mile or so back and dug in.

'We went out on patrols at night to try and locate the enemy, which we did several times, sometimes losing a man or two with anti-personnel mines, which were everywhere, but we overcame this as the engineers came in and cleared most of them. When we contacted the Germans we reported back to HQ and the artillery gave him a good stonk but he was very well dug in.

'Before we went out on patrols we had our first hot meal since we landed. Our quartermaster came up to our lines in a Bren gun carrier to dish this meal out to us.

Nothing went back to the cookhouse I can tell you. It was what we called an all-in-stew (a bit of this and a bit of that). It went down very well. As we were all very hungry we all sat in our trenches to have this meal as there was still the odd mortar bomb being fired at us. After a chat and a smoke we heard the sound of aircraft above and when we looked up we could see that these were gliders being towed to make a landing only a few miles away from us. A lovely sight but I am afraid that those glider lads got really cut up, as they were sitting ducks for the enemy.

'This day was the longest day of my life but I was spared to fight another day, thank God. I suppose one could say I was one of the lucky ones. After dark fell upon us we felt sure that the Germans would counter-attack us that evening or in the morning but nothing happened, thank God. The word got around that we had no need to worry about being pushed back into the sea. We didn't want another Dunkirk, when Montgomery sent word around that if anything happened he could lay down an artillery barrage of a 1001 guns and believe me that would be quite assuring and we all felt better for this news. That was providing none of the shells fell among our boys. Some did sometimes but that's war.'

Lebisey was the holding point for 25 tanks of the 1st Company and HQ of 21st Panzer Division commanded by Hauptmann Herr at 15:00 on D-Day. By dusk leading tanks led by Lieutenant Colonel Jim Eadie had advanced six miles form the beaches and were on the summit of the wooded hills around Lebisey. On D+1 the Warwicks were ordered to take Lebisey Ridge and village but after heavy fighting the Germans beat them back with machine guns in the woods.

The area was finally captured by the 185th Brigade of the 3rd British Division early on 8 July.

Major Eric A. Cooper-Key MC

(later Lieutenant-Colonel) commanding B Company, Ist Battalion, The Royal Norfolk Regiment.

'I landed with B Company and we had just moved off the beaches when I saw Major (later Lieutenant Colonel) Humphrey M. Wilson MC, the Battalion Second-in-command, surrounded by a group of jabbering Frenchmen. Humphrey had spent many years in India and Urdu was second nature to him. He was regaling the French in Urdu and when he saw me he turned round and said, "Eric, these bloody fools can't even speak their own language!"'

Private Nevil Griffin

(later Lance-Corporal) regimental signaller, D Company, Ist Battalion, The Royal Norfolk Regiment.

'The first clear recollection is of being on board a LCI and setting sail from Newhaven. Four hours later, when we were allowed up on deck, I was absolutely staggered by the vast armada which had gathered. Wherever you looked there were ships of all shapes and sizes. The storm clouds were gathering but they had not completely blotted out the sun, which was sending low shafts of sunlight across the surface of the sea, throwing everything into silhouette. Against this silvery background the ships looked sinisterly black.

'We spent a wretched night. Not many of us were good enough sailors to withstand the heavy sea we encountered and sick bags soon became inadequate! By morning the deck was about an inch deep in vomit and I wished I were dead! At daybreak we were allowed up on deck and never has fresh salty sea air smelt so good! The opportunity was taken to swill down and clear the foul smelling decks below, though some of the smell lingered because the leather soles of our boots had become impregnated.

'We were ordered to complete the Next of Kin and Will sections of our paybooks and a "Field Service Post card" for transmission to our next of kin. We were issued with condoms to provide waterproofing for watches and Francs and overtrousers/leggings to try to keep dry on landing. Being short my leggings could only be described as a tight fit under my arms!

'Suddenly we were told "This is it, up on deck and prepare for landing!" Up we went and took up positions on the port side of the bow superstructure. This was not really the time for sightseeing but of course we all had a good look round and truly it was a staggering sight to see so many ships so close together – literally hundreds! One or two were on fire but most were busy putting people or equipment ashore while others, having performed their task, were reversing out to sea ready to take on whatever task was next. Our ship's captain did us proud. He went so far on to the beach that when his ratings lowered the ramps for us we stepped off into only about two feet of water, which was marvellous.

'Major Brinkley, our Company Commander, ordered us ashore and down the ramps we went. Ashore on the Continent at last! It was my job to see that the No. 18 wireless set was close by the Company Commander at all times to try and maintain radio communication and not to be involved in the "Blood and Gore". I carried a standard rifle as my weapon, to the barrel of which I had tied two signalling flags in case I should need them to maintain communication. My mate Private 'Tuff' Tuffield and I went wherever the Company Commander went, just a pace or two behind. Following Major Brinkley across the beach was difficult. In addition to the weight we were carrying we had the problem of bypassing broken down or burning armoured vehicles of all sorts. Dead bodies and wounded made an additional difficulty over and above the occasional mortar shell landing near by. This short journey didn't really take very long but to me it seemed like an eternity. But at last we were clear of the clinging sand and we hurried up over the sea wall of the little French seaside town, which was just as the photographs had said it would be, crossed the road and turned away from the beach up a track alongside some houses, heading in the general direction of Caen.

The over-riding memory is of so many of my colleagues who through various causes did not see the campaign through to the end. Tuffield and I had reached the edge of Lebisey Wood in the late afternoon of Day 2 when eventually the order was given to withdraw for regrouping. As Tuff and I retraced our steps down the sloping field we became the target of a German rifleman firing from the wood. Fortunately the field was very uneven and our withdrawal was thus somewhat erratic, which put the rifleman off a bit. We reached a gap in the hedge and made for the other side. Poor old Tuff was wounded in the hand but we managed to scramble to safety on the other side. He was the first of ten signals colleagues who were to serve with me during the campaign to be replaced!

'I remember the awful carnage among the animals

during the first two or three months of our assault. I don't think I shall ever forget the sight of horses and cows bloated and putrefying but having to be left because of enemy pressure. I also remember the awful stench, which developed in the heat of that summer as a result of the carnage.'

That evening 1 Royal Norfolk was firmly established in a wooded area at the top of a gentle rise, code-named Rover, around a single building, which came to be known as Norfolk House.

Private W. Evans
I2 Platoon, B Company, Ist Battalion Royal Norfolk Regiment.

'After spending many hours on a landing craft crossing the Channel and being seasick like many others, I was glad to get on the beach. It was like manoeuvres that we had done so many times before. I could not believe it was the real thing. We had no trouble on the beach. Once off the beach we slowly advanced along narrow dusty roads with Jerry snipers banging away at us. So far we had covered two or three miles and were doing well until we came to a cornfield. Then Jerry machine guns in a small Pill Box opened up. The lads were soon being cut to pieces as the machine guns, with their tremendous rate of fire, scythed through the three foot high golden corn. I remember one of the Company cooks behind me getting a bullet in his neck. That was the day I first saw the red poppies of France in the cornfields, diving to the ground out of the machine gun fire. My nose was stuck right amongst them! They reminded me of the hell and horrors of the 1914 war which my father had talked about so often.'

Lieutenant E. G. G. Williams

'My men and I had to bury a dozen men – not a pleasant job. The sergeant's gold fillings were brilliant in the sun.'

In the period to the end of June 1944 the total number of battle casualties suffered by the 3rd British Infantry Division was 3,505, approximately one seventh of the total battle casualties of the 2nd British Army, which by that time comprised the equivalent of almost 20 divisions.

Stan Bruce

5th/7th Battalion, The Gordon Highlanders.

'We sailed to war not knowing what to expect. We were transferred from our transport ship on to a landing craft, which also had on board two three-ton Army trucks and we headed for the beaches. All went well until the time came to disembark and wade ashore. We went close in but then they decided to let the trucks off first into about three feet of water, which was no problem, but after the trucks went, that made the landing craft lighter and it also started to move into deeper water of about six or seven feet. The skipper was scared to go in any closer in case he ran aground. Now comes more Army stupidity. This idiot of an officer ordered us to take a five-gallon can of petrol in each hand and jump. We refused. If we jumped into the deeper water we would have sunk to the bottom and drowned but the day was saved by one of the sailors on the crew. He tied a rope around his waist and dived overboard fully clothed and swam ashore. The craft went a bit nearer and holding ONE can of petrol and the rope in the other hand we went into about five feet of water and waded ashore, soaking wet, and landed in France in one piece. From then on it became a hard job just to stay in one piece and not get killed. It became a test of survival, which the lucky made, and the unlucky didn't. We never got the chance to thank that sailor for what he did. I just hope he survived the war. He deserved to.

'We left the beaches and were on our way to join the battalion and then saw our first sight of the enemy. Two German planes swooped over the beaches but they did not bother us, thank goodness. When we left the beaches, there were bundles lying on the beach all covered in army blankets, which we realized were our dead waiting to be buried. A sad sight, but a common one in the future. Being British or German they had one thing in common, they all looked the same, DEAD, what for? War is so stupid.

'I was soon to get a rude awakening as on my first night the Germans decided to give me a nice welcome as they plastered our positions with mortar and shellfire. I was absolutely terrified and crouched in my duver shaking like a leaf. I really thought my end had come but the shelling finally stopped and I was still in one piece. But you could hear the cry for stretcher-bearers so some poor sod had copped it. I then understood why I was told to dig deep and if your luck was in you survived. If not, then your duver became your grave.

'The worst thing was a mortar the Jerries had named Moaning Minnie. It was a six-barrelled mortar and they landed in a straight line so if your duver was in line with the first bomb, then, if one of the next five had your name on it, that was your lot. They just filled in your duver and stuck your rifle on top of it with your name and number. I had had my first baptism of fire, but many more to come.

'Jerry kept up with his shelling and we were told to be prepared for an attack, which happened shortly after the alert. Jerry put in a big attack with infantry and tanks and we were all standing by ready to fight them off … Bill Norrie was killed. Jim Glennie and Ron Macintosh were missing with most of A Company. Jim and Ron had only lasted about three days but we learned much later that they were taken prisoner and we met again after the war. Jerry was pushed back thanks to our superiority in artillery, tanks, and of course us, the poor bleeding infantry. We always got the dirty end of the stick.'

Marine Commando Percy 'Shock' Kendrick MM

an army medic who got his nickname because most of his patients were shell-shocked.

'We sailed from England on the evening of 5 June on the *Princess Josephine Charlotte*, a Belgian packet. Our task was to land at Sword Beach and to break out on to Port-En-Bessin. Our Commando officer, Captain Walton, took us through to a junction on a coast road and told us to dig. We exposed a telephone junction box, which connected all military telephones, and we blew it up. Later, as we advanced, we had some skirmishes with the Germans. A machine gun opened up on us, injuring some of the lads. "Shock" the cry rang out from one of the wounded. As I tended to the lad, I realized I couldn't do all the necessary first aid in a prone position, but as I stood up the machine gun opened up again.

'I could see the bullets hitting the hedgerow but as they came nearer to me, the gun must have lifted. Although the firing continued, the bullets were flying about and above my head. We put in a flank attack and captured the machine gun and crew. The gunner had a right shoulder injury. I had to treat him. When I'd finished he hugged me.

'A Scout car with six Germans in it suddenly rounded a bend in the road. We dealt with it. Soon after we heard a horse galloping down the lane. As it came in view we saw it had a German rider. Sergeant Hooper stepped into the lane and fired his Tommy gun. The horse galloped off with the dead body still on its back.

'Later, we approached a small village. An elderly woman was crying by the roadside. I could see the old lady was wounded in the arm, so I tended to her and wanted to get her in the house. While I was trying to get her to understand that she should be in bed, she slapped my face! I realized she had completely misunderstood. I had no choice but to give her a morphine injection and carry on.'

John McLaughlin

Letter home from HMS 'Ramillies'

Dear Mother,

As I write this letter to you, we are lying just off the coast of France, pouring 15-inch shells into the enemy positions. It's good to see the orange flame belch forth from the muzzle of our gun. It's great to hear the one-ton shells whistling through the air, to see the clouds of dust and smoke rise where they fall, and then, to think of the destruction and panic they cause amongst the Hun, and how the morale of our troops jumps even higher than what it is when they know the Royal Navy is not far away backing up every move they make.

Perhaps I'd better explain how we felt something in our blood as every warship in the harbour weighed anchor and slowly steamed out to sea. After being at sea for about half an hour we heard the click of our loudspeakers. You could have heard a pin drop. Then came news we had been waiting for. The captain told us we were about to make history – we were going to take part in the Second Front. I felt thrilled and perhaps a little nervous. Each of us was given a signed order from General Eisenhower. He told us how important we were and wished us God speed.

HMS *Ramillies* ploughed through the water until I saw a fleet of every kind of ship the size of which I have never seen before and am never likely to see again. The mighty battleships were in the centre, cruisers on either side, with destroyers nipping around guarding the mighty brood. At the front were the all-important minesweepers and at the rear hundreds of barges carrying troops and ammunition.

During the night we split into three squadrons and by daybreak we could see the rugged coast of France. There were many enemy batteries to be silenced before the barges could get inshore. I shall always treasure the honour that fell to my ship and to my gun of firing the first shot in the colossal engagement and it thrills me beyond words to think that I had the pleasure of loading that first shell. The Germans did almost everything except hit us.

The first hour will always be imprinted vividly on my mind. But it was no time for inward emotions. There was work to be done and we did it – our guns blasting enemy destroyers as they approached to attack. The thing that struck me most was our vast sea and air superiority. Where was the Luftwaffe?

The great landing came at 7.30 a.m. Thousands of barges began to move towards the beach while our planes circled overhead. An army like this could not possibly be beaten.

I had been closed up at my gun all day. I was still there at 7 p.m., just standing meditating over the day's events. Then what seemed like a dark cloud appeared on the horizon. As it came nearer I could make out that it consisted of thousands of planes. They seemed to fly in pairs but as they moved closer I could see that attached to each plane was a huge black glider. This was the most awe-inspiring sight of the day. The enemy flak was terrific. As each plane passed over our ship the gliders began to detach themselves and glide to earth. It is easy to imagine the fear, which must have seized the enemy.

All that night we could hear the battle raging. It is raging as I write but the gunfire becomes less audible as the German war machine is driven slowly further inland.

Private T. Platt
Ist Battalion South Lancashire Regiment.

'When dawn broke we saw the coast of France and the great fleet around it and our morale soared. Our ships opened fire on the beach – it was a terrifying spectacle – then an explosion under our craft stunned my legs. We stopped 100 yards from the shore and were ordered into the water, not knowing how deep it was. A Sherman tank sank beneath the waves and two crew scrambled out. The rest must have drowned. Next was our Bren gun carrier. Its wheel got stuck in the tank. My four pals plunged in but I couldn't swim so I stood on the carrier with water up to my chest. I put my life belt on and prayed. After what seemed like an eternity, my feet touched soft sand. Half drowned. I waded through the breakers and saw men lying on the sand. I stumbled towards the nearest one and saw that his chest had been torn open. We had lost our

Bren gun so I took his rifle, ammo and steel helmet. Then I just ran for cover. Dead and wounded lay scattered all over the beach. I had swallowed a great deal of water and was violently sick. I lay in the dunes for a while. A war photographer came over to me with a packet of cigarettes. He said he had shot some film, which would be amazing, if he ever got back to England. After dark, German planes came over dropping hundreds of anti-personnel bombs. I had no sleep at all but I was still alive. God knows why, but I was.'

Leutnant Herbert Walther, 22

I2th 'Waffen-SS' Armoured Division Hitler Jugend (Hitler Youth, or HJ).

'It seems incredible that German intelligence noticed nothing of the vast preparations for the invasion and that individual precise reports from the German command posts were ignored. On the other hand, it's not that surprising because the *Deutsche Nachrichtefl Dienst* (intelligence service) was riddled with spies putting out duff information.

'I volunteered for the Waffen SS in 1940 because I wanted to join the best. And they were the finest there has ever been. We're often compared to the Royal Marines but we were better than they were.

'I was asleep when the Invasion began, when the Allied paratroopers were landing, even before midnight. The masses of troops that landed in the early morning can be said to have decided the war. They came with an armada whose size far exceeded all German fears.

'The Hitler Jugend had been alerted during the night of June 4/5 for manoeuvres on 6 June The night before, there was unusual aircraft activity and, towards morning, it was certain. We knew they were coming. We were marched towards Lisleux at first but were later switched to the west towards Caen. We soldiers in the battle units knew nothing of the confusion over higher staff but confusion there certainly was. We didn't reach Caen until deep in the night and some units didn't arrive until early next morning. We had been on the move for many hours. There were the usual technical problems and the drivers were falling asleep in their seats every time we stopped. When we arrived, the tanks were arranged in a great semicircular defensive line north of the Caen–Bayeux road, to prevent the enemy from taking the important Carpiquet airfield and penetrating the city of Caen. What did it feel like? There was no time to feel only time to do. The enemy attack was expected and it happened as expected. Our battle group leader, Colonel Kurt Meyer, known as Panzermeyer, had set up our command post at Ardenne Abbey. Its strong arches offered protection and cover and we had a good view to the coast from the towers and a gallery running all around the roof. Under cover of the gallery, we could observe the enemy tanks and infantry advancing closer to our Panzer IV tanks standing in ambush positions. To me, it was like watching a piece of theatre from a balcony seat with running commentary from the radio.

'The drama became a tragedy for the British when, on the command "Fire at will!" our tanks fired as one. Numerous enemy tanks immediately burst into flames. Others drove away in surprize and confusion, going every which way all over the battlefield.

For 40 days from D-Day to 22 August 1944 the HJ proved a major obstacle to the Allied advance.

Private Ronald Major, 21

East Yorkshire Regiment, who survived a bullet on Sword
Beach and the torpedoing of a landing craft taking him
and other wounded to a waiting destroyer.

'We went first on to Sword Beach and took a terrific
number of casualties. There were bodies and wounded
everywhere, in the sea, on the sand – so many that we had
to walk and crawl over them. The commandos who
followed us were surprized at the mortality rate and put it
down to inexperience. This wasn't the case. We had been
well trained. But heavy artillery and machine gun fire was
pouring down on us. There just wasn't anywhere to go. I
lost a lot of good mates that day. Men who gave their lives
for others.'

The 'Jocks' And The Green Berets Forge Inland

Piper Bill Millin, 21

1st Special Service Brigade.

'The image which stays in my mind is of leaving the
Hamble River and sailing through the flotilla of 21 landing
craft and the invasion fleet of hundreds and hundreds of
ships. I was in the bow of the leading group and the
troops threw their hats in the air as we passed. My
commanding officer, Brigadier Lord Lovat, 1st Special
Service Brigade, said, "You are going to lead the biggest
invasion in the history of warfare."

'"Thanks very much," was my immediate thought but though I could have refused, there was something in the way he put it that made me feel I had already volunteered. Just think, if I had turned the brigadier down, I might have ended up in the cookhouse, and then I would have missed out on the most memorable experience of my life.

'Everyone liked Lord Lovat, although we all thought that, at 32, he was bit too old for the kind of daredevilry he enjoyed. He was a typical aristocrat who would walk calmly with his head held high while all the rest of us would be ducking and diving to avoid shells. Everyone regarded him as crazy and, in retrospect, I suppose they thought that I was pretty crazy, too. I had a special relationship with him. He always called me Bill, although it would have been form to use surnames. From late 1942 to May 1944 I had been in a commando training centre, Achnacarry in the Highlands, helping to teach landing techniques to Belgians, Dutch and Americans. We were all volunteers looking for something different and exciting. One day in May 1944 he told me he was forming his own commando brigade and would like me to join and play the pipes. At that time the War Office had banned pipers in action. Lovat told me he was not bothered about the War Office and that I would be the only piper playing at Normandy. I took it as an honour and was quite happy to get away from the training centre.'

Bill Mills

Newfoundland-born landing craft coxswain, from LSI(S),
'Princess Astrid', a converted Belgian cross-Channel
passenger vessel with a capacity for 507 troops and
eight landing craft, which arrived off Sword Beach at
05:42 on 6 June with The Highland Light Infantry on
board.

'When a signal came saying we only had two and a half
miles to go our troops put their packs on and got under
cover. My crew also got down and I closed the armour
plate covers of my cockpit and opened the slots through
which I could see all around me. You could hear bursts of
machine-gun fire from the shore and the wicked snarl of
bullets ricocheting in the sea and over our boats. Some
were uncomfortably close. Occasionally a column of water
would shoot up near us and then we would hear the
sound of the gun that had fired the shell. Then 'Jerry'
started lobbing over mortar shells and putting them very
close indeed – none of the chaps were laughing and
joking then. Suddenly we were up to the outer defences.
Engines flat out. The obstacles were built of heavy timber
forming tripods, on top of which were Teller mines. It
would have been just too bad if we had touched one of
these. I felt the craft sticking on underwater obstacles and
in a moment we were up against the inner beach defences
and could go no further. I gave the order to "down ramp",
our armoured doors were opened and our troops began to
disembark. Mortar shells were bursting on the beach,
which they had to cross, and among our craft as 'Jerry' had
now got our range. On the sand, just clear of the sea, were
the bodies of soldiers who had landed a few minutes
before. Many others were in the sea itself; slowly moving

back and forth as the waves rushed in and retreated. I watched our commandos as they slowly walked through the surf and up the beach. Some didn't reach us. They would fall quietly on their faces and lie there in the water. I saw one spin about suddenly and sit down, his face covered in blood. Some chaps would throw away their packs to drag their fallen comrades ashore. I didn't feel scared any more – just numb as I wondered how much longer it would be before I got my "packet". It's a horrible feeling, the realization that death is about to strike you.'

Extract from the LSI(H) 'Maid of Orleans' ship's log.

a converted Southern railway cross-Channel passenger vessel with a capacity for 448 troops and six landing craft, arrived off Sword Beach two minutes earlier, at 05:40 with 4 Commando on board.

'At 05:40 we anchored at the lowering position and at 05:45 manned the craft. This proceeded in a most orderly manner, long practice having made each man familiar with his position in the different landing craft. As these were lowered at 06:05, we of the ship's company silently sent them our good wishes, for it will be remembered that these specially trained Commandos had been with us over a period of many months and had grown to become part of the ship's company. There was a heavy sea running at the time and so it was with a sigh of relief that the craft were seen safely away without mishap, each soldier wearing full kit and extra ammunition.

'Opposite the place where our craft landed was an enemy stronghold and the beach was swept from end to end by machine-gun and mortar fire. Many men never reached the beach and one craft had a mortar bomb fall in the centre of it while packed with troops, killing two and wounding others. Although one air-raid warning was sounded during the time the ship was anchored off the beaches, no enemy aircraft could have survived in a sky so dominated by our own aircraft. Five of our landing craft returned by 10:30 and we were genuinely pleased to see them: one had struck a submerged obstruction and returned without any steering gear. The sixth craft had been lost by enemy action ...'

Private Bill Bidmead, 20

commando, A Troop, No. 4 Commando, part of Brig Lord Lovat's 1st Special Service Brigade.

'The Highland Light Infantry and No. 4 Commando were carried across the English Channel on board *The Princess Astrid* and *Maid of Orleans*. Assault landing craft took No. 4 Commando ashore. My craft was hit and reared up almost vertically, and I was jammed between my seat and the boat under a pile of men. The ramp was kicked open and the first commando out was practically ripped in half by a burst of machine-gun fire. Still trapped, I feared I would drown as the craft began to fall back and sink. A comrade, seeing my plight, dashed back and freed me. I jumped into the sea, now neck-deep. As I waded ashore, I saw men drowning in shallow water. Wounded, their 90-lb rucksacks weighed them down.

'A Company of East Yorks had been landed earlier to clear the beach and lay white tape to mark a clear passage for us. They had not got ten yards before many had been cut down and they were ordered to dig in. It was an act of madness that only added to the carnage. I stepped over one wounded soldier whose stomach had been ripped open. I couldn't stop and help.

'I ended up in a building giving covering fire to troops attacking a German gun battery. I foolishly leant out of the window to get a better aim and was seen by a sniper who fired at me. As I ducked back inside to reload, a round whistled by me and hit the man behind me in the stomach. We carried him back on a door, but had to duck in a doorway when a German fighter flew over us with machine guns blazing. We left the wounded man there and marked his position with a small yellow pennant so he could be collected later.

'As we came back we found 30 East Yorks lying behind a hedgerow. All were dead, save one who was screaming for a padre. An oil bomb had dropped in the middle of them. It exploded burning oil and left a great black patch.'

Piper Bill Millin

Ist Special Service Brigade.

'Our job, after securing the coastal area, was to get to the bridges near the village of Bénouville on the Caen Canal and River Orne where airborne troops had already landed. We had 21 small infantry landing crafts for the assault. Lovat and I went on the first boat, LCI(S) 519, with the others following closely behind. It was stormy as we approached Sword beach and most of the men on our boat were seasick. I joined the other Commandos at the front of the craft. The German gunners were now joining in. Their fire was very accurate, and large spouts of water were shooting up around the landing craft. To our right a landing craft had received a direct hit and was burning fiercely. The occupants were scrambling into the water. No one seemed to mind the noise of the salvoes passing overhead, or the fate of the unfortunate occupants of the landing craft that had been hit. Everyone was staring ahead as the landing craft drew closer to the beaches. I could see the coast very clearly now. Two tanks at the water's edge were on fire, and a large cloud of black smoke was blowing across the dunes. It appeared that the tanks had been knocked out before they had even got as far as the dunes.

As I watched the scene in front of me, another salvo of shells from the warships passed overhead and hit a house on the seafront, throwing large chunks of masonry high into the air. There was a constant whine of bullets or shrapnel close by. We were now preparing to go ashore, and I was standing behind Shimi Lovat at the left ramp. The Commandos were now jumping into the water. One of the card players on the sea journey from England, the married man, was hit in the face by a piece of shrapnel as he stepped on to the ramp. He clung on to the ramp for a few seconds, then toppled into the sea.

There appeared to be about one hundred yards of water between the beach and us. Lovat was off the craft and wading towards the beach. I jumped off the ramp as quickly as possible, holding the bagpipes above my head, and landed in water up to my waist. I felt myself falling backwards due to the weight of my rucksack. Luckily someone pulled me upright and I struggled through the water still holding the pipes above my head. I could see Shimi Lovat just ahead of me; I was catching him up. The water was now at knee level and the beach was just a few yards away. There was a lot of noise, the sound of automatic fire, and what appeared to be mortar shells bursting on the beach away to the right. Once I could find my feet I placed the bagpipes on my shoulder, blew them up, and started to play *Highland Laddie* the regimental quick march of the Scots Guards, as I waded the few yards to the beach. Lovat turned his head towards me when he heard the pipes. He looked at me for a moment, appeared to smile, then continued on his way.

'I was not really frightened because we had practised landings so many times before but this time we were being fired on. Shells were bursting in the water. There were bodies floating in the water and lying across the beach. Two tanks were burning fiercely. It was pure noise and confusion. Commandos were rushing past me and up the beach. I stopped playing the pipes as I passed between two dead soldiers lying at the water's edge, one with half of his face blown away. They were moving back and forward with the surf. I tried to get off the sands as quickly as possible.

There was a small road leading off the beach and several Commandos were lying wounded at its entrance, their faces a strange grey colour. It was a bizarre experience to walk out of the water still playing and to be confronted with the sight of wounded British soldiers lying where they had fallen. They were shocked to see me in my kilt and playing the bagpipes. Some of them asked, "Are the medics here, Jock?" I had no idea, but I told them they were on their way. I took shelter behind a low wall and watched as a flail tank made its way towards a German position at the top of the road, its chain thumping the ground in front as it approached. As the tank drew closer I could see the Commander's steel hat just visible out of the turret as the tank came rumbling on, its front gun blasting away. I thought, "Christ! It's too wide to get up this road" and if it did make the attempt I would be crushed against the wall! I quickly got out of the path of the tank. Firing was still coming from a German position. I tried to attract the attention of the tank commander by pointing to the wounded in his path. He appeared not to notice and the tank rumbled closer and closer, eventually churning up the wounded lying in its path. As it disappeared up the road crushing the walls on either side, I looked briefly at the mangled bodies of the soldiers and dashed along the beach to join the other Commandos and Lovat. It was very traumatic watching those men die. It was horrifying. I felt so helpless.

'I joined Lovat as the Brigade Major was telling him that a message had just come through that the Airborne Forces had captured the bridge over the Orne and the Canal. This was good news for us, as we could now cross the Orne by the bridges, rather than swim across. The Brigade Major interrupted his conversation with Lovat, and looking at me as if he had just noticed me, remarked, "Piper, how about a tune?" With just a hint of sarcasm in my voice, I asked what I should play. Back came the reply, *The Road To The Isles*. "Would you prefer me to walk up and down the beach Sir?"

'"Yes, that would be fine," he replied. I placed the pipes on my shoulder and started off at a fairly brisk pace and at the water's edge. I had hardly gone 50 yards when I heard a bellowing in my left ear. "What are you fucking well playing at Piper? You mad bastard. Don't you think there's enough going on here without you attracting every fucking German in France?" It was a commando sergeant.

'... There was still automatic fire close at hand. It appeared to be coming from somewhere to our left and at the front of the column. Everyone got down in the grass. I rolled over on to my back, my rucksack propping me up. I gazed at the sky. It was a lovely morning. The sky was blue and I could hear a bird singing. Everything seemed peaceful, except for the rattle of the automatic fire away on out left.

'As I continued to stare upwards, I was surprised to see what looked like mortar bombs! They were flying in formation and heading in the direction of the beach, a few hundred yards to our rear. A few seconds later they exploded, with a crump, crump, crump. Other bombs were now coming over, also in formation. As they descended they let out a loud screaming noise that was quite frightening. This was our first introduction to the German multi-barrelled mortar. Its bombs exploded with a loud roar, followed by thick black smoke.

'The Germans certainly had the range on the beach, and the troops coming ashore at this moment were getting a hot reception.

'We were on the move again, across a few more minefields, then on to the road. There was a rifle shot close by, then another shot. The commando who had been reading the cowboy paperback on the landing craft yesterday evening, on our way across the Channel, was hit in the chest. He fell forward on to the grass verge at the side of the road. Someone turned him over on to his back, and his face had the deadly pallor all soldiers have when they have been wounded. A medic was opening his battledress blouse as we moved on. We wondered where the next shot was coming from.

'... The further we moved inland the more frequent and active were the enemy snipers. The sound of the guns and the bombardment at the landing beaches was becoming fainter.

'... Lovat asked me to play the bagpipes as long as possible as we were now approaching the area where the airborne forces had captured the bridges over the Orne. I placed the bagpipes on my shoulder to play a well-known Scottish tune called *Lochan Side*, keeping up a brisk pace on the road to Bénouville ... On reaching the Orne Bridge I looked at the brigadier. We could see the airborne troops at the other side of it. He said, "Come on". Being an aristocratic type, Lovat just carried on and never ducked down, while I was crawling through ditches. They were pleased to see us but the bridge was coming under sniper fire and I could see two of our chaps making signs for us to stop. Lovat made a wave of his hand, telling us to go on and for me to continue playing the pipes. So we both went over Pegasus Bridge as I played, and made it safely. Some of our commandos were shot while crossing the bridge but I piped my way across and shook hands with the amazed officers. A tall man appeared and said to Lovat, "Very pleased to see you, old boy." The man was Lieutenant Henry "Tod" Sweeney of the airborne forces. As they shook hands, Lovat replied, "And we are very pleased to see you, old boy. Sorry we are two and a half minutes late."'

Sapper Cyril Larkin

'A little after midday now. Then sweet music on the air – bagpipes! A company of commandos, with a piper at the head and their officer next wearing a white pullover, had reached us from the beach. What a joy for us all – temporarily. For as they crossed some of the lads were hit by the snipers. We buried one by the bridge next day. I painted Lieutenant Campbell's name on an improvized cross using a tin of paint and a brush from the café by the bridge.'

Sergeant Charles Thornton
Oxs and Bucks Light Infantry.

'By about 14:00 I was wondering when I would see England again when suddenly I heard the sound of bagpipes. "You must be mad! Bagpipes in the middle of Normandy!" scoffed Lieutenant Fox. Out of the trees stepped commando piper Bill Millin followed by Lord Lovat. He made his way on to Pegasus Bridge and shook hands with Major Howard with the words: "John, history is being made today." Meanwhile we threw our rifles in the air and embraced the 20–30 commandos who had come with him because we were so glad to see them.'

Private Bill Bidmead
A Troop, No. 4 Commando, who were shelled and mortared continuously for five days.

'That afternoon, No. 4 Commando linked up with the Oxfordshire and Buckinghamshire Light Infantry glider force that had seized Pegasus Bridge. It was still under fire and the commandos ran across in twos and threes. One officer was killed crossing the bridge. A soldier accompanying him was deeply upset by his loss and came across three German prisoners sitting beside the bridge. One cried out for water. The soldier said, "I'll give you water," and shot them. Nothing was said at the time, but the soldier was later killed himself. Funny thing; you usually found that if people went out of their way to kill someone, they generally ended up dead themselves.

'I got my head down, but someone tapped on my helmet and whispered, "Germans!" Moving forward out of a wood were dozens of coal-scuttle helmeted soldiers. Alongside me a Welsh Guardsman, Taff Hughes, picked up his Vickers K gun and opened fire. A stick grenade exploded in front of my trench. Shrapnel hit my lip and my mouth was smothered in blood. The force of the explosion flung me to the bottom of the trench and I heard someone say, "Young Bid's had it".

'The Germans made one last attack, but we cut them to pieces. We killed ten of them to one of us. A patrol went out and counted 250 German dead. Later, an 80-strong detachment of bicycle-mounted German reinforcements halted opposite our position. They were exhausted, having cycled all the way from Paris. As they dismounted and threw their kit down, we opened fire. It took 30 minutes to kill them all.'

No. 4 Commando remained in the front line for 83 days. Of its original 700-strong complement, only 70 remained unwounded.

Piper Bill Millin
Ist Special Service Brigade.

'I stayed in France from 6 June to 6 September and it was horrific ... there were so many casualties. I was very lucky. Normandy was a killing ground ... likened to Stalingrad in terms of loss of German and Allied lives. The pallor of the faces of the wounded remained strongly in my mind. There was no time to feel real emotion. It was strange to think that a friend who was alive such a short time ago, drinking a pint of beer in an English pub, was now lying in a ditch at the side of the road, with a piece of shrapnel in his head … Mac and me had only gone a few yards when suddenly there was a loud swish, followed immediately by two others, and something exploded against the side of the farmhouse, high up. This was followed by two further explosions in the cornfield to the left. I threw myself to the ground and crawled swiftly in the direction of the slit trench. As I tumbled into the trench, my heart beating wildly, I could hear Mac's feet pounding along the path towards me. There was another explosion in the cornfield and the sound of flying shrapnel. Mac suddenly landed in the trench, almost on top of me. I moved over to make room for him as he gasped, "I've been hit Piper".

"'Where have you been hit?" He did not answer. I ran my hands over his chest, and then his back. His back was sticky with blood and it was oozing all over his battledress. He did not answer when I spoke to him. I was sure he was dead. He was making no movement at all, just lying there on the floor of the trench. The explosions stopped as suddenly as they had begun, and it was peaceful again. I crawled out of the trench and went into the farmyard looking for the medics. I found them in the barn with the wounded. One of the medics accompanied me back to the slit trench to have a look at Mac. We lifted him out of the trench and carried him into the barn. The medic gave him a quick examination and said, "He is dead". He had several pieces of shrapnel in his back and in the back of his head there was also a wound. As I left the barn they were pulling a blanket over Mac's head.

'People on opposing sides were so close that you could hear them speaking and after a while, you could even distinguish who was about to fire by the sound of the bomb going down the barrel of the mortar. Jock, my friend of many years ago, had taken me off to find some shelter in a dugout, giving at least some protection from the flying shrapnel. German mortars were exploding. Two explosions in quick succession made me throw myself to the ground. They seemed so close, right behind me! ... I lay on the ground for a few moments; there were no further explosions. As I warily got to my feet I felt a compulsion to retrace my steps in the direction of Jock's trench. He lay on the grass, a large open wound at the back of his head and one of his legs was missing. His green beret lay close by. A piece of shrapnel had hit his cap badge and had penetrated the front of his skull. The cap badge with its St Andrew's Cross split in two brought a lump to my throat as I stood rooted to the spot. Stretcher-bearers were quickly on the scene, taking two wounded commandos away and leaving Jock lying on the grass. There was nothing they could do for him. No doubt they would return and place him with the other commando dead in neat rows in front of the Chateau to await burial.

'When the campaign was over, instead of going to visit my parents in Glasgow, I went straight back to Fort William to see a woman I had met during my training. I was very much in love with her. Girls had been very thin on the ground – they were generally regarded as an unnecessary distraction. When our friendship had developed I would stay at the cottage. We tried to keep it a secret but that had proved impossible. When I got back I discovered that she had died in hospital while I had been in Normandy. It was probably cancer, but no one asked about such things then. I stayed at her cottage for a few days afterwards, going out on to the hills and playing my pipes. It was my way of coming to terms with my emotions.

'I think she had known she was going to die all along. She seemed to have a kind of sixth sense about the future. A few weeks before I was given the orders to leave Scotland, she had told me that Lord Lovat was going to take me away from her. I didn't believe her at that stage, but it was all true. She also told me that Lord Lovat would be injured within seven days of the fighting, which he was. On 12 June he was hit in his back by a lump of shrapnel during an attack.

'I doubt if any pipers will play in action again. But then I doubt there will ever be another Lord Lovat.'

Simon 'Shimi' Fraser, 17th Baron Lovat, 25th Chief of the Clan Fraser, was repatriated to England after being severely wounded during 6 Commando's battle for Bréville Wood on 12 June. Lovat eventually recovered from his wounds and became Under Secretary of State for Foreign Affairs in 1945.

Beach Timetable

07:25 British 3rd Infantry Division and 27th Armoured Brigade, 18 minutes later than scheduled, go ashore with 40 DD tanks (six are lost) and flame-throwers and come under mortar fire.

08:21 They break through the enemy defences.

12:15 Panzer tanks reported north of Caen. 21st Panzer

Group commanded by Leutnant General Edgar Feuchtiger disobeys orders and attacks between Caen and Bayeux.

12:30 British 185th Brigade move inland from Sword.

13:30 Brigadier Lord Lovat's 1st Special Service Brigade, composed of four Army and one Royal Marines Commando, reach Pegasus Bridge *en route* to help other units of the Airborne Division.

14:00 Fighting on Periers Ridge overlooking Sword.

16:00 Infantry reach Bieville three miles from Caen but are stopped by tanks of the 21st Panzer Division. Infantry destroys 16 tanks.

18:00 British advance on Caen halted.

19:00 21st Panzer Division led by 50 tanks mounts massive counter-attack. Drive fails just short of the cliffs, with the loss of 13 tanks.

By nightfall six square miles of beach is under British control. 29,000 landed. Casualties, 1,000.

Order Of Battle Sword Beach
3rd British Division

Major General Thomas Rennie

8th Infantry Brigade
1st Bn The Suffolk Regiment
2nd Bn The East Yorkshire Regiment
1st Bn The South Lancashire Regiment

9th Infantry Brigade

2nd Bn The Lincolnshire Regiment
1st Bn The King's Own Scottish Borderers
2nd Bn The Royal Ulster Rifles

185th Infantry Brigade

2nd Bn The Royal Warwickshire Regiment
1st Bn The Royal Norfolk Regiment
2nd Bn The King's Shropshire Light Infantry
Divisional Troops
HO 3rd Division
7th, 33rd and 76th Field Regiments, RA
20th Anti-Tank Regiment, RA
246th Field Company, RE
2nd Bn The Middlesex Regiment (MG)
Units under command for assault phase

27th Armoured Brigade

13th/18th Royal Hussars
The Staffordshire Yeomanry
The East Riding Yeomanry

1st (Special Service) Brigade

3, 4 and 6 Commandos
45 (RM) Commando
2 Troops 10 (IA) Commando (French)
Elements of 79 Armoured Division
22nd Dragoons
5th Assault Regiment, RE
218 Bty and HQ 73
Light Anti-Aircraft Regiment, RA
1 Troop 318 Bty (of 92 Light Anti-Aircraft Regiment, RA)

263 Field Company, RE

629 Field Squadron, RE

41 RM Commando (from 4 Special Service Brigade)*

3 Troops 5 Independent Armoured Support

Battery SP, RM

Beach Groups

5th Bn The King's Regiment

1st Buckinghamshire Bn

Units of 51st Highland Division which landed on D-Day
and came under command of 3rd British Infantry Division

5th Bn The Black Watch

1st and 5/7th Battalions, The Gordon Highlanders

Plus elements of:

Royal Corps of Signals

Royal Army Service Corps

Royal Army Medical Corps

Royal Army Ordnance Corps

Corps of Royal Electrical and Mechanical Engineers

Corps of Military Police

Pioneer Corps

*41 RM Commando was an element of 4 Special Service
Brigade, which was put under command of 3.

Gold

Walt Marshall, 20

Naval Sub-Lieutenant

'On the night of 3 June I was sent with a radio operator and two commandos on a reconnaissance mission to the Normandy coast at Arromanches. We crossed the Channel in a small U-class sub and went ashore on a rubber raft. The weather was atrocious – there were heavy gales and six-foot-high seas. Our job was to find out what obstructions and explosives the Germans had planted on Gold Beach, so they could be dealt with before the troops landed on D-Day. We were noting down the positions of the steel and concrete posts that had been hammered into the sand – they looked like criss-crossing railway lines – when we nearly ran into a sentry having a quiet smoke on the beach. Luckily, he didn't see us. A little later, we were almost seen by a convoy driving along a coastal road. We all jumped into a ditch by the side of the road, and once again we had a narrow escape. We managed to discover the position of several explosives, which were taken care of prior to the invasion. Our sub arrived back at Portsmouth on the fifth. The infantry had been amassing ready for the following morning's invasion. There was such tension on their faces, I felt sorry for them – many of them young lads straight out of training. I got together sweets and cigarettes from the men on the base and threw them to those young soldiers. I was only 20 myself, but I was a veteran by then, which made me feel older.'

Franklin L. Betz
B-17 navigator, 379th Bomb Group, 8th Air Force, Kimbolton.

'We lifted off at 04:45. A fluffy layer of clouds below hampered visibility but there were some breaks and I could see the choppy dark waters of the English Channel. Droning steadily toward the continent, I gasped when a huge opening in the clouds revealed ships and boats of all sizes dotting the water as far as I could see. Hundreds – no, there must be thousands, I thought. Although no one type of ship could be identified from nearly three miles high, I was to learn later practically the whole spectrum of powered vessels from battleships to motor launches made up the invasion fleet.

'Landing ships, carrying thousands of troops, tanks,

guns, vehicles and ammunition, were positioning for the dash to the Normandy beaches. Barrage balloons swayed lazily above the ships to which they were attached by stout cables.

'More holes appeared in the clouds and the awesome spectacle continued to unfold. I rose from my seat in the navigator's cramped work area in the left rear of the B-17G's nose to get a better view from the right waist window. Fascinated, I saw puffs of white smoke from the huge guns of battleships and cruisers aimed toward the mainland and a moment later massive explosions could be seen a short distance inland where the shells landed, kicking up a fountain of dirt and debris. That, I reflected, must be a mixture of steel and stones, flesh and bones when the targets were hit.

'The Fortress, swaying gently, throbbed on. No sign of Me 109s or FW 190s but *our* "little friends" were out in force. The Lightnings, Thunderbolts and Mustangs, their invasion markings – black and white stripes on wings and fuselages – very prominent, were providing an aerial umbrella for the landing forces. Strafing the enemy positions up and down the coast and for some miles inland, they were determined to help the GIs embarking on the great crusade. The white-capped wake of hundreds of circling landing craft, awaiting the order to head to the shore, contributed to the drama of the scene.

'The cloud cover required a blind bombing technique using radar. According to my log we were close to the target; gun positions near Arromanches roughly midway between the Cherbourg peninsula and Le Havre. The bombs dropped from the bellies of the bombers, disappearing in the clouds to devastate and disrupt the enemy's fighting capabilities far below. The briefing officer was right. "There would be meagre flak, if any at all," he had said. There was none. The German guns were busily exchanging fire with the mighty invasion fleet massed in the Bay of the Seine and stretching for miles into the Channel. We touched down at 09:26 and I could sense an air of excitement on the base when I dropped to the ground from the plane after the pilot parked it in the dispersal area.

'"How was it, Lieutenant?" asked the crew chief in charge of keeping the Fortress flying, an intense look on his leathery face, weathered by the winds of his native Texas.

'"What I saw through the breaks in clouds was an unforgettable sight," I replied.

'There was no time to say anything more. A truck pulled up to take the crew to interrogation, after which we had to get ready for the afternoon flight, my 30th mission. B-17s continued to peel off from the formation and land as the sun shone brightly through the cloud covering that was breaking up. It was a good omen.'

Lieutenant Jim Tuffell

commanding an LCT carrying DD tanks of the 4th/7th Royal Dragoon Guards.

'There was no doubt in my mind that to launch these crack troops would have even worse results than the charge of the Light Brigade at Balaclava.'

231 Brigade, which was to capture 'Jig' sector to the right and 69 Brigade 'King' on the left, attacked on a two-battalion front with the 1st Hampshires on the right and the 1st Dorsets on the left. Fire from strongly defended positions at Le Hamel and Asnelles-sur-Mer, and a smaller strongpoint

near Les Roquettes covered 'Jig' Sector. Defences at La Riviere and Hable de Heurtot on the coast protected 'King' Section. Higher ground inland had defences at Mont Fleury and Ver-sur-Mer. Le Hamel presented a formidable target for the Hampshires. The beach was flat and sandy, bounded by a belt of low sand dunes. A gentle slope led to the sea wall of German 75-mm guns overlooking the shore. These were to enfilade the entire beach. Machine gunners and riflemen were stationed in every building overlooking the shore.

Unnamed officer in the Dorsets

'We had to move across the sand at some speed so that the "Deballiker" mines, which were designed to pierce between the legs, only hit one in the fleshy part of the behind. Most of us had seen men shot before but nothing like the damage done by Spandau fire and 88s. Men were blown apart and in the case of machine gun fire, men were hit a dozen times at once – not a chance for them to live. We had been trained in most all aspects and actually pretty well knew what to expect. However, it was not enough to bolster you for this kind of carnage. I took a few minutes on the beach to comprehend, adjust and move forward. Some did not …'

Lieutenant Irwin
Commander of an LCA assault group watching the East Yorks land and rush the beach.

'We were 50 yards away and saw it all. One man was wounded. Just like a rabbit. Up and down and up they crawled to the sea wall, which had to be stormed like a Middle Ages fortress. Germans on top of the sea wall were chucking hand grenades on to our soldiers below.'

Citation,
CSM Stan Hollis, Green Howards

the only man to win the VC on D-Day.

'During the assault on the beaches and the Mont Fleury battery CSM Hollis's Company Commander noticed that two of the pillboxes had been bypassed, and went with CSM Hollis to see that they were clear. When they were 20 yards from the pillbox a machine-gun opened fire from the slit, and CSM Hollis instantly rushed straight at the pill-box, recharged his magazine, threw a grenade in through the door and fired his Sten gun into it, killing two Germans and taking the remainder prisoner. He then cleared several Germans from a neighbouring trench. By his action he undoubtedly saved his Company from being fired on heavily from the rear, and enabled them to open the main beach exit. Later the same day, in the village of Crépon, the Company encountered a field gun and crew, armed with Spandaus, at a hundred yards' range. CSM Hollis was put in command of a party to cover an attack on the gun, but the movement was held up. Seeing this, CSM Hollis pushed right forward to engage the gun with a PIAT [Projector Infantry Anti-tank] from a house at 50 yards' range. He was observed by a sniper who fired and grazed his right cheek, and at the same moment the gun swung round and fired at point blank range into the house. To avoid the falling masonry CSM Hollis moved his party to an alternative position. Two of the enemy gun crew had by this time been killed, and the gun was destroyed shortly afterwards. He later found that two of his men had stayed behind in the house, and immediately volunteered to get them out. In full view of the enemy, who were continually firing at him, he went forward alone using a Bren gun to distract their attention from the other men. Under cover of his diversion the two men were able to get back.

'Wherever fighting was heaviest CSM Hollis appeared, and in the course of a magnificent day's work he displayed the utmost gallantry, and on two separate occasions his courage and initiative prevented the enemy from holding up the advance at critical stages. It was largely through his heroism and resource that the Company's objectives were gained and casualties were not heavier and, by his own bravery, he saved the lives of many of his men.'

Ken Mayo
'B' Squadron, Nottinghamshire (Sherwood Rangers)
Yeomanry, 8th Armoured Brigade.

'Within weeks of arriving back in England from the Middle East and in the short period before D-Day, I was to be physically thrown in at the deep end on the very secret Sherman (Duplex Drive) Tank. The DD was capable of swimming ashore from two miles out using its twin propellers and yet within minutes of reaching land, becoming a fighting tank. Intensive training found us ready. We loaded on board an LCT in Southampton Harbour on 2 June.

'I shall always remember our sailing from the Solent at midnight 5 June; we were on our way. The sea was very rough, little sleep was possible and in common with all aboard I was violently seasick. As dawn broke, we were amongst hundreds of ships of all sizes – then the Naval Bombardment started, shells and rockets screaming overhead with the RAF Fighter Bombers adding to the din. The whole coast was a pall of exploding missiles.

'We approached Gold beach and due to rough seas closed to 1,000 yards to launch at approximately 07:20 hours. Action stations were called – all crews were in their places. I had "netted in" the radio and our supporting canvas super-structure was inflated. The LCT ramp was lowered and we launched into a very choppy sea, then the shells and other incoming fire started to reach towards us but missed. I saw two of the Sherman "Flail Tanks" brewing up on the beach and wondered about our reception. We finally grounded on the beach, engaged the tracks, deflated the canvas sides and "hey presto" were ashore.

'The infantry of the 1st Hampshires were taking all possible cover on the beach from the withering fire from the pillboxes and the 88s on the high ground, which knocked out the tank on our right, a terrible sight to see the crew gunned down as they baled out. We then returned the fire from the pillbox, with success.

'At last the sappers taped off exits from the beach and we all began to move off through the sand dunes. When about 50 yards into our lane, there was a loud explosion. We had hit a mine, which damaged our nearside track. We were immobile. This didn't prevent us using our fire power to shell the many targets which presented themselves in support of the advance and to try and winkle out the snipers who were proving a real menace.

'I heard on my radio that our forward units were into Le Hamel and heading for Bayeux. Orders were given for us to sit tight and await the fitters so we closed down and gave what help we could on the beach. There was considerable congestion.

'Late that afternoon, we were standing beside our tank,

discussing the damaged track, when an armoured bulldozer came towards us widening the beach exit. Within a few feet of us, there was an almighty explosion. All went black and I was flung through the air into a minefield. I crawled towards the shouts of the crew and they bandaged me the best they could and took me to the nearest Field Dressing Station. I spent a very restless night in the open wrapped in a blanket with 'Jerry' strafing the area. Next day it was Hospital Ship to Portsmouth.

'After treatment and leave it was return to the unit and to discover the "Bocage" and to witness the destruction of Falaise. I was however, shaken to hear that the Regiment had already lost nearly a quarter of its Tank Commanders and many crewmen. A terrible sacrifice!'

Sergeant Robert 'Bob' E. Palmer MM

(later Battery Sergeant Major) who commanded No.I gun in 'F' Troop, 5II Battery, I47 Field Regiment, RA (Essex Yeomanry), which was equipped with Sexton SPs and was part of 8th Armoured Brigade attached to the 50th (Northumbrian) Division.

'One minute you would be seeing your mate and talking to him; the next you were having to put a field dressing on him, realizing it was too late and being thankful it wasn't you.'

During the day Bob was responsible for the destruction at Asnelles-sur-Mer of an 88 mm gun in an enormous and very strong emplacement, an anti-tank gun and two heavy machine guns, each in a fortified house. The 88 had already accounted for six British tanks. It held up the advance from the beach until it was destroyed at a range of 300 yards by a 25-pounder SP gun commanded by Sergeant

Palmer, who was awarded the Military Medal and was decorated by General Montgomery at a small place called 'Jerusalem'.

Major Peter Selerie
'B' Squadron, Sherwood Rangers Yeomanry.

'There was quite a shambles on the beach. Out of B Squadron's 19 original tanks, only five were still mobile. We paused on the outskirts of Le Hamel and were overtaken by one of the AVRE Churchill tanks armed with a Petard that looked like a short and wicked piece of drainpipe sticking out of the turret. It appeared that the Sergeant commanding it was the sole survivor of his troop. He joined our five tanks and confronted the back of a pillbox that housed an 88-mm gun firing along the beach. The gunner dropped a petard through the back door and blew the place up. We noticed a stream of enemy fire coming from a farmhouse. Then petard fired and something like a small dustbin hit the house and it collapsed like a pack of cards.'

The AVRE gun was a 290-mm mortar, which fired a 40-lb projectile. Only NSRY achieved their D-Day objective in capturing Bayeux on the morning of 7 June, with the assistance of the Commander of the AVRE Sexton tank, which opened the way.

Lieutenant H. Foster
A Canadian, serving with the Dorsets.

'You had the feeling of "what am I doing here?" Of all the thousands in uniform, how come I'm right at the front of what we knew was the biggest assault in history. There was another misgiving, which was more or less general that we would not return. This produced a deep calm, something observed in others.'

Ronald Scott, 20

radar operator, on the minesweeper HMS 'Ready', part of the 18th Flotilla which left the Solent on 5 June, in a letter home to his family.

'Five mighty cruisers were silhouetted against the streaks of light where the sun would soon rise. I don't think I have ever seen anything so impressive; it thrilled me through and through. Slowly the vessel nearest us brought its powerful guns round. Then – Boom! Boom! Two resounding crashes. They sounded to me as if they said, "WE'RE HERE!" for they were the first shots fired in the invasion. Then all the other ships opened fire and it became one series of ear-splitting salvos after another ... I think that night was the most dreadful one I have ever been through ... In the dawn half-light, our task completed, we were free, more or less, to steam up and down, having a good look at everything. There was a terrific bombardment at one end of the bridgehead and when we got there we found two battleships firing away for all they were worth. We were right up close to one – so close we could even hear the sigh of the shells as they left those massive guns. Just before dusk, in the distance, we saw one solid mass of aircraft; wave after wave of troop transports towing gliders – hundreds and hundreds of them. I have never seen so many aircraft all at once. They seemed never-ending and stretched far back into the distance ... We sweated blood when we first went in, but it was very exciting too. None of our ships was affected by mines so we knew we had done our job properly.'

Leutnant Wolfgang Fischer

3/Jagdgeschwader 2.

'In the early hours of 6 June, about 05:00 hours, on the warning of the invasion we were ordered to Criel, just outside Paris. There in all haste our "Dodels" were prepared and we took off at about 09:30 hours for our first low-level attack on the landing fleet in the English sector of Caen–Bayeux. The landing craft provided excellent targets for the aircraft of our *1* and *3 Staffeln*.

'On the evening of the first day we only had three serviceable FW190s. Hauptmann Huppertz landed at about 20:00 with eight FW190s of his *III Gruppe*. Together with the three aircraft of our *I Gruppe*, he was going to lead an attack on the beachhead and upon freight-carrying gliders. From our *I Gruppe* flew Leutnant Eickhoff, Oberfähnrich Bär and myself. We took off shortly after 20:30 and approached at low level the great road bridge over Risle, west of Bernay. There we saw 12 Mustangs shooting-up a German supply column. We were too late to help, so Huppertz led us away in a left turn at about 1,200 metres. We headed for a light evening haze. It was then that we saw the other "Indians". We dodged away from eight Mustangs, then we caught four more. I got mine in a high reverse turn as he approached the bridge. He fell on fire into a wooded bank on the Risle and set a tree on fire. I then observed Huppertz and his Katchmarek attack another aircraft. The fire was devastating and the Mustang disintegrated. Eickhoff and Bär each scored an *Abschuss*. After landing at Senlis, two reporters sent in confirmation of our victories, for they had seen the whole battle.'

Fischer's combat career ended abruptly on 7 June, when his FW190 was shot down by AA gunfire while attacking shipping off the British beaches. He survived to become a prisoner. His commander, Herbert Huppertz, was credited with five Mustangs destroyed on 6 June.

Lieutenant John Milton
6th Battalion The Green Howards.

'... We had several skirmishes during the day but the talk that night was inevitably of the gallantry of our Sergeant Major, Stan Hollis, who was subsequently awarded the only D-Day Victoria Cross.'

Lieutenant Basil Heaton
86 (Herts Yeomanry) Field Regiment RA.

'I was the junior officer in a troop of four self-propelled guns. Our role was to bombard the beaches from the sea (the run-in shoot) and then go ashore behind the first wave of infantry. We opened fire at 06:50, closing on the shore at the rate of 200 yards per minute, and landed at 08:05 in support of 69 Infantry Brigade. We landed just below the Ver-sur-Mer lighthouse and in front of the dreaded Mont Fleury Battery. The 6th Green Howards attacked this gun position with great gallantry and CSM Hollis won a VC. On their left the 5th East Yorks took the lighthouse and by 09:00 our guns were clear of the beach and deployed in this area. By nightfall the brigade had advanced seven miles to come within sight of the Caen–Bayeux road. We spent the night in Crépon preparing a fire programme for the dawn counter-attack. The beachhead was secure.

'The sun went down three times that day. And we were very young.'

Many outstanding acts of gallantry were performed. Two

Victoria Crosses and ten American Medals of Honor were awarded between D-Day and D+12.

Eric Broadhead
9th Battalion Durham Light Infantry, I5Ist Brigade aboard LCI(L) 50I.

'Monday 5 June passed with an awful tension although somehow we had loads of fun whistling to Wrens on the dockside. At 21:00 we were issued with seasickness pills. That was enough. We knew by morning we should be in less peaceful waters. That evening *501* weighed anchor and slid slowly down the river into sailing position. We sat on the decks, looked towards the shore, still calling to any female that could be spied, but behind all these joking habits, much deeper thoughts passed through the minds of everyone aboard.

'As darkness fell, we went below decks and lay on our bunks fully clothed. Outside the wind was howling even more as we turned out to sea. I dozed off before we really turned on full steam, only to be awakened by a horribly sickly feeling inside. *501* was rolling in every imaginable direction; the seasickness pills had failed if ever anything did fail, and there was only one thing to do, that was to lie still; even that was dreadful and only served to make one feel worse.

'Time passed. I felt more ill than ever before. It was beyond dawn and it was only a few hours before we must engage an enemy of unknown strength. About 05:00 I made a supreme effort and crawled on deck. The Yankee sailors manning every gun were dressed in sheepskin clothing and all carried a revolver as only a Yank dare wear it, Hopalong Cassidy style. The lovely fresh air on deck was worth a million pounds. The scene was unforgettable. Over a vast expanse of the Channel there were ships of every type – from small Naval MTBs and Landing Craft to HMS *Rodney* and her escort. Overhead an array of the immense power of the RAF roared through the skies, each and every plane heading for France. The sea was rolling and in the morning sunlight it was a picture that could not be forgotten. I was on deck less than half an hour. Looking at the sea only served to send me back to lie on my bunk.

'The rough sea complicated the landing. Around 07:00 we were ordered to dress with all kit. We were below decks wondering what was going on. Heavy Naval gunfire could be heard. *501* had landing ramps, which dropped down from her side into the sea, or the beach where it was possible for her to nose far enough in. It was when these ramps dropped we knew the voyage was over. We scrambled up on deck. The kit we had was terrific. Our waterproof jackets came up to one's chest from one's feet. I tore these as I struggled on deck. Only a matter of yards away was the French coast but it was too far to keep dry. As we scrambled along *501*'s decks, Naval personnel were shouting, "Get ashore!" Ships were everywhere like a traffic jam. Down the ramps we went but this only led into the ship in front, across its decks. Then came ten horrible yards between ship and shore with water in between. Over the ship's side, still dizzy from seasickness, and into water four feet deep, each one let out a gasp as the water swirled around. We struggled for shore. It was the hardest ten yards I ever did but we all got ashore, mighty thankful to be off *501* and her terrible motion, even if the harbour was the beaches of Arromanches. It was a godsend that all this took place with nothing more than heavy naval gunfire. It became apparent that the enemy had been taken by surprise, at least in our particular section of the attack. One thing was supreme; the water had brought me round like a footballer's magic sponge. Seasickness was gone. We were ashore. After five minutes regrouping as a battalion, I saw a German soldier for the first time. The lads who beat us ashore were bringing him in as a prisoner. The last few hours had brought us 80 miles from Southampton to what was to become one of the greatest beachheads ever.

HMS *Rodney*, a 16-inch gun battleship, part of the Bombarding Force reserve, left the Solent at 02:53 on 7 June and ran down and sank LCT 427 *en route* for Sword then Juno. On 11 June *Rodney* and another reserve battleship, *Nelson* arrived off the beaches and pounded targets ashore until 18 June.

Wing Commander A. H. D. Livock

controller on HM LSH (Landing Ship, Headquarters) 'Bulolo', the converted Australian (Burns, Philip) liner built in 1938, which arrived off Gold Beach at 05:56 on 6 June.

'The regularity with which large formations of our own aircraft of every type flew over reminded one of Clapham Junction during a Bank Holiday weekend'.

Bulolo was damaged by a bomb near the operations room at 06:05 on 7 June and her upperworks were superficially damaged when rammed by *Empire Pitt* on 15 June.

Private Ken McFarlane

Anti-Tank Platoon, the Ist Battalion Dorset Regiment,
23Ist Infantry Brigade, 50th Northumbrian Division.

'... It was a bit bumpy in a flat bottom LCT and then the Padre came on board and told us that we were not landing until the morning (6 June), blessed us and left. I sat in the Carrier all night waiting for dawn. At first light I stood up in my seat and looked at all the ships. We seemed to be marking time. The day passed slowly, as we didn't seem to have much to say to each other, another day being tossed about. We all said, "Roll on morning."

'As Tuesday dawned there was a flurry of activity. Sitting in a Bren Carrier the field of view was limited but I could see planes overhead. Then at last we started a square run for the beach. Suddenly there was a big bang from the stern and we started to go in at an acute angle, and then when the ramp went down, the matting was washed along the beach. The first carrier drove off on the angle and turned turtle. We drifted a few feet then the boat marshall waved me to go out. I stood up on my seat and said that the tank was supposed to go next. He said, "Bollocks, get out now", so I shut my eyes and eased off the ramp with my heart in my mouth. As the next bit had been practiced so often, I carried on as a drill, over the sand, through the gap, on to the beach road, turn right, forward a few yards and wait for my gun crew to join me. This they did eventually. My sergeant, Lofty Dawson, said, "Get the waterproofing off." While I did this he joined the crew in the ditch. I asked Lofty what the puffs of smoke were all over the sky.

'"Airbursts," he said.

'"What were they for?" I asked. When he said that they

were shrapnel shells, I shrank as low as I could to finish the job without being too big a target … My D-Day was a very long day. I had no watch but time just seemed to stand still.'

Private Reginald 'Punch' Burge
the 2nd Battalion, The Devonshire Regiment.

'We knew that we were destined for France when we were issued with French money. Our vehicles were water-proofed, our Bren Gun Carriers had extra sides, a metre in height, fitted and all were loaded to the hilt. My carrier was filled with .303 ammo, 2- and 3-inch Mortar Bombs, petrol in jerrycans and a roll of wattle fencing tied to the front. We sailed on 5 June and on the morning of the sixth we approached Gold Beach (Jig sector). The tide was so strong we drifted over towards the Canadian sector and landed broadside against the obstacles which had mines attached to the tops. The ramp was lowered and we could see bodies of the commandos who had gone in ahead of us to clear the mines. On being given the order to disembark I drove off, turned left and reached the beach safely although two carriers were immediately drowned in deep water. We pushed on up the beach amid the chaos and the noise of the naval bombardment and the rocket barrage, which was really terrifying. We were ordered to keep going forward and we made our way down the country roads. As we turned on to the main road we hit a mine on the grass verge, which knocked out a front bogie. Nobody was injured so we shortened the track and drove on. We pushed on until the evening when we regrouped at Le Hamel with the Battalion Mortar Platoon and the Anti Tank Platoon. On the seventh we pushed on to Port-en-Bessin to help 47 Marine Commando who were having a bad time. By the 11th we had reached the crossroads at La Belle Epine where I was directed towards an apple orchard. I reached the orchard and on turning into it came face to face with a dug-in Tiger Tank. That was the lot for me. When I came to I was in hospital in Basingstoke in England.

'I was one of the first in on D-Day and there were bodies all washed up on the beach. How we got on the beach I don't know. It makes me wonder why I am still alive. Why wasn't I one of those who was killed?'

QM Sergeant Robert Fitzgerald

aboard an LST.

'We could hear firing in the distance as we approached the shoreline, which we reached at about 05:00. I remember remarking at the time on the absence of an aircraft though one did appear, dropped two bombs and flew off in a hail of anti-aircraft fire from our ships in the vicinity. I asked one of the crew if the plane was a Stuka? In a very broad scouse (Liverpool) accent he said, "It were and I just shook my fist at him and said, You did not get me at Liverpool or London and you ain't going to get me yet, and with that the beggar missed!" I remarked that with this sort of spirit we were going to win this war.'

Major R. J. L. Jackson

6th Battalion, The Green Howards.

'The beach was completely deserted as we approached and I remember being puzzled by the comparative silence. At every step we expected to be fired at but were not. The lack of opposition became eerie. Then, after about 200 yards, we must have reached a German fixed line. Suddenly they threw everything at us. The mortars took us first and I was hit badly in the leg. My radio operator and policeman were both killed outright by the same explosion.'

Private Reg Shickle
2nd Battalion, The Cheshire Regiment.

'A young naval officer addressed us over the tannoy and told us that the shoreline along Gold Beach was planted with steel girders with mines attached. He added that when he was a few miles from the shore, he intended to "put his foot down" and get us as close to the beach as possible. "Meanwhile, gentlemen, get some sleep; I'll let you know when."

'"Hear this! Hear this!"

'I realized I must have dozed off. How, I don't know, for the noise was tremendous. It came from the battleships all around us, and the shells and rockets that were firing towards the beach. Two hundred yards, 100 yards. Then crash! Our craft came to a shuddering halt amid a loud explosion. A jeep that should have been first off was no more. In its place was a gaping hole in the deck. The ramp went down. With the engine of my Bren carrier roaring, I rammed it into first gear, let off the brakes and shot over the hole into the sea. Its tracks gripped the beach and we moved slowly forward. An eternity then fresh air. On the shore, Hagerty, one of my crew, was looking dumbly down at his leg. His foot had been blown off. This was our first casualty. This was the invasion of Normandy.'

Private Dennis Bowen, 18

5th Battalion, The East Yorkshire Regiment.

'I was a soldier of the wonderful 69th Brigade; a battalion of East Yorkshire and two battalions of Green Howards – my heroes – who had already defeated the Germans. How could we lose or come to any harm?

'The struggle across Gold Beach, the casualties, the heat, noise and exhaustion of the fight were absolutely indescribable. I know I should have died of fright alone without the calmness under fire of these wonderful fighters wearing the ribbon of the Africa Star who taught me to survive that day.'

Bill Davey, 19

Commando Combined Operations Unit.

'Our job was to land on 'Jig' Beach at first light with the advance units to clear away, repair or blow up any shipping hindering landing craft and troops. Because everyone was stacked up we had to wait until late afternoon before we could go in. We passed the time playing cards and my mate Eddie and I cut each other's hair. At first it seemed like a Boy Scout outing to me. I was a bit worried and apprehensive, but I don't think it occurred to me we might get killed. We finally rode in alongside a destroyer with its aft guns blazing – the finest sight I've ever seen. Six shells dropped round our landing craft as we neared the beachhead and underwater obstacles that couldn't be seen because of the high spring tide holed the ballast tanks.

'We immediately came under fire. I will never forget the sheer noise. There was so much going on, with mortar shells banging and guns shooting all round, I went temporarily deaf. It was a warm day and so we stripped everything off. We all had to make do with cheap-looking swimming belts to keep us afloat when we jumped in the water. On the beach we were told by the naval officer in charge to get to work immediately but mortar shells were exploding everywhere.

'I crawled round to safety behind a tank that had had its tracks blown off. To my surprise, I found the tank's two crew crouched there eating tins of pears out of an 'A' Compo Box. They shared the pears with me and told me to keep my head down. Compos were officers' rations and they had the best food. They included tins of soup with heat trips down the middle. In about three or four seconds you had real hot soup. There were Compo Boxes lying about all over the place, left behind by the dead and wounded, so you just took what you found.

'After the shells stopped I joined my mate. He was sheltering against our landing craft. Soon our unit got together and did what we came to do, like digging dead soldiers out of the sand and rolling them in grey army blankets. This was the worst job. We were ordered to cover up our dead soldiers, but to leave the enemy lying, for morale purposes. There were bodies everywhere. At one point I sat down on what I thought was a log with a blanket on it. It was only when I saw a boot sticking out I realized there was a body underneath.'

Gold Beach Timetable

07:25 British XXX Corps', 50th Infantry Division and 8th Armoured Brigade: hit a defensive wall of 2,500 steel and concrete obstacles with strong German troop emplacements behind on a three-mile stretch of coast. They come under heavy artillery fire.

As with all the British beaches, success hinges on the speed with which tanks can be put ashore. The tanks of 8th Armoured Brigade are landed by the 15th LCT Flotilla under Lieutenant Commander Porteous. (They subsequently land the 7th Armoured Division and many hundreds of tanks and armoured vehicle reinforcements until Mulberry is fully operational.) For the six assault regiments on Sword, Juno and Gold with DD tanks the weather is considered too rough to launch. However, this is not communicated to two regiments – the Nottinghamshire (Sherwood Rangers) Yeomanry, which launches from 1,000 yards out (and the 13th/18th Hussars, which launches from 4,000 yards out at Sword Beach). The remainder are landed dry on the beaches and cause some delay in supporting the infantry regiments. Four of the first five flail tanks on to the beach at Le Hamel are knocked out, burn furiously, and bulbous black clouds of smoke envelop the leading troops and obscure the beach.

C and D Companies, Royal Hampshires, having reached the sea wall east of Le Hamel, exploit a gap in the coastal wire and minefield belt and push inland in depth, outflank and capture Asnelles.

By 08:00 this movement is under way.

By mid-morning landings of the follow-up assault bring the 7th Armoured Division – The Desert Rats – ashore.

By nightfall British forces hold five square miles and almost reach the Caen–Bayeux road. 25,000 men land. Casualties, 1,000.

Order of Battle Gold Beach

**50th British (Northumberland) Division
Major General Douglas Graham
69th Infantry Brigade**
5th Bn The East Yorkshire Regiment
6th Bn The Green Howards
7th Bn The Green Howards

151st Infantry Brigade
6th Bn The Durham Light Infantry
8th Bn The Durham Light Infantry
9th Bn The Durham Light Infantry

23Ist Infantry Brigade
2nd Bn The Devonshire Regiment
1st Bn The Hampshire Regiment
1st Bn The Dorsetshire Regiment

Divisional Troops
HO 50th Infantry Division
61st Reconnaissance Regiment, RAC
357th, 385th and 465th Btys, 90th Field Regiment, RA
99th and 288th Btys, 102nd Anti-Tank Regiment, RA
233rd, 295th and 505th Field Companies, RE
235th Field Park Company, RE
2nd Bn The Cheshire Regiment (MG)
Units under command for assault phase

8th Armoured Brigade
4th/7th Royal Dragoon Guards Nottinghamshire Yeomanry
(Sherwood Rangers)
24th Lancers

56th Infantry Brigade
2nd Bn The South Wales Borderers
2nd Bn The Gloucestershire Regiment
2nd Bn The Essex Regiment
Elements of 79th Armoured Division
2nd County of London Yeomanry (Westminster Dragoons)
2 Troops 141st Regiment, RAC
6th Assault Regiment, RE
86th and 147th Field Regiments, RA
394th and 395th Btys

I20th Light Anti-Aircraft Regiment, RA

73rd and 280th Field Companies, RE
1st RM Armoured Support Regiment
47 RM Commando
GHQ Liaison Regiment

Beach Groups

2nd Bn The Hertfordshire Regiment
6th Bn The Border Regiment

Plus elements of:
Royal Corps of Signals
Royal Army Service Corps
Royal Army Medical Corps
Royal Army Ordnance Corps
Corps of Royal Electrical and Mechanical Engineers
Corps of Military Police
Pioneer Corps

Juno

E. J. Thompson
aboard the destroyer HMS 'Kempenfelt', a gunfire
support vessel in Assault Convoy JIO escort.

'Captain M. L. Power told the assembled ship's company that our target was some six-inch shore-based guns, the position of which was known exactly from air reconnaissance. There were some larger guns and possibly some shore-based torpedo tubes, but these would be looked after by the cruisers and battleships and that we must not be distracted from our allocated target. He also told the ship's company that the six destroyers in the flotilla would be anchoring for accurate bombardment about two miles off shore with the anchors on the "slip" for quick getaway. If after firing a few salvoes there was no response from the shore defences we would raise anchors and again anchor accurately closer in. If we were badly hit he would beach the ship and "whatever happened – if the bridge or gun control got shot away" we were to keep on firing under local control if necessary.

'HMS *Kempenfelt* led her flotilla in some time before the invasion fleet arrived. Early morning mist was around but it was only shallow, as a steeple and water-tower were all too clearly visible at that range, sticking up through the mist ... The First Lieutenant looked up at the gradually clearing shore and said cheerfully "La Belle France!" The anchored destroyers then fired several salvoes without any reaction at all from the shore, so according to plan the anchor cables were connected up and a new position taken up close in shore ... Still there was no response. Rocket launchers "wooshed" off their rows and rows of rocket salvoes. Invasion barges passed through and it was not until they were touching the sand that the sparks of rifle fire could be seen coming from all the windows of the buildings along the seafront. We wished we could lower our urns and flatten them, but we continued to fire at our allotted Shore Battery positions – and got not a single shell back. After the experience of Anzio and the build-up we had been given it was quite an anti-climax ...'

Lieutenant Roy Clark, 33
RNVR, Commander, LCT 770, 36th Flotilla.
'I was having a game of pontoon when the signal arrived for our part in D-Day to begin. Just after midday we

slipped our moorings and set off for the Normandy coast. On board LCT 770 we had sections of the 9th Canadian Brigade as well as armoured vehicles. A Canadian major asked me, "Will we need our Wellingtons?" meaning would his troops get their feet wet?

'I said, "No, we will take you all the way to the beach."

'The Solent was jam-packed with every type of vessel imaginable; it was as if you could walk across the water, there were so many. I suppose I was a bit nervous when you think I smoked 60 cigarettes that night.

'We were travelling at about four and a half to five knots when at about 01:30 the bombardment started. I reckoned it was about 40 miles away by the flashes I could see in the sky. I reached my waiting position off "Mike Green" beach near Courselles-sur-Mer. There were cruisers, battleships and destroyers all around us. It was daylight by now, the sea had quietened a little and it was quite warm. I reached my waiting position but there was so much congestion in the water we had to put back our beaching from 09:50 to 03:10. For five minutes before we hit the beach I gave the two 1,000-hp Davey Paxman diesel engines (originally used to power tanks) everything we had and ran full speed for the shore.

'I came up on the starboard quarter of Des Lewis's LCT 632, which went in first. It hit a tetrahedra, a metal triangle with a teller mine attached. The mine exploded but LCT 632 carried on. Des, a New Zealander, shouted, "We've got the bastards, Nobby! We've got the bastards!" He was of course referring to the Germans. (I didn't see Des again until 1950 when I heard his booming voice in a bar at the Waterloo Hotel in Wellington.) There was tremendous German activity, especially from snipers, while we were getting our lads on to "Mike Green". We were stuck there for four hours until high tide refloated us.

'After an hour or so, while we were having lunch, three German aircraft came in from the southeast. For some reason they took a liking to us, probably because we were a sitting target. I went to the bridge in time to see their bomb doors open. Though the bombs missed us by about 25 yards LCT 770, all 360s tons of her, was moved 18 inches, though all the explosions did was to cover us in mud and shingle. I had a very good port gunner and he opened up on one of the bombers with his 20mm Oerlikon cannon. The bomber went down over the hills inshore. Half a dozen other vessels were firing too so we never claimed it. It was like shooting pheasants, when everyone is tempted to claim the downed bird!

'An LCE opened up on a German-held bungalow right on the beach. I was flashed up by Aldis: "Can you fire into those dummy windows? I can't do any good." We opened up with the starboard Oerlikon and filled the windows with shells and tracers. A bunch of Germans came out with their hands up. We continued firing and at the same time soldiers in the sand dunes were firing as well.

'Finally, the high tide refloated us and we reached our waiting convoy position to join a convoy heading back to Stokes Bay.

'Three months later, I was sitting in the Oasis restaurant at Arromanches and got talking to a Frenchman, André Andelhof. He asked, had I been on D-Day? I told him that I beached my LCT a mile or so from where I was now sitting but before this a 75mm gun on shore had begun firing at our flotilla and the big shells began exploding around us. Using outstretched hands the Canadian major looked up at me on the bridge and pointed this way and that to indicate where each shell was coming from and I interpreted them. We steered "port", and a shell exploded where we had been; then "starboard" and "ahead". Each shell missed but they had our range. They were going to sink us. Then suddenly, the firing miraculously stopped.

'André listened to my story and said that he was in the Maquis. He asked me what was my craft? I told him LCT 770 with a big "P" on the side. André said that they saw a craft in danger and his resistance group had crept up on the German gun position. It was a hot day and the German gunners had their helmets unstrapped and hanging on the back of their neck. André's men twisted the German gunners' helmets and throttled them all.

'The Oasis had very few bottles of wine left that night.'

Sergeant Leo Gariepy
Canadian 6th Armoured Regiment.
'The German machine-gunners in the dunes were absolutely stupefied to see a tank emerge from the sea. Some ran away, some just stood up in their nests and stared, mouths wide open. To see tanks coming out of the water shook them rigid.'

Jim Gadd
bulldozer operator.
'Our instructions were that the bulldozer operators had to start the machines up around 06:00 so the engines were warm when we entered the water. Mine would not start but when the ramp went down and the Centaur in front of me pulled off I was able to use the manual start. The bulldozer to my left started to approach the ramp. We were under

heavy fire from those who were supposed to be too dazed to fight back, when the operator misjudged his alignment going down into the sea and slid sideways blocking the exit. I was called on to get in position to tow the beleaguered machine back up the ramp in a straight line.

'Because of the noise and the poor visibility I had sitting down in the turret looking through the bullet proof visors, I had to stand up and expose my head like a coconut on a stand. A Canadian engineer, crouched behind perched on the Hyster winch, gave me instructions to get the towrope in place. I had just managed to right the machine in front and off it went when I was hit in the face with such force it left me slumped into the bottom of the turret dazed and bleeding. A voice called out to me, "Are you OK? Would you like a spare operator to take over?" My answer was "No". I was not being brave but climbing out of the turret would make me a sitting duck.

'Whatever the missile was that hit me had been fired from the pillbox directly in front of us. I examined my wound. It had slit my left cheek and I had small abrasions above my left eye and right cheek. I took my field dressing out and tied it round my face in the manner of one suffering with a toothache, tying the knot on the top of my head. I then went down the ramp into the water making for a place to give cover to my Canadian ground crew so that we could regroup and try and make out how best to tackle the job we were sent to do. Of the four bulldozers that landed from my craft two operators were badly wounded by mortars. One was the one who had blocked the exit. Another had struck a mine. (It was a few days before I had time to go into a field dressing station to have my wounds seen to; they were not life threatening.)

'We were being pinned down by the fortification that was directly above us. The Canadian captain got in touch with the two Centaurs and they made their way up behind the Germans and put the fortification out of action. My crew and I started to dismantle the obstacles and mines so that we could get at the telegraph pole devices. I was able to flatten them but we were unable to explode the explosive heads because they had too much pitchblend around the nose caps to protect them from the seawater.

'On D+1 we moved inland where I was being used to remove German and our own damaged vehicles and remove other debris cluttering the road to Caen. Then we got the message that a *Panzer* group was trying to cut us off so we had to fall back to the beach.

Malcolm Cook, 19

Wireman LCT(A) 2306, IO3rd Flotilla Second Support Squadron.

'As we passed the battleships the bombardment was going on and great belches of smoke were coming from their guns. The LCT(R)s were firing their salvoes of rockets and again there were great clouds of black smoke. A flight of Spitfires got caught in the salvo and one burst into flames and fell away to our port side. We passed the LC(A) carrier ships lowering their craft full of infantry and some were already heading for the beach. We had gone to action stations and would soon be at beaching stations. The noise was ear-splitting and expectations were at high pitch. The troops were prepared and alert. We were approaching the shore and Berniers-sur-Mer was on our port side. I saw shot hitting the church spire. To starboard was open land with a farmhouse in the distance. Bofors fire and tracer was going in to the farmhouse. The craft was lodged on the obstacles and as the waves came along it would lift the bow and then it would drop down on to the obstacles puncturing the hull. The rear of the craft was slewed to port and the props were also fouling the obstacles and stalling. The stokers were desperately trying to restart the engines. You could hear the "thunk" as they engaged. (In fact the propeller blades were being torn off: of the three shafts there was only one blade out of 12 which survived...)

'There looked to be a very bad situation on shore. A large number of men could be seen under the shelter of the sea wall. They were without arms or helmets and looked in a critical position. These men were survivors from damaged LC(A)s, which had sunk attempting to navigate through the obstacles. One of the army officers on board us tried to swim ashore to see if he could help but he was washed back and dragged onboard exhausted. As the LC(A)s went in the Germans opened up and one to starboard lost many men. Perhaps 20 or more men fell in an arrowhead. One or two struggled to get up and then fell back.

'We were in a bad situation sinking slowly on to the beach. Then there was an almighty explosion on the port side and the craft heeled over to starboard. We had hit a mine. The engine room was flooding and we were going down on to the beach. The skipper gave the order to "abandon ship". Then realizing we were on the bottom he belayed the order and we watched the water come up the tank deck and up to the mess deck door. But it came no higher. Someone said to come and help a chap in the water. They said the firing had stopped. He was an LC(A) coxswain, a Royal Marine. His craft had sunk and he was swimming for dear life. We had to lower a man down to grab hold of him and then dragged him up the side, got him down below with a blanket and a tin of self-heating soup. He was saying, "You saved my life. You saved my life."

'The Canadians had secured the beach and we had a look round. Everywhere there were dead men lying in all sorts of positions. Mostly Canadians, you could see the darker green uniforms. Damaged craft and debris, what a spectacle of despair and sadness.'

These craft were equipped with Centaur tanks mounting 95-mm howitzers on special ramps at the forward end of the tank deck. Their job was to give fire support to the troops on the beach, an idea that evolved from the disaster at Dieppe when initial troop landings were decimated by enemy fire.

Unnamed Canadian Officer

'At about 07:15 we could see the long low line of white cliffs. Already great columns of smoke were rising. The Air Force was doing its job with a vengeance. The battleships were throwing in their share of stuff. Things were beginning to liven up. At about 08:00 our craft formed line and we were going in. I was on the verge of descending from the bridge when a shell tore through our rigging and another burst in the water a few yards away. It had no restraining influence on me. I almost jumped from the bridge and I had on my "light assault jacket" which weighed at least a hundredweight.

'Most of the fellows were ready to go in, their Mae Wests giving them all an outlandish shape. I was very interested in the expression on their faces. Some looked like a wounded spaniel, some were quite nonchalant about it. Others made a feeble effort at gaiety. What amused me most was a fat boy trying to whistle but the best he could do was blow air with a squeak now and then. Just between ourselves I was pretty scared myself about that time. Those last few moments were pretty awful. It was the waiting that was hard. We were coming under pretty intense small arms fire by this time and everyone was down as much as possible.

'At last the gangways were run down and it was a case of get up, get in and get down. I manoeuvered into position to be as near as possible to the front. I wanted to be one of the first to land; not because of any heroics, but waiting your turn on the exposed ramp was much worse than going in. A sergeant and a corporal started down. I was third. The sergeant couldn't touch bottom but pushed away and swam in towards shore. The corporal started to follow and I plunged in but the weight of my "light" jacket, filled with enough canned goods to start a grocery store, pulled me under, in spite of my Mae West. I got back on to the ramp and the skipper, very sensibly, decided to pull off and try and come in a bit better. A couple of sharp cracks in the water near me made me jump on to that ramp in a hurry. While I was floundering about in the water, the corporal got into trouble. There was a terrific backwash and only quick action by a brave Merchant Navy lad saved him from drowning.

'The next run at the shore put me in about three foot six inches of water. A naval fellow with a life belt went in with a rope and I followed. I must have been a ridiculous sight, holding on to my pistol in one hand and a bag of my valuables (mostly cigs) in the other, as well as trying to hold on to the rope. Some of the men had great difficulty getting ashore, particularly the short ones. One poor chap was crushed to death when the ramp broke away in the heavy seas and slammed him between it and the side of the ship.

'I didn't lose much time getting to the back of the beach where there was a bit of protection, and wriggled out of my assault jacket. I swore then and there never to wear that thing again. Many of the assault troops had already crossed the beach and were fighting forward towards their objective, a ridge a few hundred yards back from the beach. The houses along the waterfront were well stocked with snipers, having been bypassed by our forward troops. If, as the radio announced later, it was an unopposed landing, God forbid that anyone should ever have to go in on an opposed one! Our beach was littered with those who had been a jump ahead of us. A captured blockhouse being used as a dressing station was literally surrounded by piles of bodies. Many of the lads on our LCI never got ashore. A Spandau opened up just when the water was full of men struggling to get ashore.

'I crawled and ran to the place where I was to meet the rest of our little organization. This was accomplished without mishap except that a tin hat, much too small for me, which I had borrowed from a poor chap, was knocked from my head by something or other, which I neither saw nor heard.

'The afternoon and evening of D-Day was devoted to "delousing" the houses behind our beach, and quite a job it was. We were a bit clumsy at first and lost quite a few because of it, but soon it became more or less a drill. We found ourselves in little groups, nothing intentional or premeditated on anyone's part. I had a small group of two sergeants and six sappers. They had plenty of guts and were simply eager when we formed a plan to "do" a certain house. By dark most of the houses in our immediate vicinity were clean. My loot up to that point was a swastika flag, which I had torn from the wall of a sort of HQ or Mess. Some of the houses just refused to be deloused so we burned them. We set one on fire, which had caused us a lot of grief, and when it really started to brew one young 'Jerry' made an effort to escape through a window. He got partly out when a gunner on an LCT saw him. A streak of about 50 Oerlikon rounds hit him. He hung there for a couple of days until a burial party found him ...'

Mike Crooks

RN Chaplain.

'On Monday the long wait ended. The engines of our American LST at anchor in the Thames Estuary came alive, the rumble of the anchor chain, the engine room telegraph and we were off. The LST was fitted out as a hospital ship (of sorts) for the return journey, with rows of folding bunks on each side of the tank space and an operating table in the Ward Room (Officers Mess). It is impossible to describe the feeling of relief. It was strangely exhilarating. The sense of brooding suddenly evaporated and gave way to smiling faces, jokes, light-heartedness and rudery. Out to sea we went, past North Foreland, Ramsgate, the Goodwins, much too far out in the Channel for my liking. There was France on our left with all its heavy coastal artillery. They must presently blow us to pieces but strangely not a shot was fired. Two destroyers passed at speed laying a welcome smoke screen. On and on we went in this ever-growing, awe-inspiring fleet heading for "Piccadilly Circus", the area south of the Isle of Wight where the ships from the East met those from the West and were joined by a monumental armada from Portsmouth, Southampton and the Solent. This was something the world had never seen before, the biggest invasion in history – 4,000 ships. The Spanish Armada had 130!

'Night came and another day – D-Day. Looking from the bridge we saw men moving about, some sitting on top of the covered wagons, one playing a banjo, one having a haircut, gunners swivelling their weapons – a spirit of nonchalance. Then came the voice of the BBC Home Service at full volume throughout the ship: "Under the command of General Eisenhower, allied Naval Forces began landing allied armies this morning on the Northern coast of France." The already high spirits went even higher – jubilation! But this was short-lived for we were approaching a large curious-looking object in the water and passed close by it. It was the underside of an upturned landing craft. It had a sobering effect, and your imagination is as good as mine.

'Soon we were at our appointed landing place and were ordered to anchor offshore until the beachhead was secure as we were carrying highly secret equipment which must not fall into enemy hands. My church pennant was now hoisted. Canadian and British troops had stormed the defences and we listened to the battle further along the beach and just behind the rising ground in front of us. A signal came from ashore, "Send in your chaplain". Three US sailors delivered me ashore in one of our assault craft.

On grounding they dropped the ramp and I was about to step into the water when I was suddenly swept off my feet by two large sailors and planted dry-shod on the sand. Then they began to dance about with boyish delight at being on Juno Beach on D-Day. I thought, "I wish to God they would do it somewhere else!"

'I went on my way up the beach walking (like that Old Testament character Agag who "walked delicately".) There was a Sherman Flail Tank going to and fro exploding mines. I was astounded at the number of them, mostly small but occasionally a big one when the tank would immediately stop (and the chains hang limply down) whilst the driver had time to recover from the blinding blast and concussion right in front of his face. Things were relatively quiet apart from sniping. Of course there were artillery shells, mines and booby traps and occasional hit-and-run raids by enemy aircraft. It was no place for German pilots that day for we had 11,000 aircraft in the sky.

'My first encounter was with three Canadian soldiers who had been in a slit trench, five of them, when a bomb landed in one end. When it exploded so did a petrol bowser across the road. These three men had no hair on their faces, no eyelashes, no eyebrows and no hair below the line of their helmets. Their faces were scorched scarlet. They were in a sorry state, scarcely knowing where they were. I asked about the other two. Couldn't find a trace of the first. Of the second all we could find of him was in a sack on the ground. You could pick it up with one hand.

'Having stayed with them for a time I moved on to the wounded on stretchers, (the majority of them were Germans as they had suffered a fearful bombardment from sea and air before our landing) and then on to the burial of the dead. (These casualties were later exhumed and moved to war cemeteries.)

'There was much work to be done that day, "The Longest Day". The briefest survey must include my admiration for the doctors and sick bay attendants.'

'I had at least 16 Channel crossings in the ensuing weeks. I vividly remember the rows of dead German soldiers all carefully laid out on the ground by our orderlies with the contents of their pockets and identity discs in bags attached to their uniforms, subsequently to be sent to their next of kin. They looked so young compared with our more mature soldiers. I remember the farmyards and paddocks near Courseulles, where horses and cattle lay dead in the fields, pigs with their feet in the air and groups of cows still alive crying out pitifully to be milked.'

'There were two exciting days and infernally noisy nights with vehicles, tanks, armoured cars, pouring ashore past our high and dry landing craft in a constant stream, everybody blazing away with their guns at the sound of aircraft passing over. It is impossible to describe the volume of noise, and flak going up like a firework display to end all – and of course our own shrapnel coming down like rain. We were all in danger of being killed by our own gunfire.'

Lieutenant Brian Lingwood

RNVR, LCI(s) 526, 202nd Flotilla, suffered 87 per cent casualties.

'After the final pre-D-Day exercise in Bracklesham Bay, we learnt that six of our craft were to embark 48 RM

Commando and land them on Nan Red beach on the left of the Canadians in Area Juno. My own craft *526* (Sub Division leader) and *536* (Laidlaw) were to carry HQ Group 4th RM Commando Brigade. Our two craft were to land 10 to 15 minutes after the main group at a point, as we should see fit, some 300 yards to the west.

'On D-1 the whole flotilla sailed under the command of our Flotilla Officer, Lieutenant Commander Georges C. C. Timmermans DSC RNR (later Commander in Charge of the Belgian Navy). Our group also included some LCT. The next morning, on arrival off the Normandy coast, our LCT(s) detached and circled the headquarters ship HMS *Hilary* until zero hour. Commander Timmermans' six craft sailed and headed for the beach and at the appointed time my sub-division turned away to make our final run in to Juno beach. On watching our FO's approach to Nan Red beach, I soon realized that his group was in serious trouble.

'*540* could be identified bows down offshore and as we drew closer, we could see *513* and *539* both sinking. Underwater mines and obstructions were causing most of the craft casualties, whilst a strongpoint along and just behind the seawall was causing casualties to both the Marine Commandos and the crews aboard these craft. In *526*, I signalled *536* of my intention to pick a spot where the curve in the seawall afforded some protection from the strongpoint and to land close by an abandoned LCT(v) *2283* on our port side. The CO of the LCT (Lieutenant Collins) was the only survivor on board his craft and the LCOCU he was landing had apparently all perished with his crew. Most of the men of the LCOCU could be seen lying at the water's edge, together with their scattered equipment. Through the carnage Churchill AVRE tanks with the aid of bridging material were struggling to get over the seawall, at the same time leaving a white taped mine-free path.

'The beach was now in confusion and it was poignant to see the ashen faces of the more seriously wounded, packed so close together, seeking every vestige of shelter under the sea-facing walls of the houses, with their accompanying medics holding plasma drips, magnificently ignoring the mayhem around them. The upper floors of the houses under which they were sheltering were still occupied by the enemy, since from this direction, short menacing bursts of automatic fire prompted us to keep our heads down. Not so fortunate in my craft was the leading commando Marine Casson; the poor fellow was shot in the neck and died instantly before reaching the port ramp.

'A.R. Keen DSM, a member of the ramp crew, was hit in the leg in several places but steadfastly stayed by the port ramp to assist its retrieval on our withdrawal from the beach. Matters were now being made worse by mortaring and some of these were falling uncomfortably close. One in particular fell between *526* and *536* and this helped to hasten the departure of the remaining group of wireless carrying commandos, who left behind two portable motorcycles and a quantity of PIAT ammunition. We received an encouraging wave from Laidlaw (CO *536*) but it was noticed that his first lieutenant, Sub Lieutenant Cobbe was supervising the ramp crew with the upper part of his uniform turning crimson. He had been shot in the upper arm and had declined to get attention until forced to do so by his own weakness.

'A. B. Dixon, the port Oerlikon gunner, was firing into

the upper storeys of the houses on the sea front and he concentrated on one room in particular, where he had noticed movement. When later on Major Peter Wood RM visited us, he told us that his troop had discovered several dead in this room together with an assortment of weapons. He was convinced that one of the dead was in fact, a female.

'We now concentrated on unbeaching but discovered that we were taking in water in No. 2 troop space. I gave the order for our engines to be put half and then full astern but we were seemingly stuck. Just to help matters, at that point the port engine intake manifold blew. The crew worked magnificently to stem the leak and despite only having one engine, we got off. We proceeded slowly seaward and managed to reach the LSI *Prince Henry* and with the aid of a Neil Robertson stretcher, we were able to get A. R. Keen, now in much pain, transferred to obtain medical attention. *Prince Henry*'s priority was to disembark troops and for this reason, they would not accept the body of Marine Casson and we gave him a rather impromptu burial at sea the next day.

'We were ordered to embark fresh troops and we were inclined to feel sorry for them as they descended the scrambling nets down the side of the ship, for they were weighed down with equipment and weapons. The first soldier to step on board our craft with his metal studded boots promptly slipped on our steel deck and fractured his ankle. He was just as promptly re-transferred on board his ship and that presumably ended his D-Day.

'We were to land these troops in *Gold* sector but the prospect caused us some disquiet, since water was coming through our makeshift repair and the craft was becoming unmanageable allied to the fact that only one engine was operational. Having accomplished our task, I decided to dry out on the beach, pump and bail out the water and attempt further repairs. That afternoon while we were stranded on the beach, we were straddled by four bombs from a German bomber, a bomb splinter hitting the side of the bridge, fortunately without other mishap. However, two soldiers jumping from a Rhino ferry that had just landed were killed outright, their bodies lying on the beach until they were covered by the sea ...'

R. S. Haig-Brown, 22
93rd LAA Regiment, Royal Artillery.

'With our LST now a hundred yards off the Normandy shore, tanks unlashed and all ready to go, the front doors were opened. The ramp lowered and down into the sea went the tanks; long since carefully water-proofed and tested as well they needed to be, for the water was all of five feet deep. To the left and right were other LSTs, some disabled having hit mines, but we managed our dash to the shore without any problems, weaving our way on the sea-bed between steel spikes, sticking up at all angles and put there by the Germans to deter us. Like hounds at a hedge row, looking for a way through, we were soon up on dry land, stationary with guns at the ready to beat off the German airforce which never came, and the drivers – pulling savagely at the waterproofing so that the engines could once again run as their makers had intended. Suppose that in all that movement, on something never before tried in world history, to have been only half an hour late, was something of a triumph for the masterly organisation which we saw throughout.

'My first real shock was to see not one but perhaps a hundred of our men dead, lying at the water's edge, their bodies rolling unnaturally on the sand as the tide washed around them. Devastation was everywhere. Nothing was in one piece. Tree trunks snapped off by shells were strewn across the road. Every building was wrecked by the earlier bombardment of the Navy. Cows lay awkwardly, legs in the air, dead or dying from bullets and shrapnel which had ripped through the air not half an hour before. Overhead was the fierce crack of the Navy's 21-inch shells on their way inland to stop the Germans from coming forward at us. The noise was unbelievable, made worse, if possible, by Frenchmen in berets worn like skull caps, running here, there and everywhere, too bewildered to know what they were doing.

'Bill Lean, my troop commander, met up with me and together we walked down the village street, now in ruins, the road so jammed with debris that we could not see the tar, to get to the church and spy out the land for the best gun positions. A shell had hit the church steeple and now there was a gaping hole six feet across. Up there was a German sniper. Before long we heard the familiar crack of rifle fire over our heads but we seemed immune because of our training with live firing and the sound was not so unusual. "Do you know something kid?" said Bill beaming all over, "I think someone's firing at us." But we just walked on and to this day I have no idea why we did not bother to take cover. It never occurred to either of us. However a few minutes later a well-aimed Bofors round put a stop to that little nuisance and I heard no more shots.

'Our job was to reach two bridges, one over the Orne

canal at Bénouville, and the other 100 yards to the east, over the Orne river. We were to protect them from air attack as they were the only road link between the beach and the 6th Airborne Division who had landed to the East of the river. As it turned out we did not see a German aircraft for at least a week. The bridges lay on the other side of a minefield. As I had been on the course I was told to organize a way through for the tanks. In their methodical way the Germans had every minefield marked with barbed wire and on the top strand hung a notice saying, "*Achtung Minen.*" If the writing sloped to the left it was a dummy. To the right it was an anti-personnel field. Upright meant an anti-tank one. The way I wanted to go was through an area with upright lettering so I knew I was looking for buried mines and not those showing on the surface. I knew exactly what to do until I came across the first mine. I had never seen one like it before. Even if I knew all about German mines I was not prepared for this and all the others to be British, captured at Dunkirk in 1940 and used against us now. I had no idea how to handle any of them.

'When eventually I did clear a way through no one would volunteer to drive the first tank down my taped path. "You cleared the way, sir," said the troop sergeant major, "and if you don't mind", he added with a huge grin, "perhaps you would prove it is all right by taking No. 1 down there yourself?"

'On my first run down the lane, and at the end of it, it was necessary to turn sharp left; in doing so on sandy ground, a track broke under the strain of the earth which built up against the tank's side. It could not be easily mended where it was, so I hunted round for a Royal Engineer's road-laying tank, and asked the Major with it if he would pull my helpless tank to better ground. To do so meant going down my cleared lane, but the tracks of a Churchill tank differ from those of a Crusader, and although I had managed it successfully, the wider tank ran over a mine I had managed to miss, wrecking it and killing the driver.'

Reverend R. M. Hickey
chaplain to Canada's North Shore Regiment, whose work on D-Day won him a Military Cross

'A feature of Juno was a concrete wall, which provided good cover for assault troops who reached it. But the wall was 50 yards from the water's edge and many perished on the open sands in between. The beach was sprayed from all angles by enemy machine guns and now their mortars and heavy guns began hitting us. The noise was deafening. All the while enemy shells came screaming in faster and faster. As we crawled along we could hear bullets and shrapnel cutting into the sand around us. When a shell came screaming over you dug into the sand and held your breath, waited for the blast and the shower of stones and debris that followed.'

Hickey crawled along the sand towards a group of three badly wounded men. He had just reached them when a shell landed among them, killing the three wounded but sparing the padre. He reached many others before they died and identified their religion from a disc worn around the neck.

'Whether Catholic or Protestant, I would tell the man he was dying and to be sorry for his sins, and often I was rewarded by the dying man opening his eyes and nodding to me knowingly. I will never forget the courage of the stretcher bearers and first aid men that morning.'

Hickey helped to put the wounded on stretchers and carry them to the shelter of the sea wall.

Private Jim Wilkins

The Queen's Own Rifles, 3rd Canadian Infantry Division.

'... We watched one salvo go high over the beach just as a Spitfire came along. He flew right into it and blew up. That pilot never had a chance and was probably the first casualty on Juno Beach. Overhead we can hear the roar of large shells from battleships, cruisers and destroyers. Beside us is a boat with pompom (anti-aircraft) guns shooting away at church steeples and other high buildings, which had observers who were spotting for the German ground troops.

'Soon we were only 500 yards from the beach and were ordered to get down. Minutes later the boat stops and begins to toss in the waves. The ramp goes down and without hesitation my section leader, Corporal John Gibson, jumps out well over his waist in water. He only makes a few yards and is killed. We have landed dead on into a pillbox with a machine gun blazing away at us. We didn't hesitate and jumped into the water one after the other – I was last of the first row. Where was everybody? My section are only half there – some were just floating on their Mae West's.

'My Bren gun team of Tommy Dalrymple and Kenny Scott are just in front of me when something hit my left magazine pouch and stops me up short for a moment. The round had gone right through two magazines, entered my left side and came out my back. Kenny keeps yelling "Come on. Come on!"

"I'm coming, I'm coming," I yell to him. We are now up

to our knees in water and you can hear a kind of buzzing sound all around as well as the sound of the machine gun itself. All of a sudden something slapped the side of my right leg and then a round caught me dead centre up high on my right leg causing a compound fracture. By this time I was flat on my face in the water – I've lost my rifle, my helmet is gone and Kenny is still yelling at me to come on. He is also shot in the upper leg but has no broken bones. I yell back, "I can't, my leg is broken – get the hell out of here." Away he goes and catches up to Tommy. Poor Tom, I've got ten of his Bren gun magazines and they're pulling me under. I soon get rid of them and flop over onto my back and start to float to shore where I meet five other riflemen all in very bad shape. The man beside me is dead within minutes. All the while we are looking up at the machine gun firing just over our heads at the rest of our platoon and company and then our platoon Sergeant and friend of mine, who had given up a commission to be with us was killed right in front of me.

'Finally I decided that this is not a good place to be and managed to slip off my pack and webbing and start to crawl backward on my back at an angle away from the gun towards the wall about 150 feet away. I finally made it and lay my back against it. In front of me I can see bodies washing back and forth in the surf. Soon, one of my friends, Willis Gambrel, a walking wounded, showed up and we each had one of my cigarettes, which surprisingly were fairly dry. Then he left to find a first aid centre. A medic came along and put a bandage on my leg. I had forgotten all about the hole in my side. Then two English beach party soldiers came along carrying a five-gallon pot of tea. "Cup of tea Canada?"

"Yes sir" – and they gave me tea in a tin mug. It was hot and mixed 50/50 with rum. It was really good.

"Okay?" he said and as darkness fell on 6 June, I was soon asleep.

'By this time all that was left of my platoon of 35 men was one lance sergeant, one wounded lance corporal and six riflemen. All the rest were dead or wounded. Field Marshal Erwin Rommel had been right – it had been and will always be the longest day. Altogether The Queen's Own Rifles lost 143 men killed or wounded.

'Lest we forget.'

A. W. Sadler

'June 5 1944 was my 24th birthday, celebrated aboard an American-crewed landing ship. I was the driver of an ambulance jeep. But as I was about to drive from the ship on to a landing craft a naval officer attached a trailer full of ammunition to my towbar. What about the red crosses on my vehicle? What about the Geneva Convention? But at such a moment how can you start an argument with a superior officer? About 30 minutes later we were on Juno beach behind Canadian infantry and armour. Flame-throwers had been directed against German pillboxes and blinded soldiers in them. Many of them were doomed. They were treated by medics and seated in deckchairs. There was nothing else that could be done for them.

Sam Earl

48 Royal Marine Commando.

'Most of us preferred to sit on the deck despite the cold wind and rain. The hyscene tablets issued did little to prevent sickness, which affected the majority of the commandos. The beach was clearly recognizable from the air photos. We passed close to the beach control ship and continued inshore. We had been told the tide would be low enough for the craft to beach below the beach obstacles. Actually the beach obstacles were under water and only a narrow strip of beach remained visible; consequently several craft hit obstacles which were sunk. There was a heavy swell and a vicious tidal stream, which carried away and drowned men. Mortar and shell fire became intense. MG fire started from the beach, Some commandos were killed by small arms fire on the craft before landing. The enemy had held his fire until we were beached and had us cold.

'The landing craft ramps failed because of the under water obstacles. Many officers and men attempted to swim ashore, a high proportion of these were lost through drowning. I got ashore. After running up the beach with two of my mates. We stopped near the sea I looked my left and saw many dead and wounded men. Another commando came running towards me but he didn't quite make it; he was killed with small arms fire. Another commando was running behind him, stopped and seeing he was dead picked up his rifle, which was a sniper's rifle. He got down on one knee and started firing at the strong point. He fired two rounds but was killed by small arms fire. His name was Lance Corporal Appleyard MM. He was awarded the MM in the Sicily landing. The commando who was standing on my right was also killed. I think his bullet saved my life. I moved along the sea wall and tripped over a wounded Canadian. I thought he was dead. Another Canadian threatened to shoot me. I never had time to say I was sorry. My troop commander had been shot in both arms and was unable to carry on. One of the men gave him a cigarette and lit it for him.

'A quick reconnaissance showed that the beach exit to the right was free from aimed (SA) fire except for occasional shots, as this was the quickest way to the assembly area. On the way to the assembly area a commando was sitting on a bank. He beckoned me. I ran over to him seeing he had a field dressing on his neck. As I asked him if he could walk a shot came from a house which killed him. A tank was there; a Canadian stood beside it crying. He said all his crew in it were dead, blown up by a mine.

Passing a small house, which had a shell hole in the roof, I saw an old man inside. I went inside to look around. There was an old man and old woman crying. A young woman who was also crying offered me a piece of brown bread. As I walked from the house she followed me to the gate. Two German prisoners were being marched past with hands on head; one of them saw the young woman. He stopped and said something to her as he was being marched down to the beach. He kept looking round at her. I think they were sweethearts.

'The assembly area was much quieter. It was found possible to reorganize. We advanced to Langrune according to plan where we started working on the beach defences between St Aubin and Langrune. We cleared the houses up to the strongpoint; we rushed the crossroads and gained the houses on the far side. By the end of this action 48 Commando strength had been reduced to 223 men, the total casualties being 217 men. Seventy per cent of all casualties occurred on the beach and in the landing craft. On D+2 one troop was sent to bury the dead in the garden of a house near Nan Red beach. A year later this cemetery was moved by the War Graves Commission to Bayeux.'

Unnamed Canadian Officer

'... The night of D-Day was a weird fantastic thing. The wind had died down. Several buildings were burning viciously. Others were just smouldering. An ammunition DUKW, hit in the early evening burned brightly and crackled with the detonations of exploding ammo. All night we "stood to" as we fully expected a counter attack or German paratroops and with the sea at our backs we had no alternative positions. I got terribly cold but there we all were. Jerry bombers were constantly overhead and dropping everything that would drop. Our AA was magnificent both from the ships and the shore and more than one Jerry plane came down in blazing pieces. Big guns helped to make the night a veritable hell, particularly those across the mouth of the Arne. It was the longest night I ever knew but at last day began to break and D-Day was a thing of the past. So much for D-Day, D+1 and up to D+10. Every day had its full quota of incidents. The shelling of our beach continued non-stop day and night for 70 days, but it was remarkable how few casualties there were for so much shelling.'

Juno Beach Timetable

Local naval commanders delay H-Hour from 07:35 to 07:45 until the tide is so high that landing craft can clear the treacherous reefs off shore. However, delayed by a choppy sea, the leading assault craft head in almost 30 minutes later than scheduled and are borne by the tide for several hundred yards through the belt of heavily mined obstacles. Twenty of the leading 24 landing craft are lost or damaged. Only six of 40 Centaur tanks mounting 95-mm howitzers manned by Royal Marines make the shore.

Canadian 7th Brigade, the Royal Winnipeg Regiment and the Regina Rifles are first ashore on the right flank of Juno, West of the Seulles River, followed a minute or two later by the Canadian 8th Brigade and 8–10 DD tanks manned by the Canadian 1st Hussars. On the left, ahead of the armour and running the gauntlet to the sea wall, is the Queen's Own Regiment of Canada, the North Shores and the Canadian 8th Brigade. Losses are significant but the survivors move quickly and are already involved in heavy fighting at Courseulles, Bernieres and St Aubin as the delayed DDs struggle ashore.

By 09:30 Flail tanks open exits on both sides of the Seulles and the worst of the craters has been bridged by fascines and bridging tanks.

11:15 St Aubin falls to Canadians.

20:10 Taillerville captured by Canadians.

By end of day 12 lanes are clear and Canadian follow-up units – the 7th Brigade on the right, the 9th on the left – are past the assault troops, as planned, and heading for Caen. 21,500 men of the 3rd Canadian Division and 2nd Armoured Brigade and British troops storm seven miles inland. The Canadians make the most progress of all the beaches and at nightfall are within sight of Caen while two battalions are only three miles from its NW outskirts.

Casualties, 359 killed, 715 wounded.

Order of Battle Juno Beach

3rd Canadian Division
Major General Rodney Keller

7th Canadian Brigade
The Royal Winnipeg Rifles
The Regina Rifle Regiment
1st Canadian Scottish Regiment

8th Canadian Brigade
The Queen's Own Rifles of Canada
Le Regiment de la Chaudière
The North Shore (New Brunswick) Regt

9th Canadian Brigade
The Highland Light Infantry of Canada
The Stormont, Dundas and Glengarry Highlanders
The North Nova Scotia Highlanders
Divisional Troops

HO 3rd Canadian Division
12th Canadian Field Regiment SP, RCA
13th Canadian Field Regiment SP, RCA
14th Canadian Field Regiment SP, RCA
32nd Bty, 4th Canadian Light Anti-Aircraft Regiment, RCA
16th and 18th Canadian Field Companies, RCE
Cameron Highlanders of Ottawa (MG)
Units under command for assault phase

2nd Canadian Armoured Brigade
6th Armoured Regiment (1st Hussars)
10th Armoured Regiment (Fort Garry Horse)
27th Armoured Regiment (The Sherbrooke Fusilier Regiment)

4th (Special Service) Brigade
48 RM Commando
1st Section, RM Engineer Commando
C Sqn, Inns of Court Regiment
19th Canadian Field Regiment SP, RCA
62nd Anti-Tank Regiment, RA
HQ 80 Anti-Aircraft Brigade
372, 375 Btys, 114 Light Anti-Aircraft Regiment, RA
321 Bty, 93 Light Anti-Aircraft Regiment, RA
5th Canadian Field Company, RCE
26 and 80 Assault Squadrons, RE
72 and 85 Field Companies, RE
3 and 4 Btys, 2 RM Armoured Support Regiment
Beach Groups
8 Bn The King's Regiment
5 Bn The Royal Berkshire Regiment

Plus elements of:
Royal Corps of Signals
Royal Army Service Corps
Royal Army Medical Corps
Royal Army Ordnance Corps
Corps of Royal Electrical and Mechanical Engineers
Corps of Military Police
Pioneer Corps
Royal Canadian Army Medical Corps

A Foothold On
The Continent
Of Europe

Winston Churchill

in a telegraph to Stalin on the afternoon of 6 June.

'Everything has started well. The mines, obstacles and land batteries have been largely overcome. The air landings have been very successful and on a large scale. Infantry landings are proceeding rapidly and many tanks and self-propelled guns are already ashore.'

Lieutenant Eugene Fletcher

pilot of 'Government Issue' (BI7 Flying Fortress)
assigned to the 4I2th Bomb Squadron, 95th Bomb Group at
Horham, Suffolk.

'We had arrived in England – or rather, Valley, Wales – on
D+1 via ATC. The airport was just a runway in the Welsh
farm country. Upon deplaning, knowing the invasion was
in progress and wanting some information about the war, I
walked over to a Welsh farmer not far from the runway,
and asked if there was any news from the Continent.

"'Aye, 'tis a great contest going on over there. 'Tis a
great contest." These were the first words to greet my ears
in the ETO.'

Les Barber

tank driver.

'The stench of war was everywhere. The scene on the
beach was one of destruction, with houses alight and
knocked-out tanks burning. I saw a commando first-aid
post with quite a few wounded lying out on stretchers.
The commandos were clearing houses of snipers and odd
pockets of Germans. The captured Germans looked as if
they had suffered badly, and some were helping their own
badly wounded down the road. We were on the extreme
left of the seaborne forces at Ouistreham, on the River
Orne. The area faced high ground and we were shelled
heavily. But one enemy tracked vehicle showed itself and
was quickly disposed of. Suddenly the most magnificent
sight appeared in the sky – swarms of bombers towing
gliders. Many were hit and were crash-landing. My first
day in France ended in a noisy night, with incessant
gunfire.'

Marjorie Jefferson, 19

probationer nurse, Leeds General Infirmary.

'After 24 hours off, Ward 1, women's medical, had changed beyond recognition. As I opened the ward doors I could hardly believe it. First of all it was the untidiness that hit me. Every bed and locker was overflowing with khaki; greatcoats, kitbags, remnants of tattered uniforms and army boots under every bed. The beds themselves were filled with the pride of the army – glider pilots, parachutists, commandos, soldiers of the first wave of the assault troops to land on or behind the beaches. They were all so masculine. Splintered arms and legs stuck out from the beds at the most peculiar angles. I can remember the faces of many of them: the four Cockneys who each spoke a different London dialect. I can even remember their wounds. The tank sergeant with the burnt hands. The young football fanatic with a shattered knee, the quiet, older, glider pilot who survived three days and nights wounded in a dyke but was soon to die of a coronary. And there was the boy who became one of my favourite patients. He was only 19 and one of his feet had been blown off. But he was always so cheerful and nearly drove us mad singing: "Mares eat oats and does eat oats and little lambs eat ivy."'

Patricia Gent

a land-girl near Blandford, Dorset.

'I was ploughing fields when above the noise of my tractor I heard a strange drone in the sky. It was a sight I'll never forget. Over the horizon were so many aircraft they blotted out the sky. As the sound got louder I was so afraid that I hid in a ditch. That evening they were bringing casualties into a nearby army hospital and we land-girls volunteered to help the wounded. One American soldier insisted on giving me a little present to show his appreciation. He said it was something to remember D-Day. It was a Purple Heart medal awarded to US soldiers wounded in action.'

USN Nurse Helen Pavlovsky
stationed at The Royal Victoria Hospital at Netley.

'... And then the casualties came. I was an operating room supervisor. We started out with one operating room theatre and then we required another because we just couldn't handle all the casualties. When I say theatre I mean several rooms, each room with its own surgeon and nurse, and corpsman (enlisted Navy medical personnel). It was one big unit. The first casualties came into my downstairs operating room and kept on coming. We had no place to put them so we put them out in the halls and everywhere. We never thought about food, sleep or anything else. The doctors, as well as the nurses and corpsmen were taking care of patients. Finally sleep had to be rationed because no one would leave their work. We lived on sandwiches and coffee for a long time. As the casualty load lightened, things got back to a decent pace.'

Sara Marcum
a ward nurse originally from rural Kentucky who, after graduating nursing school in January 1943, joined the Navy Nurse Corps.

'A lot of the casualties were suffering from "shell shock". Some of them didn't know who we were. They thought we were Germans and they wouldn't tell us anything except their names and serial numbers. They were classified as mentally ill. Some of them were just farm boys and the shock of war was just too much for them.'

Elizabeth Hillmann
American Army Nurse.

'I had a 30-bed surgical ward; 27 of my patients who had been severely wounded on 6 and 7 June were critically ill. All were 19 and 20 years old – younger than I was. Some had fingers and arms blown off. One had his buttocks blown off. Some had stomach wounds. It was one almost constant nightmare. We were fighting death. One 19-year-old boy from Texas had been in a tank and all but his face and the top of his head and the palms of his hands were burned. Before he was picked up he had lain there so long he was covered with maggots. He told me, "I can stand the pain of the burns but the crawling maggots are driving me almost insane." The doctors, the sergeant and myself immersed him in warm, sterile, saline solution but never got them all. A tall young black man read from the Bible to him. This white Texan and the black Southern soldier talked about God together. I had the Miraculous Medal and I asked him if I could put it on his finger. I so wanted him to live. He whispered to me, "Don't worry, don't worry, I am ready to go and when I die, I want you to write to my parents and tell them I was prepared and I knew I would see God."

'So I did.'

Sapper Harold Merritt
689 Road and Airfield Construction Company RE.

'Our convoy of ten tank landing craft arrived on the evening of D-Day. The battleships and rocket craft were firing continuously. There was a scare while we were under a smokescreen as a plane flew overhead, but it turned out to be a Spitfire. We landed early next day ... Unfortunately, my mate, Fred Bone from Chesham, had to endure many months of torment. He had lost his false teeth overboard.'

Orv Iverson
9th Tactical Air Command Signals Section.

'In England we had been told that in France we would be driving on the left side of the road like in England. I soon discovered this was incorrect.

'As I drove my load of radio equipment up the hill from the beach I noticed other six-by-six trucks with stretchers placed from bench to bench with soldiers on them. At first I thought they were wounded GIs being taken back to England. Then I realized they were the dead GIs being removed from the battlefield. Also I noticed six-foot-high piles of bloodied blankets all around. As I drove on farther I met a truck heavily loaded with German bodies, piled in a criss-cross, helter-skelter fashion, being taken to a bull-dozed burial place. Inland the road was lined with dead soldiers and also dead bloated cattle with their legs outstretched.

'One dead soldier with curly hair really hit me emotionally. He looked just like a dear friend from high school days.'

Flight Sergeant Roland 'Ginger' A. Hammersley DFM

RAF Lancaster air gunner, 57 Squadron.

'After debriefing and a short rest period, we found that we were again on the battle order with another evening briefing. The RAF was to be thrown into the battle to establish the beachheads and we were to prevent movement of enemy reinforcements to the battle area. The flight out to the target (bridges in Caen) was uneventful and we made our attack from 5,000 feet as briefed. Then, without any warning, our Lancaster was raked with cannon and machine-gun fire, with a short reply from Sergeant G. Jennings, the rear gunner. Ron Walker, the pilot put the aircraft into a dive to starboard and commenced to corkscrew away from the area. There was no more fire from the enemy aircraft, identified from the astrodome by the navigator, Flying Officer M. A. Crombie, as a Ju 88. Ron called all the members of the crew to check if all was well. There was no reply from Tom Quayle in the mid-upper gun turret, so I went back along the fuselage to see what the problem was, only to find that he had been killed in the action. His wounds were such that he must have died instantly.'

Lieutenant Abel L. Dolim

Diary entry, navigator, 332nd Bomb Squadron, 94th BG.

'Wednesday 7 June. We crossed the invasion coast on the way to bomb a railway bridge over the Loire River at Nantes. The English Channel was positively jammed with ships and boats of all descriptions. Several landing craft were burning on the beaches. The fields near the coast were littered with Horsa and CG-4 gliders, all painted with the same black and white invasion striping we carried on our fuselage and wings. We took flak at Tours and then began our bomb run from the south of Nantes. Halfway down the bomb run, it became apparent we were on a collision course with a B-24 group. The enemy was beginning to pound us with 88s so we elected to do a "360" and came up behind another B-24 group. The second bomb run was good. We hit the target just at the southern approach to the bridge and there was a very large ball of flame in the marshalling yard – gasoline! We took more flak on the way out at Rennes and at Guernsey Island, where we were clobbered at only 11,000 feet.'

Les Bulmer
pilot, 2I Squadron.

'21 Squadron was out whenever weather permitted, patrolling behind the battlefront looking for anything that moved. The night of D-Day we were briefed to patrol the Caen–Lisieux–Boisney road to stop German reinforcements reaching the beachhead. We were told that there was a corridor across the Channel in which every aircraft must stay on outward and return flights. Our night-fighters were patrolling on either side of the corridor and were likely to regard any plane that was found outside the designated area as hostile. As we left the English coast a hail of flak went up from a ship in mid-Channel, right where we were headed. Pretty shortly, down went an aircraft in flames – it looked like one of our four-engined bombers. It seemed that one of our own ships (the Royal Navy got the blame) had parked itself right on the path that every aircraft going to and from the Continent that night would be following. And, in true naval fashion, it let fly at everything that went over. We decided to risk the night-fighters rather than fly through that lot and did a wide detour. Whereas before D-Day there had been almost total darkness, now over France there were lights everywhere and most of the Normandy towns burned for several nights. Navigation was much easier; you just flew from one fire to the next.'

Seaman G. E. Jacques
aboard a landing craft at Sword beach.

'I spotted an airman in the water. We tried to rescue him but he was numb with cold. The boat got stuck on a mud bank and my skipper shouted to let the airman go. He threatened to shoot me if I didn't. He had a gun trained on me. Then the ship turned and sliced the chap's head off.'

Fellow Officer recalling a conversation with Lieutenant Denis J. M. Glover DSC
RNZNVR, Commanding Officer, HM LCI(S) 516, in the wardroom of LCI(S) 519 alongside a sunken blockship in the Arromanches Gooseberry.

'After D-Day floating bodies were plentiful off the Normandy coast. One, in particular, had been washed to and fro in the anchorage for days. We manoeuvred alongside and got lines round it and heaved it inboard. The head was nearly skeletonized and things crawled on the deck from the sodden bundle that had once been an RAF pilot. Everyone, even my coxswain, felt pretty sick.

"Come on you bastards," I said. "Rip off those clothes; let's see the poor devil's papers." Then we weighted his feet and I forgot all about that lovely prayer book of mine down below. As we slid him into the sea I just said: "Oh Lord God, we commit these sorry remains to the sea from whence they came."

'There was a silence in the wardroom. We could see that Denis was deeply moved and we knew the moral courage it had taken to perform that act.

"I sent the papers to NOIC Arromanches," he went on, "so some poor mother will know what happened to her son. And afterwards I issued a tot of rum all round and entered the fact, and the reason therefor, in the log."

"What about your crew?" I asked.

"Oh," said Denis, "they just said 'You can offer us as much rum as you like, Sir, but we don't want any more jobs like that.' But it did the bastards good."

'Denis's eye beamed, our glasses clinked ...'

Glover's and Lieutenant J. F. Ingham RNZNVR's handling of their landing craft, LCI(S) *516* and LCI(L) *110*, respectively, under heavy fire while negotiating mines and underwater obstacles in order to put Commandos ashore at Ouistreham resulted in both being awarded the DSC. On the beach Lieutenant R. Crammond RNZNR's work as naval liaison officer with the Commandos earned him a mention in dispatches and a Croix de Guerre. Lieutenant N. Watson, commanding MTB *453* and Lieutenant C. J. Wright, commanding MTB *454*, engaged *E-boats* in six separate night engagements and both were awarded the DSC.

Antonia Hunt, 14

an English girl who was left behind by her parents in Nazi-occupied France.

'... It had happened! Excitement in Paris was at fever pitch. The news was patchy, because the BBC stations were jammed. People rushed round in the streets telling everyone they met the latest news. Soon it would all be over – unbelievable. There were rumours that all the water supplies for Paris were going to be blown up, as well as the gas mains and electricity. Diana and I spent a whole day frantically filling empty wine bottles with water, adding one grain of permanganate to each one. We were unaware that the General in charge of Paris, General von Choltitz, was having a bitter struggle with Hitler and the Gestapo. He too loved and appreciated Paris and felt it should be left intact, whereas Hitler wanted to raze it to the ground.

'The rest of June was glorious, making up for the bad weather of the landings. Diana and I prayed and hoped and willed the Allied Armies to succeed in their advance. All over France, Resistance organizations were doing all in their power to help by disrupting communications. For a week or so it had appeared to be touch and go, but now the advance seemed to consolidate. I wondered if my father was with them. Everyone hoped the British would liberate Paris, though that was still a long way off.'

Mike Henry DFC

air gunner, IO7 Squadron, Hartford Bridge, June I944.
'After D-Day, the radio in the mess did a roaring trade, especially with the French crews. We were all eager to know how the Allied front was moving, although a few of us semi-privileged people could walk into the ops room and see the current situation chalked up in Chinagraph on the talc-covered, large-scale map. I shall, however, never forget the day when the liberation of Paris was so dramatically announced. I was standing by the radio

looking out into the ante-room. There was a large circle of attentive faces, French, British, Canadian, Australian and New Zealand, all-agog for latest news. After the pips the announcer, in calm measured tones, said, "It has just been announced that Paris was entered this morning by American troops; Paris is liberated ...". There was a moments pause, during which a pin would have been heard if dropped, broken by the first strident but stirring notes of the *Marseillaise*. Looking round the sea of faces I saw many an unashamed tear. I, too, had a lump swelling in my throat. It was truly a wonderful moment.'

Bill Stafford,
2nd Tactical Air Force advance party.

'Our destination turned out to be Gosport with its Mulberry Harbours where there were a large number of flat-bottomed tank landing craft awaiting us. We drove our wagons right on to the far (stern) end of the craft and chained them down. The tanks followed us on and we chained these down as well. The fumes, perspiration and stench were multiplied tenfold and the condensation dripped from the underside of the upper deck so much that it resembled being in a thunder storm. We were still completing these tasks when we set sail and we did not see the leaving of our shores. When we had finished chaining we were allowed to our quarters, a long passage, about three foot six inches wide, running the length of the craft with bunks in tiers of three joined at the foot and head. From end to end there was the stench of sweaty bodies. I had just taken off my boots when buckets of steaming hot tea came round. A cheer went up and we all filled our pint mugs. I took my first gulp. It was made with "connie onnie" (condensed milk). I made a hasty dash topside and spent the rest of the crossing hanging over the rail wishing that I had never been born.

'As we neared the Normandy coast we were ordered back on to our vehicles ready to disembark. A shudder went through the landing craft as we hit the beach. The ramps dropped down, the tanks thundered off and then it was our turn. Juno beach was littered with wrecked and abandoned tanks, trucks, jeeps, guns, and even clothing and personal effects. All evidence of the hellish time that they had experienced. Hundreds of army personnel were busy extricating gruesome remains from the wreckage. It was enough to make you sick. Our sight of this was very brief and up the beach into a very narrow country lane we went. Progress was rather slow. We had to be very cautious because our front line was still only about six or seven miles ahead and we could hear the noise of gunfire up ahead.'

Pharmacist Mate Frank R. Feduik, 19
USS LST 338.

'On 8 June we got orders to unload our cargo on Omaha beach. There was just chaos and confusion everywhere. I don't think we hit the right part of the beach. We saw a lot of people completely lost who didn't know where they were. I didn't see any Navy corpsmen or Navy aid stations. But I did see a lot of Army medics. They established their aid stations wherever they could. We saw bodies – some were our troops, some were theirs. I saw people with arms and legs missing, parts of bodies. You just couldn't understand it – guys not even making it to the beach, some of them impaled on iron rails that were in the water.

Some were washed ashore. It was complete mayhem, terrible.

'After unloading our cargo, our LST was filled with wounded. We treated the wounded, mostly by applying tourniquets and giving morphine. Then we would mark the patients as to what time you had given the morphine to tell when they were due for the next shot. I remember one soldier. I knew he was in pain so I checked him right out. His leg was missing. He had stepped on a mine right on the beach. I gave him a morphine shot and told him he would be okay for a couple of hours. He jumped up and looked at the stump. I don't know where he got the strength. He said, "I'm a farmer. What am I going to do?" I pushed him back and told him he would be okay. He just screamed. He was only 20 years old.'

Leutnant Herbert Walther, 22
12th Waffen-SS Armoured Division Hitler Youth (HJ).
After winning the Iron Cross he became an American PoW.
'We were soon given a taste of what our fate was to be in the coming weeks, when a rain of fire suddenly came pouring down. Such an unrelenting concentration of material had never been seen in such a restricted area in the whole of the war. The enemy's artillery was far superior to ours in numbers, excellently positioned and they had observation aircraft. But the unforgettable factor for anyone who was there was lying just off the coast and battering the division thunderously. The whistling of the heavy shells and the explosions was just devastating.

'I came across a young lad who had been very badly wounded in the back and chest. My driver and I heaved him into my car and laid him on our coats, trying to make him comfortable. He knew he was dying and with his last breath he asked me to find his company commander and ask him to pass a message to his mother. He said, "Tell her I died for my beloved Führer and for my Fatherland and that I tried to be brave. Tell her she shouldn't cry because she can be proud of her son."

'I am not ashamed of the tears I cried. The boy gave me his hand and I held it until he died. I then went to sleep. When I woke, I saw we were parked under a great oak and there were several fresh graves under it. I saw from the date on the boy's cross that he had fallen on his 18th birthday. I cried my eyes out. In the Falaise Pocket, I tried to escape. My driver was burning and I had a bullet in the arm. As I ran along a railway track, I was hit in the leg and then, 100 metres further, again in the back of the neck, like a hammer blow below my right ear. The bullet came out through my cheek.

'I was choking on blood and there were two Americans and two French soldiers looking down at me. The French wanted to finish me off but the Americans bandaged my leg and then operated on me for more than five hours. They removed 13 bullets.

'I know one thing; if the army had not been left by the *Luftwaffe* and the navy to fight alone, the invasion would have turned out very differently. But we had run out of planes.'

Stan Bruce
5th/7th Battalion, The Gordon Highlanders.

'... Every day another face would vanish ... 'Jerry' opened up, killing our Bren gunner, who was just a wee bit in front of me. We all hit the deck and returned fire into the woods where the firing came from. You did not aim but just fired where you thought 'Jerry' was to make him keep his head down. The Bren gunner was a very nice chap called Bill Hughes, another Desert veteran. The 'Jerry' who had opened fire came out with his hand up shouting, "*Kamerad, Kamerad.*" I just heard Bert shout, "You Bastard," and he shot him dead. This kind of thing happens in the heat of battle. Your blood is up and you do things like that. I suppose 'Jerry' did the same. Bill Hughes had paid the price. So had the 'Jerry', whose body was still lying there next morning.'

S. Davies
one of 30 crew of the British MoWT (Ministry of War Transport) 'Freeman Hatch' making its second run to the Omaha Beachhead with stores and ammunition on I3 June.

'As a lovely morning dawned, a lone German came out of the sunrise and an aerial torpedo hit our escort, the HMS *Boadicea*. Within seconds she sank. There was a mass of bodies and fuel oil in the water. Our captain ordered us into the lifeboats to pick up the survivors. There were only 20 out of 300 men.

Boadicea was hit in the forward magazine by an aerial torpedo at 04:45.The fore part of the ship disintegrated and afterward sank rapidly.

Field Marshal Gerd von Rundstedt
Commander-in-Chief West, I0 June.

'Field Marshal Wilhelm Keitel, head of Armed Forces High Command, rang me from Paris in a panic. "What shall we do?" "Make peace you fool."

Von Runstedt could make no decisions during the invasion – only Hitler could issue direct orders.

'As commander-in-chief in the West my only authority was to change the guard in front of my gate. I asked Supreme Command in Berlin for authority to commit two divisions into battle but the answer was "no action". Hitler was asleep in bed with Eva Braun at the Berghof and no one dared disturb him.'

Von Rundstedt and Rommel wanted to withdraw behind the Seine but Hitler decreed that 'There should be neither a fighting withdrawal to the rear nor a disengagement to a new line of resistance. Every man will fight and fall where he stands.' Von Rundstedt was sacked two days later.

General Montgomery

'We have gained a foothold on the continent of Europe.'

Extract from 'Behind The Lines in Normandy' by Lieutenant Commander R. D. Franks DSO

Royal Navy, Force 'S', 28 June 1944.

'With the minimum of delay, we set out and left our unattractive beaches behind. We drove along the coast through Lion-sur-Mer, Luc-sur-Mer, St Aubin and so on, to Courselles. Most of the houses were damaged, with rubble lying about and "*Achtung Minen*" notices everywhere. At Courselles I walked through the town to the beaches. The volume of craft and shipping lying off this beachhead is many times greater than Sword. They are fortunate in having a kind of harbour, or rather a sort of tidal cutting, where large numbers of small craft could shelter. The mass of shipping to seaward is an incredible sight. We examined an immensely strong strongpoint, more complete than any of ours. We had to withdraw when craft started asking for orders from me and I had to say "I was a stranger 'ere." The town was pretty unprepossessing. We passed the local tart no less than three times in our wanderings, making a different date each time: she was most unattractive. The only shop we could find was full of sailors and soldiers and seemed to be selling the most awful trash in cheap jewellery and seaside souvenirs, so we went on. Another memory is of Courseulle's drains, which were evidently out of action. We picked up the car and drove west along the coast, past the edge of Gold beach where there seemed to be an incredible number of DUKWS, and then via a rather long diversion inland to the Mulberry at Arromanches. This was impressive, though we would see it better from a boat. The combination of sunken merchant ships (Corncobs) and concrete towers (Phoenix) appeared to give a lovely shelter and it must be much steeper to here as some of the coasters were right close in, being unloaded rapidly by DUKWs. The Whale piers with their Spud pierheads were interesting and when the second is complete there should be a great speed-up in unloading.

'We met one of our former American correspondents who told us about his first visit to the American beaches Utah and Omaha. The latter was apparently very hot and he said they had only succeeded in getting 150 yards inland by the evening of D-Day.'

A. B. Lol Buxton

Higher Gunner on HMS 'Goathland', part of Assault Convoy S5, which left Portsmouth harbour at 13:20 on 5 June and arrived off Sword on the 6th.

'I shall never forget what I saw and experienced that day. It was absolute hell. All you could see was dust and smoke and flames, and the pungent smell of cordite hung in the air. We were lucky to survive. Every time I return to Normandy, I know what a fantastic feeling it is to be alive. Yet it is tinged with sadness and emotion when we visit the British cemetery where 4,000 men are buried. It was about survival, a case of kill or be killed, getting on with what you had to do. 6 June 1944 was one of the proudest days of my life.'

Jack Woods

who volunteered for action on 23 May 1942, his 18th birthday. Two years later, as part of the 9th Royal Tank Regiment, he landed in a Churchill tank on a beach in Normandy.

'We went straight into what became a veritable tank war of attrition. Landing on 21 June, by which time the allies were well established but being held up by German forces, we were to be quickly in action in the battle for the Odon River and the capture of Caen. The losses were hellish. After Caen, we were involved in the crossing of the Orne River, among other things supporting the 7th Battalion Royal Norfolks, and then the crucial crossing of the Seine, which effectively ended the Battle of Normandy. By this time, the pursuit of the Germans was swift, so the "heavies" were switched to clearing up the channel ports like Le Havre and Dieppe. Still to come were Arnhem, the Ardennes,

Rosendahl and the corridor to the Rhine. Every time there was the fear of the unknown. There was the dreadful fear of moving into attack, though once in action you had to concentrate on the task in hand. Everyone had their own way of dealing with it. I liked to be alone. Normandy is a funny place. You never get over it. You can hear it, feel it. The smell never gets out of your nostrils. I went back in 1984 and when I went to the cemetery at Bayeux my mind went straight back to 1944. I could smell it then. I could see it all so clearly. I was not at the cemetery any more. I could suddenly smell the tanks burning, a terrible smell, the smell of death around you all the time. It was very traumatic. I'm not alone in feeling this way.'

British Mulberry Harbour Project

The first designs were made at Kingswood School in Bath. The codeword came from a tree standing in the grounds. Up to 45,000 workers, based in companies all over Britain, were involved in the construction of the Mulberries, round the clock. Most of them had no idea what they were building.

Mulberries consisted of four miles of piers and six of floating roadway from 15 pier heads. They were towed in sections and submerged on D+1. Each enclosed more than five square kilometres of water with a breakwater of concrete caissons each five storeys high and weighing

6,000 tons. 200,000 tons of old ships known as Gooseberries were towed from Scotland and sunk alongside the Mulberries to act as breakwaters.

From drawing board to construction Mulberry took less than a fifth of the time it took to build Dover harbour which had half the capacity. In eight months two artificial harbours and five Gooseberry breakwaters including: 400 Mulberry units totalling 1.5 million tons and including up to 6,000-ton Phoenix concrete breakwaters, were built. Fifty-nine old merchantmen and warships were sunk in line as blockships for the Gooseberries to provide protection to the innumerable small craft immediately after D-Day, before the Mulberries were properly laid and in operation. All were in place by 10 June.

The Mulberries were designed to deal with up to 12,000 tons of stores and 2,500 vehicles a day, as well as Atlantic storms and dramatic tide differences.

The largest Phoenix caissons weighed more than 6,000 tons and were 60 feet tall. More than 200 different types were made, using more than a million tons of concrete and 70,000 tons of steel.

Steel pontoon bridges, which rose and fell with the tide, created the roadways and piers. Vertical columns 90 feet tall and weighing 36 tons anchored them to the sea bed.

Admiral Tennant had a force of over 15,000 men to tow the harbours over, 'plant' and maintain them. It took 160 tugs to tow the Mulberries across the Channel.

By D+2 the blockships were in position and the Gooseberry harbours were operating. The placing of the 1.5 million tons of gear for the Mulberries was under way and by D+13 the major work was done. By the end of June 1944 they had landed 875,000 men on the beaches.

19—22 June: A storm (the worst during any June for 40 years) batters the Mulberries and they start to break up. The weather wreaks five times the amount of damage caused by enemy bombardment after D-Day. Many landing craft and DUKWS are lost and a total of 800 are driven ashore. American Mulberry 'A' off St Laurent is wrecked and its parts used to repair the more carefully laid British port at Arromanches off Gold beach, which is gravely damaged. It is to last another ten months, landing 2.5 million men, 500,000 vehicles and four million tons of supplies.

30 June: *Neptune* officially ends in the British sector.

3 July: *Neptune* officially ends in the American sector. However, the shuttle service of men and supplies continues unabated. By these dates, ships had conveyed to France more than 800,000 personnel, in excess of 130,000 vehicles and at least 400,000 tons of stores. In the words of *Neptune*'s commander in chief, Admiral Sir Bertram Ramsay, it was 'the greatest amphibious operation in history'.

PLUTO

Early 1942: Construction begins on a network of pipe lines, 1,000 miles long, to carry petrol brought across the Atlantic to the relatively safe ports of the Mersey and Bristol Channel to London and the South and East coasts.

PLUTO (Pipeline Under the Sea): A three-inch diameter steel pipeline is laid to carry fuel across the Channel.

RE and RASC troops are trained to operate the pumps, which are camouflaged as garages, bungalows and teashops. Special ships with large holds carry the huge heavy coils of pipeline. Barges join the main line to the beaches. By D-Day the PLUTO Force has over 100 officers and a thousand ratings.

PLUTO covers 770 miles of the seabed and pumps 210 million gallons of fuel from England to the Allied forces.

Once Cherbourg falls and sea-lanes are cleared through minefields, a submarine pipeline is laid from the Isle of Wight and petrol pumped to France. Later, as the British and Canadian Corps move north along the coast, more lines are laid across the Channel until the point is reached when over a million gallons of petrol a day passes through PLUTO to the Allied Armies in France.

In the days after D-Day more than 112 million gallons were pumped through.

When salvaged after the war it supplied the plumbing needs of 50,000 houses and yielded 75,000 gallons of high-octane petrol.

PLUTO cost £3,000 per mile to construct, and once salvaged was sold at £2,400 per mile.

The Beachhead Is Won

6 June—3I August: RAF flies 224,889 sorties and loses 2,036 aircraft (983 of which are from Bomber Command and 224 from Coastal Command). Aircrew Killed/Missing in Action total 1,035 from 2nd TAF and ADGB (Air Defence of Great Britain), 6,761 from Bomber Command and 382 from Coastal Command. In this same period, D-Day to 31 August, 21st Army Group suffers 83,825 casualties.

7 June onwards: 65,000 men and 19,000 vehicles leave Weymouth and Portland to reinforce the initial landings.

8 June: Omaha and Gold beachheads joined. Twelfth SS Panzer attacks Canadians at Port-en-Bessin and Bretteville l'Orgueilleuse.

9 June: Counter-attacks on British by élite German Panzer Lehr Division beaten back.

IO June: Utah makes contact with Omaha. Montgomery establishes his HQ in Normandy. First RAF base established on French soil.

12 June: Carentan liberated, joining up Utah and Omaha landings. All five beachheads joined up. British 7th Armoured attacks towards Villers-Bocage. 330,000 men and 50,000 vehicles are ashore. As US Seventh Corps fights its way across the Cotentin, the rest of US First Army thrusts forward around St Lô. Further East the British and Canadian Corps of British Second Army battle their way around Caen against fierce German counter-attacks.

30 June: By the end of June 875,000 men have landed in Normandy, 16 divisions each for the American and British armies. Although the Allies are well established on the coast and possess all the Cotentin Peninsula, the Americans have still not taken St Lô, nor the British and Canadians the town of Caen, originally a target for D-Day. German resistance, particularly around Caen is ferocious, but the end result will be similar to the Tunisian campaign. More and more well-trained German troops will be thrown into the battle, so that when the Allies do break out of Normandy the defenders will lose heavily and lack the men to stop the Allied forces from almost reaching the borders of Germany.

Lest we forget

Glossary

AA Anti Aircraft (or Ack Ack)

AAC Army Airborne Corps

ABC Airborne Cigar (radar jamming device)

ACM Air Chief Marshal

ADGB Air Defence of Great Britain

AEAF Allied Expeditionary Force

AGRA Army Groups Royal Artillery

APA U.S attack transport

A/S Anti-Submarine Escort Groups

ATC Air Transport Command (USAAF)

AVM Air Vice Marshal

AVRE Armoured Vehicle Royal Engineers

BBMF Battle of Britain Memorial Flight

BEM British Empire Medal

BG Bomb Group

Bn Battalion

Bty Battery

CASEVAC Casualty Evacuation

CG Group Captain

CO Commanding Officer

Conc. Area Concentration Area

Corpsman U.S Enlisted Navy Medical Personnel

CSM Company Sergeant Major

D+1 etc Days following D-Day (D+1 7th June)

DD Duplex drive

DFC Distinguished Flying Cross

DFM Distinguished Flying Medal

DR Dead reckoning

DSR Distinguished Service Cross

DSO Distinguished Service Order

DUKW(s) Duplex drive amphibious truck 2 1/2 tons

DZ 'O' Drop Zone

E-boat German torpedo boat

ETO European Theatre of Operations

Flt Lt Flight Lieutenant

F/O Flying Officer

Fos Forward Observers

FPU Pak(t) German tank mounted gun

GH Gee-H Navigation System

GP General Purpose

H+30 etc H-Hours following at intervals after the first hour
   of landing

HAA Heavy Anti-Aircraft

HE High Explosive

KIA Killed in Action

KSLI King's Own Scottish Light Infantry

KW Krzyz Walecznych (Polish Cross of Valour)

LBW Landing Barge

LCA Landing Craft, Assault

LCE Landing Craft, Equipment

LCF Landing Craft, Flak

LCI Landing Craft, Infantry

LCI (L) Landing Craft, Infantry (Light)

LCOCU Landing Craft Obstacle Clearance Unit

LCR Landing Craft Rockets

LCT (A) Landing Craft Transport, Assault

LCT (R) Landing Craft Transport, Rocket

LCV Landing Craft, Vehicle

LCVP Landing Craft Vehicle Personnel

LFC Lieutenant 1st Class

LI Light Infantry

LSI Landing Ship Infantry

LST Landing Ship Tank

LZ Landing Zone

M-1 Rifle (AM)

MC Military Cross

MG Machine Gun

MIA Missing in Action

MiD Mentioned in Dispatches

MM Military Medal

MoWT Ministry of War Transport

MPs Military Police

MTBs Motor Torpedo Boats

NCDU Naval Combat Demolition Units

NOIC Navy Officer in Command

NSRY Nottinghamshire Sherwood Rangers Yeomanry Oerlikons Guns (Cannon)

OR Other Ranks

Pay parade Means by which the forces were paid on duty

PFC Private 1st Class (U.S)

PIAT Projector Infantry Anti-Tank (British hand-held platoon anti-tank weapon)

Pongos Service slang for British soldier

PPI Scope Pilot's Position Indicator

RA Royal Artillery

RAAF Royal Australian Air Force

RAFVR RAF Volunteer Reserve

RAMC Royal Army Medical Corp

RANVR Royal Naval Reserve

RCAF Royal Canadian Air Force

RE Royal Engineers

REME Royal Electrical and Mechanical Engineers

RM Royal Marines

RN Royal Navy

RNR Royal Navy Reserve

RNVR Royal Navy Volunteer Reserve

RNZAF Royal New Zealand Air Force

RNZVR Royal New Zealand Air Force Volunteer Reserve

RV Rendevous

SHAEF Supreme Headquarters Allied Expeditionary Force

S/Sgt Staff Sergeant (U.S)

S/L Squadron Leader

SP/SPs Specials (tanks)

'Stick' A number of paratroopers dropped in sequence

TAFs Tactical Air Forces

TRIDENT Code name for Washington Conference, May 1943

U/I Unidentified

USN United States Navy

USNR United States Navy Reserve

VM Virtuti Militari (Polish)

W/C Wing Commander

Wg Cdr Wing Commander

W/Op Wireless Operator

Window (on aircraft) Strips of metal on aircraft used to confuse enemy radar

WREN Women's Royal Navy Service

Acknowledgements
and Contributors

Ray Alm; Ed "Cotton" Appleman; James Roland Argo; Peter Arnold; John Avis; Les Barber; Harry Barker; Mike Bailey; Carter Barber; Neil Barber, author of The Day The Devils Dropped In; E. W. D. Beeton; Franklin L. Betz; Bill Bidmead; Rusty Bloxom, Historian, Battleship Texas; Lucille Hoback Boggess; Prudent Boiux; Dennis Bowen; Tom Bradley; Eric Broadhead; Stan Bruce; K. D. Budgen; Kazik Budzik KW VM; Les Bulmer; Reginald 'Punch' Burge; Donald Burgett; Chaplain Burkhalter; Lol Buxton; Jan Caesar; R. H. "Chad" Chadwick; Noel Chaffey; Mrs J. Charlesworth; Chris Clancy; Roy Clark RNVR; Ian 'Nobby'

Clark; P. Clough; Johnny Cook DFM; Malcolm Cook; Flt Lt
Tony Cooper; Lt-Colonel Eric A. Cooper-Key MC; Cyril
Crain; Mike Crooks; the late John Crotch; Jack Culshaw,
Editor, The Kedge Hook; Denis Glover & R.D Franks
accounts c/o Rupert Curtiss papers, Warren Tute/Russell
Miller/Frank and Joan Shaw collection, D-Day Museum,
Portsmouth Museums and Records Service; Bill Davey; S.
Davies; Brenda French, Dawlish Museum Society; John de
S. Winser; Abel L. Dolim; Geoffrey Duncan; Sam Earl;
Eastern Daily Press; Chris Ellis; Les "Tubby" Edwards; W.
Evans; Frank R. Feduik; Ron Field; Wolfgang Fischer;
Robert Fitzgerald; Eugene Fletcher; Captain Dan Flunder;
John Foreman; Wilf Fortune; H. Foster; Lieut-Commander
R. D. Franks DSO; Jim Gadd; Leo Gariepy; Patricia Gent; Lt
Commander Joseph H. Gibbons, USNR; Bill Goodwin;
Franz Goekel; Lt Denis J. M. Glover DSC RNZNVR; John
Gough; Peter H. Gould; George 'Jimmy ' Green RNVR;
Albert Gregory; Nevil Griffin; Edgar Gurney BEM; R. S.
Haig-Brown; Leo Hall, Parachute Regt Assoc.; Günter
Halm; Roland "Ginger" A. Hammersley DFM; Madelaine
Hardy; Allan Healy; Andre Heintz; Basil Heaton; Mike
Henry DFC, author Air Gunner; Vic Hester; Reverend R. M.
Hickey MC; Lenny Hickman; Elizabeth Hillmann; Bill
Holden; Mary Hoskins; Ena Howes; Pierre Huet; J. A. C.
Hugill; Antonia Hunt; Ben C. Isgrig; Jean Irvine; Orv
Iverson; George Jackson; Major R. J. L. Jackson; Robert A.
Jacobs; G. E. Jacques; Marjorie Jefferson; Bernard M. Job
RAFVR; Wing Commander 'Johnnie' Johnson DSO* DFC*;
Percy 'Shock' Kendrick MM; the late Jack Krause; Cyril
Larkin; Reg Lilley; John Lincoln, author of Thank God and
the Infantry; Lt Brian Lingwood RNVR; Wing Commander
A. H. D. Livock; Leonard Lomell; P. McElhlnney; Ken

McFarlane; Don McKeage; Hugh R. McLaren; John McLaughlin; Ron Mailey; Sara Marcum; Ronald Major; Walt Marshall; Rudolph May; Ken Mayo; Alban Meccia; Claude V. Meconis; Leon E. Mendel; Steve Mendham; Harold Merritt; Bill Millin for kindly allowing me to quote form his book, Invasion; Bill Mills; John Milton; Alan Mower; Captain Douglas Munroe; "A Corpsman Remembers D-day" Navy Medicine 85, No.3 (May-June 1994); Major Tom Normanton; General Gordon E. Ockenden; Raymond Paris; Bill Parker, National Newsletter Editor, Normandy Veterans; Simon Parry; Albert Pattison; Helen Pavlovsky; Charles Pearson; Eric 'Phil' Phillips DFC MiD; T. Platt; Franz Rachmann; Robert J. Rankin; Lee Ratel; Percy Reeve; Jean Lancaster-Rennie; Wilbur Richardson; Penny Riches; Helmut Romer; George Rosie; The Royal Norfolk Regiment; Ken Russell; A. W. Sadler; Charles Santarsiero; Erwin Sauer; Frank Scott; Ronald Scott; Jery Scutts; Major Peter Selerie; Alfred Sewell; Bob Shaffer; Reg Shickle; John R. Slaughter; Ben Smith Jr.; SOLDIER Magazine; Southampton Southern Evening Echo; Southwick House, HMS Dryad, Southwick, Portsmouth; Bill Stafford; Allen W. Stephens; Roy Stevens; Mrs E. Stewart; Henry Tarcza; Henry "Buck" Taylor; June Telford; E. J. Thompson; Charles Thornton; Robert P. Tibor; Dennis Till; Edward J. Toth; Walt Truax; Jim Tuffell; Russ Tyson; US Combat Art Collection, Navy Yard, Washington DC; Thomas Valence; John Walker; Herbert Walther; Ed Wanner; R. H. G. Weighill; Andrew Whitmarsh, Portsmouth Museum Service; "Slim" Wileman; Jim Wilkins; E. G. G. Williams; Deryk Wills, author of Put On Your Boots and Parachutes! The US 82nd Airborne Division; Jack Woods; Len Woods; Waverly Woodson.

Index